TRAIN

Also by Tom Zoellner

A Safeway in Arizona

Uranium

The Heartless Stone

An Ordinary Man (with Paul Rusesabagina)

TRAIN

Riding the Rails That Created the
Modern World—from the Trans-Siberian
to the *Southwest Chief*

Tom Zoellner

VIKING

VIKING
Published by the Penguin Group
Penguin Group (USA) LLC
375 Hudson Street
New York, New York 10014

USA | Canada | UK | Ireland | Australia | New Zealand | India | South Africa | China
penguin.com
A Penguin Random House Company

First published by Viking Penguin, a member of Penguin Group (USA) LLC, 2014

LIBRARY OF CONGRESS CATALOGING-IN-PUBLICATION DATA
Zoellner, Tom.
Train : riding the rails that created the modern world : from the Trans-Siberian
to the Southwest Chief / Tom Zoellner.
pages cm
Includes bibliographical references and index.
ISBN 978-0-670-02528-2
ISBN 978-0-670-01717-1 (export edition)
1. Railroads—History. 2. Railroad travel—History. I. Title.
HE1021.Z64 2014
385.09—dc23   2013036816

Printed in the United States of America
10 9 8 7 6 5 4 3 2 1

Set in Adobe Garamond Pro with Glypha LT Std
Designed by Daniel Lagin

CONTENTS

My heart is warm with the friends I make,
And better friends I'll not be knowing,
Yet there isn't a train I wouldn't take,
No matter where it's going.

—Edna St. Vincent Millay

INTRODUCTION

Twenty years after I saw her, I still remember the young woman across the aisle from me on a train through a snowstorm in Pennsylvania. She was half visible in the overhead lamp, wearing a college sweatshirt and holding an open book on her lap. Whatever she was reading was making her cry softly. I couldn't see the title and I was too shy to ask, but the sight of her wiping away tears—emotionally transported into one world as she was physically transported in another—made me feel my individuality dissolving.

Snowflakes struck the dark windows without a sound, but unseen wheels hummed, and outside realities could be subsumed for a while in this linear realm of motion and warmth, five hours from Pittsburgh and nowhere in particular. We were standing perfectly still, yet moving over parallel lines of steel, and she seemed like a ghost in the dim light. I can't ride on a train at night without remembering her, wishing I had talked to her, strangely grateful that she remained a cipher.

Railroads anywhere, but especially in America, have the power to invoke odd spells like this, a feeling that might be called Train Sublime: the tidal sway of the carriages, the chanting of the wheels striking the fishplates (to me it sounds like *dear-boy, dear-boy, dear-boy*), the glancing presence of strangers on their own journeys and wrapped in private ruminations. These secret pleasures of a railroad summon forth a vision of a sweet pastness, a lost national togetherness. The train is a time traveler itself, the lost American vehicle of our ancestors, or perhaps our past selves.

We live in a society that was *made* by the railroads in ways we never think about anymore: our imported food, the beat of our music, our huge corporations and their methods of stock financing, our strong labor unions, our abstract notion of time and our sense of everyday connection with people who may live far out of sight but are made neighbors through mechanical means. Under the skin of modernity lies a skeleton of railroad tracks.

But in the light of the modern world, trains are not nostalgic playthings—not by any measurement. They serve unromantic needs and hard economies.

On an average weekday morning, approximately 100 million people across the world are boarding trains: from Paddington station in London, from the magnificent Victoria Terminus in Mumbai, from the tawdry and run-down Tirana Railway Station in Albania, the Baltazar Fidelis platform on the Jundial line outside São Paulo, the flying saucer of Beijing's sparkling new South Station, tiny one-room depots or lonely platforms scattered in the countryside all over Laos, Belgium, South Africa and Japan and eighty-six other nations, to say nothing of the 13 trillion tons per kilometer of cargo they haul each year. Global commerce would instantaneously crash without them.

And passenger trains are still alive and breathing even in America, though we have sacrificed most of them in favor of the long-haul plane ride and interstate car travel. A quasi-federal agency called Amtrak has kept overland trains in a state of reliable mediocrity since 1971, and it was on the creaky old *Pennsylvanian* when I first spotted the woman in the snowstorm. At least two dozen major cities have working commuter rail tentacles out to their suburbs—about 3 percent of Americans use them to get to work, mainly in the Northeast. I am one of those 100 million who ride the train as a matter of routine. And I do it from the famously car-happy city of Los Angeles.

My trip to my workplace takes a reliable forty-seven minutes, and I don't do it as an act of rebellion against the oil companies or as an ideological protest against my car. I do it because it is relatively cheap and it saves me from the freeway. And while I usually tote a book, I more often stare out the window at one of the truly ancient vistas of California: a corridor lined with pipe-fitting yards, crinkled tin warehouses, oil pumpjacks and homeless encampments.

Anyone who rides an American train can see that old industrial hardpan where the money is made without pretense and which was often—especially in the West—the first line slashed on the map before any major population showed up. And in this case, it's the tracks of the old Atchison, Topeka and Santa Fe that came through in 1885 to steal some orange-hauling business from the Southern Pacific. This right-of-way is now leased by Metrolink, a perfectly decent commuter rail line that runs to three counties and is shockingly underused. When I tell people I take the train to work, I often get a confused look. *Is that even possible?* And then a look of envy. *You can read. You can do work. You can listen to your iPod.*

All of those things, yes. But the clacking motion of the train, the way it shudders as if being pulled by a spinnaker sail—its uncanny, unlikely grace—often compels me to watch the old light-industrial panorama spool past, and I feel transported into a lulling sense of mystery, a sense of past and present merging into a single continuum. This is a private feeling, but on the train one is almost never alone.

"The world was so much smaller than we thought," wrote Charles Dickens at the dawn of the railroad era in Britain. "We were all connected. . . . People supposed to be far apart were constantly elbowing each other."

The very first rail passengers felt a sense of oceanic awe, even verging into dread, at their first sight of a train. A locomotive was the world's first true "machine" ever put on wide public display—a golem of gears that made loud gasps of expiration much like an animal's breath. Watching it creep forward came as a shock to the psyche, for this wagon was not pulled by a living animal, which would have been readily understandable. This was a grotesque and ghostly apparition. When crowds gathered in 1825 to watch the debut of the world's first real railroad—the Stockton & Darlington of northern Britain—the correspondent from the *Morning Herald* reported that multiple spectators "fled in affright" from the locomotive and others looked at the train with a "vacant stare," as if in a trance.

This experience was repeated thousands of times. Wherever the train would be introduced, observers responded with confusion and even horror. The editor of the *Cincinnati Enquirer* saw crowds "dumbfounded at the strange and unusual spectacle" with "distended eyes" in 1846. Another newspaper said witnesses at LaSalle, Illinois, "stood dumb with amazement" when the first engine of the Illinois Central came through. "Many of them looked as though they had come out between the shakes of the fever and ague," noted the reporter. The *Bengal Hurkaru* newspaper said the test of a locomotive near Calcutta astonished nearly all present with "its snort and its whistle and its fiery speed." Some made motions to bow and worship. Others considered the whistle "the voice of a demon" and believed that its sound would curdle milk, its smoke would kill birds and its vibrations dry up women's fertility.

Riding on this vehicle brought another wave of incomprehensibility. Never before in human history had people been able to travel without the use of an animal or a boat or their own muscles. And here was the countryside passing at a steady rate of fifteen miles per hour, a speed that was fascinatingly alien to the consciousness. Searching for any comparison that would make sense, journalists determined that a locomotive was traveling at one-quarter of the velocity of a cannonball on the battlefield. Excited merchants in America and Europe began to pool their financing to connect their own cities and villages to the grand colossus of new tracks, but when the school board in Lancaster, Ohio, received a request to let a classroom be used for a chartering meeting, the official response was this: "If God had designated that His intelligent creatures should travel at the frightful speed of 15 miles an hour, He would have foretold it through His holy prophets."

No object out the window could be watched for very long. Trees, flowers, houses, horses, waving children—all of them receding as quickly as they were seen, gone down the backward-spooling time funnel. Travelers complained of headaches and nervousness, plus a new condition that doctors came to call "railway spine," a disorder resembling fibromyalgia that nagged at people long after they disembarked. "The rapidity and variety of the impressions necessarily fatigue both the eye and the brain," reported the British medical journal *Lancet* in 1862.

The flickering quality of the landscape made the foreground virtually disappear and brought a new method of "seeing" into the vocabulary of the brain. In many ways the advent of the railroad in the mid–nineteenth century helped prepare humanity for the coming of the motion picture at the end of the century. Henry David Thoreau noticed the accelerating speed of life even inside his cabin on Walden Pond, where he could not avoid hearing the daily passing of the Boston & Maine:

> The startings and arrivals of the cars are now the epochs in the village day. They go and come with such regularity and precision, and their whistle can be heard so far, that the farmers set their clocks by them, and thus one well-conducted institution regulates a whole country. Have not men improved somewhat in punctuality since the railroad was invented? Do they not talk and think faster in the depot than they did in the stage-office?

The world has since accelerated to a velocity that would have astonished Thoreau. Gargantuan amounts of data are sent around the world in a millisecond, a kind of magic that staggers the imagination as much as the first sight of the train had startled the residents of Darlington in 1825. Yet underneath that electronic skin coating the world is a stubborn physicality—and a constant need to move people and things from place to place. The best tool for this purpose known to humanity does not require any reinventions.

The remarkable efficiency of rail is why nations like Spain and Korea have spent billions of dollars on a new generation of high-speed trains to get citizens from home to work: a mammoth savings of fuel. China has built a network of these same trains linking all corners of its vast territory, and Saudi Arabia is finishing a line to speed pilgrims to Mecca. Transportation planners have known for decades that rail corridors are far more elastic than roads for handling increases in population: they don't choke up as quickly, they require far less maintenance and they can be more easily plowed into city centers than can a new freeway.

The American economy, meanwhile, is more dependent on overland rail transportation than ever before: an average freight train can carry the contents of about 280 trucks by burning far less oil. About 40 percent of the national cargo is carried on trains, which are envied around the world for their efficiency. Smooth wheels sliding down a smooth artery of steel is a trick of physics that remains the best-known way to move heavy material. A train is like a broom or a hammer: an object of elegant and simple design that never became obsolete. The farmers and merchants of the early nineteenth century were amazed that a long string of heavy carriages could carry up to twenty thousand tons of whatever material they desired. That function still powers the world.

And yet the value of trains remains obscured. The train suffered a blow to its image during the highway-building phase of American history, and it is still regarded as a charming antique, an object of art for eccentrics and a last resort for the poor. Approximately 98 percent of the American public has never set foot on a city-to-city train.

An incident out of Maryland could function as a parable here. A track crew for the Baltimore & Ohio Railroad was digging a trench in August 1898 when a worker's shovel glanced across bone-white stone, too large and too smooth to be any ordinary piece of granite. The workers brushed away the dirt and saw it was a carved marble block about the size of a steamer trunk. Several layers of roadbed fill had been tossed over it and packed down by decades of spring rains. The block had been lying at a depth of six feet. Tombs of Egyptian pharaohs have been found lying closer to the surface. They brushed more dirt off the marble block and read an inscription on the side: FIRST STONE OF THE BALT & OHIO RAIL ROAD.

Here was a truly embarrassing discovery. Executives soon certified what the track crew suspected: this was the ceremonial cornerstone that had been laid on July 4, 1827, amid speeches, sashes, whiskey and marching bands to mark the launch of what had been America's first true railroad.

On that day the last surviving signer of the Declaration of Independence, Charles Carroll, had been persuaded to put on his top hat and knee breeches and come out to make what proved to be the last speech he ever delivered. He was one of the richest men in America, a prominent lay Catholic and a plantation owner who had introduced a bill in the Maryland Senate calling for a gradual end of slavery (though he never freed his own slaves), and he had also strong-armed the B&O's charter through the same body—an act of legislative aggression that marked the first use of the term "railroading." Like thousands of other Baltimore citizens, he was an investor in this plan to extend iron strap rail over the Allegheny Mountains toward the rich farmlands of Ohio and to use this bizarre-looking specimen from the British coalfields as an alternative to digging another canal.

The morning of July Fourth had been sunny and warm, and a crowd of fifty thousand people gathered to watch a band play a song that had been specially commissioned for the occasion, "The Rail Road March." In the rich and lengthy history of music associated with railroads, this ranks as the very first train song:

> *Here are mountains to be leveled,*
> *Here are valleys to be filled,*
> *Here are rocks to be blown and bridges, too, to build!*
> *And we're all hopping, skipping, and jumping*
> *And we're all crazy here in Baltimore!*

The crowd gathered around a pavilion decked with red, white and blue bunting—this was the Fourth of July, after all—to watch a group of Masonic elders ritually measure the First Stone with their rulers and sprinkle its surface with wine and oil. Nobody commented on the irony of a stone's being laid as a stationary symbol of a moving system (a cornerstone of *what*, precisely?). Carroll was handed a shovel, and he placed his buckled shoe onto the lip, pressed it down and made a turn of the soil for the First Stone.

"I consider what I have just now done to be among the most important acts of my life, second only to my signing the Declaration of Independence, if indeed it be even second to that," he said, a sound bite for the ages. And while he spoke it in a moment of promotional fervor, he was not far from wrong. America was a young country wealthy only in wilderness at the time of his speech, but the railroad created the financial strength of a rising world power.

The tracks of the B&O wouldn't reach the Ohio River for another twenty-seven years. And at some point—probably during the frenzied rebuilding after the Civil War—the cornerstone was covered up in heaps of dirt by a careless track crew near the Mount Clare shops and was lost underground for seven decades.

Our connection with railroads is like that First Stone: a submerged national foundation, covered with the residue of time and forgetfulness, waiting for rediscovery.

Already there are strong signs of a railroad revival. Thanks to high gasoline prices and the inconvenience of air travel, that old lumbering dowager Amtrak is enjoying some of its most profitable years in a generation, and state legislatures are demonstrating a willingness to reinvest in dormant train corridors. Cape Cod in Massachusetts is now seeing its first rail service since 1995, and plans are being made to extend new lines to places like New Bedford and Springfield in hopes of triggering a real-estate boom. The state of New Mexico built a commuter train from Albuquerque to Santa Fe that sees nearly a million one-way passengers a year, and Amtrak's *Hiawatha Express* from Chicago to Milwaukee now runs full seven times a day. The Obama administration committed $8 billion to fund a new generation of high-speed trains, and California has already started construction on a line that will whisk passengers from L.A. to the Bay Area in just 160 minutes. If the train is an artery into the past, it is also a route into the future, especially in a world of shaky oil politics and potential climate change. There may be no more exciting time to be railroading than today.

I wanted an up-close view of this underappreciated marvel, and I could think of no better means of getting one than by boarding trains across the world—especially the long-distance ones—and talking to fellow passengers all along the way. I wanted to see the flickering landscape through their eyes, to understand how the world's rails continue to exert a formative influence on how people live and how our cities, economies and mentalities still bear the watermark of the first real "machine" unleashed on humanity. Each of these journeys had something important to say about the past and future of railroads; each was a physical road that led to the heart of an idea.

I began by riding a series of trains all the way across Britain, the birthplace of the steam engine, and I chose to do what is still possible there in this motherland of railroads: to travel from tip to tip by train, from the northern shores of Scotland to the southwestern corner at a spot in Cornwall called Land's End.

Then I went to India to see the inner workings of the state railway company, an astonishingly vast enterprise that stands as the eighth-largest employer of humans on the globe. I went out with track-repair crews, almost wandered into the path of a stray locomotive and rode with pilgrims and myriad other souls on an express from the capital at New Delhi to Hinduism's holiest city at Varanasi.

In America I stepped on in New York and stepped off in Los Angeles, following the routes of the long-vanished carriers that built up a younger country. There is a movable mini-city of people who go to sleep every night on American trains—an invisible shadow country—and their late-night conversations in the club car are like echoes of an old national exchange. We think of railroads as if they were a Disneyland exhibit (in fact, the famous theme park was almost completely inspired by a train—more on that later), yet they are anything but a nostalgic toy. A culture of tremendous vitality and wealth lies within the American train, waiting to be unlocked.

I went to Russia to experience the immense tedium—mingled with danger—of the Trans-Siberian Railway, a project of Czar Alexander III that cemented the nation's status as a two-continent power and sent millions to the prison gulags of the country's far east. I never did get to finish this journey because of a stupid and unexpected wound incurred halfway through, but even that incident felt in step with the violent history of this train, as well as the darker side of railroading in general.

In China I rode the bullet trains that will cost the quasi-Communist government up to $400 billion in an all-out effort to make their nation the leading transportation power of the world, which poses a formidable challenge to the United States. I also became a passenger on the staggering line up to the heights of the Tibetan plateau, the highest railway in the world. Surveyors called it impossible. The Dalai Lama considers it a tool of cultural genocide. And it has effectively killed the dream of Tibetan independence.

The journey next led to Peru, to the prow of a locomotive on the *second*-highest railroad in the world—a corkscrewing path through the Andes that had been the brainchild of a charming con artist who nearly brought this South American country to bankruptcy. A burst of new capital has made it the latest of the old freight roads being reinvigorated across the world to accommodate a new economy dependent on physical logistics.

The book concludes in Spain, where an audacious gamble on a system of high-speed trains has changed the way an entire nation travels and helped inspire a similar gambit in the United States, one whose outcome is still uncertain.

Writing about the railroad has seemed at times like a pursuit from Herodotus: that capturing the true historical and contemporary impact of the railroad is to risk writing about the entire modern world and everything inside it. No one book on this subject will ever carry the authority of an encyclopedia, and I have had to mercilessly limit my scope. Paul Theroux once wrote that every country's railroad functions as a rolling metaphor for that country, and it was mightily tempting to ride as many trains in as many places as I could, but time, money and space limited me to seven of the most important. The building of the transcontinental railroad in the United States has received exhaustive scrutiny elsewhere, and I chose to mention it only as a matter of context. City subways and trolleys descended from the same common ancestor, but they occupy an entirely different ecosystem and deserve books of their own. The result is a narrative history–cum–travelogue—and not anything that should be mistaken for comprehensive treatment. And there certainly will be even more to be said about railroads in the coming years.

This series of journeys may have been inspired by that nameless woman in a Pennsylvania snowstorm, but it also happens to touch a recollection from childhood. Many intellectual questions can be reduced to a sensory element if you look hard enough, and my interest in the train is rooted in a sound as much as a sight.

I can recall being taken to see my grandmother in the small town of Frankfort, Kansas, and being laid to sleep in an upper room of a white house with tall elms outside, a place far removed from where I had grown up in the throwaway strip-malled fringes of Tucson, Arizona, where cars were the only game in town. Frankfort was one of thousands of American towns that owed their existence to the railroad, having been created as a watering stop on the prairies nearly overnight in 1867 by the executives of a start-up called the Central Branch.

The curtains swayed in the open window, and it was raining outside. From the tracks of what was now the Union Pacific five blocks away came the horn of a coal train heading through town, past the grain elevator, past the one bar with its lighted beer sign, past the lumberyard and over the iron trestle that crossed the river and away out into the fields still trailing that one lonely note, which seemed to me one of the most beautiful and mysterious sounds I'd ever heard, the lowing call of another world of the already-past that came back to me when I saw a woman crying quietly in her book during a snowstorm and which I still feel today when I hear the sound through windows at night.

TRAIN

BEGINNINGS

Pentland Firth to Land's End

The village of Thurso on the northern coast of Scotland has had a train station since 1874, the day when the tracks arrived here near the shore of the North Sea and could go no farther, and the scene at the stone depot at the end of town has been more or less ageless ever since. A time traveler from that year would find almost nothing foreign here today, except perhaps for the plastic chairs in the waiting room and the padlocked bathrooms out on the platforms.

Thurso looked to me like an Alaskan fishing village: there was a squat Anglican church also made of stone, a village green the size of a shuffle-board court, a hotel that sold single-malt scotch for three pounds a glass, a few chip shops, a dock for cod boats, a shingle of beach shaped like a scythe blade. This outpost on the edge of Pentland Firth is the topmost point in the British rail system, same as it was during the reign of Queen Victoria, and still lonely enough that a stranger waiting here under the wooden shed in the first light of the morning is considered an unusual sight.

"Your first time here?" a younger woman asked me, and I acknowledged that it was.

"Oh, you're going to like this train," she told me. "The toilets often freeze over this time of year."

"Just cross your legs and you'll be fine," a middle-aged man next to her suggested.

"I've been stranded on this line before," said the woman. She had a ponytail and a slightly upturned nose. "Snow blew over on the tracks, and we stalled out. They had to rescue us with a snowmobile. But I don't think it's going to snow today."

The temperature was a few degrees above freezing, but I was grateful for the first rays of sunlight shining on the platform. I had spent part of the early-morning darkness trespassing on a lonely tip of grass called Dunnet Head—the northernmost point on the British mainland—and now was heading for Land's End, 595 miles to the south, which was the southwesterly tip of the island. I wanted to cover as much of Britain as possible on the rails. And truly, any logical assessment of the railroad must start in Britain, where the train was invented in fits and starts by several restless and talented people at the beginning of the nineteenth century who all happened to be working on the same problem—namely, *how can we keep water from seeping into our mine shafts?* Out of this nuisance came a brilliant accident: a new coal-fired vehicle of astonishing power that would kick-start the industrial revolution and change almost every aspect of modern living.

The British were the champion railroad builders of the nineteenth century, shipping their locomotives and steel rails all over the globe and especially to the places where they thought it could make them money or win their wars. They built trains to miserable sugar plantations in Jamaica, sweltering rubber farms in Malaysia, lonely cattle stations in Australia. British rail surveyors opened vast wheat fields in Canada. The queen's hardy subjects unified her domains in India with railroad rivets, fought the Crimean War with jerry-built tracks to the front and domi-nated eastern Africa with a ridiculous imperial railway from the Indian Ocean into Uganda, a line known as the "Iron Snake" or the "Lunatic Express," which killed twenty-four hundred African laborers and Indian coolies shipped over to a jungle teeming with mud, disease and maraud-ing lions. "If a Briton wished to swagger—and at times this duty is incumbent upon him—he might challenge the world to match our achievements in this line," bragged Rudyard Kipling.

Britannia may have ruled the waves, but it was also master of the timetable. And while today's rail system back at home in the United Kingdom—a shrunken version of what it used to be—might no longer be the subject of swaggering, the train still plays a life-giving role in forgotten villages like Thurso. The train is a diorama for what Britain used to be, and what it still may become.

The 8:41 train pulled up precisely on time, and it was not an auspicious entrance. The Far North Line was just two cars long: a "diesel mobile unit," or DMU, powered by a petroleum engine that sounds like a lawn mower. These are not elegant vehicles. But they are nevertheless the standard workhorses of the British rail system, especially on the rural routes. Conductors nicknamed them "flying bricks" when they were introduced in the 1950s. The end of the front carriage is a cockpit for the driver, about the size of an outhouse. There are but two controls: a throttle and a brake. In the carriages there are twin rows of bucket seats sheathed in purple upholstery and an overhead luggage rack that looks barely large enough to take a handbag.

About a dozen morning passengers shuffled into the frigid cars and soon we were off into the grasslands, Thurso retreating behind us.

The northern reaches of Scotland are expansive and bleak; they reminded me of Arctic prairies. The only real mountain I saw was a single high lump with a pooling of clouds at its summit that looked like a hat. Speckled here and there were puddles in the grass, and the woman who had earlier warned me about the freezing toilets now gestured out at the damp plain.

"See that?" she asked me. "That's a proper peat bog."

She said her name was Dani, and she worked as a warden at a nature reserve. Part of her job was getting rid of the nonnative trees that sucked water from the ground and turned the fragile peat to dust. And every tree out here in this part of Scotland was an invited guest.

"The government encouraged people out here to plant them to make better use of a barren land," she said. "And it's been a disaster." Some of the poorer locals still harvested the peat in tufts to burn in their stoves when they couldn't afford electric heat, but there wasn't much of it to go around.

I wanted to talk to her longer, but she had to get off at Forsinard. The train wound through more peat bogs and then started to follow the course of the river Thurso* through a valley that the conductor told me had been the scene of a minor gold rush fifty years before. And before that, it was the 1871 route surveyed by the old Sutherland and Caithness Railway, whose original path we were following today through the far north. I paced the length of the train and back, stretching my legs for the journey. WE LOVE OUR BABY BUMPS, said a headline propped in front of somebody's face. The papers that month were obsessed with the pregnancy of the Duchess of Cambridge.

Sprawled in a window seat across the aisle was a fortyish man with a buzz cut and an earring. His hands were stuffed into his pockets, and he looked miserable. I decided to talk to him anyway. Ray was a martial-arts instructor who was traveling to Inverness, four hours away.

"I like this train," he said. "Except it's effing *freezing* in here!" This comment was aimed at a passing conductor, who smiled and muttered vaguely about repairs coming next week.

Ray was ethnically Irish but living on the northern shore of Scotland in his ex-wife's hometown, mainly due to the kids. He was out of the house today to pick up a four-wheel-drive Jeep that was for sale on the Internet; it was decrepit and shabby-looking, but it would get him through the winter. After he relaxed a bit in my presence, he told me a uniquely Irish story about a death in the family.

Six days before Ray was to be married, his father was run over and

---

* The name is derivative of the Norse god Thor. Vikings had used this part of Scotland as a raiding base.

killed by a nun on an errand. The nun, of course, was horrified, and Ray, of course, was devastated. But forgiveness was a part of his vocabulary even though he wasn't a practicing Catholic. At the funeral he went up to her and said, "Hey, accidents happen." Then he went to embrace her, and she went stiff as a flagstone. "I don't think she had ever been touched by a man. She didn't know what to do. I thought she'd explode. Then I had an evil thought: maybe I should have given her butt a little squeeze."

"Did you?"

"No. I just now thought of it. It is kind of an evil thought." His eyes wrinkled at the corners as he giggled.

The train passed a field of frost-covered grass and a few hillocks where fat-butted sheep were grazing. Some of the ewes bore purple lines on their backs. This was a marker to tell the farmer when to expect lambs; the rams all wore leather harnesses around their bellies affixed with thick stubs of chalk, and every time one mounted a ewe, he left a trail of purple.

We were creeping past a stand of lichen-coated trees—the apparent scourge of the Scottish grasslands—when a text came beeping in for Ray. It was from the guy who was selling him the four-wheel drive: *the roads are treacherous*. And he didn't feel safe driving to Inverness.

Ray's face went pink, then darkened. The whole trip had been a waste, and it was barely sprinkling outside. "*Treacherous?*" he fumed. "What does that mean?"

He spent the next twenty minutes staring out the window and sighing loudly, and I let him be, looking at tufts of red-colored weeds choking the valleys of frigid creeks and then onto a plain dotted with pine trees and the wreck of a stone castle, a physical remnant of the people here who had struggled to raise barley against the rain and who were now a part of the soil. One particular hill covered in bleak grass stood poised against the gray clouds in a way that made my heart leap a little; a seeming infinity of space lay behind the hill and the sky. At Lairg there was a stone cottage, a row of Quonset huts, a few oil tanks and a warning sign: NO MATCH, NO FLAME.

Ray eventually perked back up, and we spent the last twenty minutes to Inverness talking about the perils of buying cars, watching the scrap-metal yards and oil docks go by. He had decided to make the best of the squandered journey and do some Christmas shopping at the mall, which was the only one operating in the Scottish Highlands. We crossed the river Ness and scooted under the canopy of the train shed. And then we shook hands and said good-bye. I hoped he would eventually get his Jeep.

On the afternoon train to the oil-soaked harbor of Aberdeen, I sat across from the retired headmaster of a school for special-needs children. She had a helmet of white hair and earrings in the shape of a sheriff's badge. "I suppose you've seen how good our country's railways are?" she asked me. "I'm speaking sarcastically, of course. The delays are unconscionable."

We passed duplex cottages with tiny yards, and as we got closer to the city, a glassy British Petroleum tower and a series of Georgian town houses with their chimney flues marshaled tight, as neat as cigarette packs. The next train out of Aberdeen wasn't for an hour, and I stepped outside to look at the ships in the harbor. To get there I had to pass through a shopping mall that smelled of pizza and cinnamon. The jewelry stores were doing a fine pre-holiday business among the petro-rich. There was a hill covered with official medieval buildings of lead-colored granite, and in a clearing was a thirteenth-century stone cross a few paces away from a set of hideous Harold Macmillan–era council flats and a plaque on the wall marking the place where the city gate once stood. It has been locked, said the sign, IN TIMES OF PLAGUE, PESTILENCE AND PERIL. I checked the time and had to run back to the station, darting between rush-hour traffic

I made the Edinburgh train with one minute to spare and found myself sitting across a table from an attractive brown-haired woman wearing a business-casual sweater and shiny black shoes. She was holding a thick binder of what I came to learn were tax documents. This train was stuffed with people who looked like fresh escapees from a cubicle farm; this was primarily a business commuter route. As we crawled out of Aberdeen, the descending sun made burnt-orange patterns on the rooftops.

"You're coming from work?" I asked the woman across the table.

"The start of a new job, actually. We were just at a training session." After a few years on the queen's payroll as a revenue official, she had become a consultant advising companies how to pay as little tax as possible.

"The revolving door," I said.

"Indeed. A long tradition here."

The trip was long, and the twilight had disappeared into full night, and she spent the rest of the journey telling me about her life: how she had read literature and French at St. Andrews and not really mixed with the posh class (she missed Prince William by a year), then worked for the EU in Belgium for a while but disliked its politics. She asked thoughtful and bemused questions about what I did for a living and what I hoped to find in Britain.

I liked the way she laughed and her soft accent, and I thought of what it had been like to be twenty-five in a suit-and-tie job and feeling simultaneously pleased with the grown-up accessories and yet feeling vaguely like an impostor. She dropped a studiously casual reference to a boyfriend—lucky man, I thought—deep into the conversation as we were approaching Edinburgh, and it might have depressed me in another context, but this was the train, which has its own set of mingled desires and cruelties. The limited journey, the purring rhythm of the rails, the intimate anonymity, the pulling power of an unseen locomotive have always given rail carriages an atmosphere of flirtation. Victorian pulp literature, especially the underground variety, was obsessed with the railroad and the possibilities it offered for assignations and stolen kisses; the moving parlors of the coaches were an escape from the routines of ordinary life. The 1945 movie *Brief Encounter* depicts a doomed three-week unconsummated affair between a married doctor and a suburban housewife who have a chance meeting in a railway depot. But the rushing of steam locomotives in different directions functions not just as a symbol of unbound libido but also of frustrated yearning. To be sharing a train with a charming stranger is to be set free for a short time but also to be enchained by the realities of what lies outside the timetables.

Which came all too soon. We trundled over the Firth of Forth on the graceful curve of the Tay Bridge—a replacement for one that had collapsed under the weight of a train in a wretched 1879 disaster—and then passed the runway lights of Edinburgh Airport and luminescent cones of security light outside the air-cargo warehouses. The hillsides were terraced with firefly winks that each signaled a comfortable town house and a family within. The tax girl lived in a neighborhood close to the Haymarket station but rode with me all the way into the main Waverley station. I had an impulse to ask her to dinner and miss the next train to Newcastle. But she had a boyfriend. And who knew what she was thinking, if anything, about this random traveler across from her? So I kept it to myself.

The tracks passed underneath the volcanic plug that was the base of the Edinburgh Castle, a multilayered fortress built there to repel invaders in the twelfth century. Suspected witches used to be dunked into the loch below the castle, and it became a reeking garbage pit, but it had been drained in 1759 to accommodate a public garden and then a row of railroad tracks eighty years later. The tracks seemed to snap perfectly within the valley, as though Scotland had been waiting for them to appear all along. The occasional loose chunk of lava still tumbles down from the castle heights, and the railway has had to mount netting to keep the rocks from hitting the trains.

"My dad always used to have a joke," she told me. " 'Why would they build a castle like that next to a railroad track?' "

"Nice one."

We collected our bags and walked out under the roof of Waverley station, which looked like a greenhouse. There were hundreds of plate-glass triangles overhead.

"Good luck with the tax man."

"Thanks. Good luck crossing Britain." After the banalities a smile that lasted a few seconds longer than it should have. And then she was gone. *Maybe in another time, another life*, I thought lamely, and silently wished her well. Then I went over to the next platform to board the Newcastle train.

Out of Scotland then and into England and into the dark Northumbrian countryside; past Berwick-upon-Tweed, Alnmouth and Morpeth; toward the river Tyne and into the coal-bearing regions that had blackened British skies for six hundred years. It was this coal, in fact, that made the railroad possible.

Early Victorian writers who didn't quite know what to make of the snuffing, chuffing, fire-eating locomotives they saw often reached for satanic imagery. One of them was the historian Thomas Carlyle, who never forgot his first rail journey. "To whirl through the confused darkness, on those steam wings, was one of the strongest experiences I have experienced," he wrote. "Out of one vehicle into another, snorting, roaring we flew: the likest thing to a Faust's flight on the Devil's mantle."

These metaphors were dramatic, but they were correct in naming the railroad as an essentially chthonic machine, born underground. The primary fuel for its engine, the most important cargo, its entire economic reason for being—all of these critical elements were a direct result of the velvety rock that lay in shallow deposits under the soil of northern England.

Bizarre-looking plants covered the surface of the landmass that would eventually be known as Britain, which was then located somewhere near the equator. The steamy climate of the Paleozoic era of 360 million years ago created ideal growing conditions for a palmlike tree called the *Lepidodendron*, which had scaly bark and grew as high as a ten-story building. Its leaves were typically the length of a tennis racket.

When it fell into the swamp and died, as they all did, it disintegrated with other plants into a spongy mass of decaying pulp that was attacked by bacteria like micrococcus and streptococcus and transmuted eventually into oxides of carbon, pressed into ebony bands. The temperature and time required to make coal is remarkably feeble by geological standards. According to some estimates, two hundred degrees and thirty years is all it takes to start the transformation from dead vegetation to fuel.

These black folds would lie there until peasants around the mouth of the river Tyne in northern England in the twelfth century noticed that the strange ebony rocks made an uncommonly good substitute for wood. As the easy surface deposits of coal disappeared, the people of Scotland and northeast England sank shafts to tap new veins. The work was supervised mainly by priests of the Roman Catholic Church, which owned most of the land. A team of diggers known as hewers would shovel away the turf and then pickax a hole in the shape of a square, which would be broadened into an octagon if the seam proved rich.

A coal mine in the sixteenth century was a dizzying series of slopes and passages, with wooden planks covering surprise drop-offs. Tunnels called "drifts" could zigzag in multiple directions. Visibility was limited to what could be seen by the weak glow of a candle, and workers had to learn to half swing their picks while crouched in a flickering crawl space less than four feet high. Women were often employed to tote the coal up to the surface in baskets that could weigh as much as 170 pounds; this journey was repeated possibly two dozen times a day.

Children suffered most. They were customarily taken into the pits at the age of eight, often clinging to their fathers' backs and made to pull coal carts out of the grim maze of drifts. The child thus became the "locomotive" in a primitive type of railroad.

"Chained, belted, harnessed like dogs," was how an angry parliamentary commission described colliery children in 1842, "saturated with wet and more than half-naked—crawling on their hands and feet and dragging their heavy loads behind them." The vision was "disgusting and unnatural" to the author. The typical punishment for perceived laziness was a "purring," which meant being kicked in the ribs.

The air in London grew thick and nasty as coal's popularity increased, and the central part of the city became a smoke-choked rookery of breweries, dye houses and lime burners, all of which had come to depend upon a healthy stream of Newcastle coal to keep their cauldrons flaming. But the hazards of breathing the aboveground smoke were nothing compared to the air quality inside the mine shafts. The labyrinths underground were roosts for all varieties of deadly gases, of which the most feared was called "firedamp." Coal is perpetually emitting a low level of flammable methane gas, sometimes called "marsh gas," which is harmless in small quantities and blows away in the open air. But the new caverns became traps for these invisible fumes that built and built until the moment they touched a candlewick. Small explosions of firedamp could scar a face; larger ones could snuff out hundreds of lives.

Sometimes a brave employee—known as a "fireman" and justly paid fivefold wages—would walk halfway down a suspect corridor and dig a grave-shaped trench with a pick. He would then lie in the hole, pull a wooden board over himself, shove a lighted candle through the front crack and hope for the best. Another delicate test was to raise a candle to the ceiling ever so slowly, until the top of the flame danced a telltale blue, known as "the ghost." The candle was then quickly pulled away and snuffed out.

The average life span of a miner was hard to calculate, but in that profession forty was considered old and seeing sixty was almost unknown. "Toiling underground was made even more hellish by the miners' dread that the inexplicable disasters that plagued them were due to demons and goblins haunting the mines," wrote the historian Barbara Freese. "It could not have helped that the mines were filled with eerie signs of past life—like the perfect imprint of a fern deep below the surface—that defied everything the miners believed about the history of the world." The itinerant Anglican preacher John Wesley found some of his most eager converts in the unhealthy demimonde around Newcastle in the eighteenth century. Fires burned for years in some of the galleries, and the snow melted in strange patterns up above. The editors of the *Newcastle Journal* sarcastically told their readers in 1767 that coal-mine disasters were becoming routine, "yet, as we are requested to take no particular notice of these things, which, in fact, could have very little good tendency, we drop the further mentioning of it."

One peril that mine owners *did* happen to take seriously was flooding. Some of the bigger mines had punched nearly one thousand feet below the surface, far underneath the aquifer, and so the walls themselves were bleeding water, to add to the torrents that came during the rains and invaded every twist of the honeycombing passages. Bucketing the water out of these rooms was a task even more despairing than hauling coal, because the water had no end.

This cursed water also came loaded with an intrinsic trick, familiar to anyone with a teakettle. When it boils, it transforms into a gas and balloons to several times its prior mass as liquid. A powerful spasm of energy results: not just from the freakish blossoming of the steam but also the sucking power of the empty space that it leaves behind. As the saying goes, nature abhors a vacuum. But in order for steam to do any effective work, it had to be imprisoned inside a tight chamber. Otherwise it just melted away into the air.

Among the first to grasp the idea was Denis Papin, a Protestant who had been chased out of Catholic France. He published a 1675 article with the name "A New Method of Obtaining Very Great Moving Powers at Small Cost" and dropped hints* that he was working on "a little

---

* He said this in a letter to his onetime laboratory colleague Gottfried Liebniz, the metaphysical philosopher who would become famous for his cheerful formulation that this earth was the best of all possible worlds.

model of a carriage." But he could not find a strong enough metal to keep steam from leaking away. The model was apparently lost.

The next man to pick up the idea was an energetic self-promoter named Thomas Savery, who borrowed from Papin's drawings and marketed his own water-pumping device he called the Miner's Friend. "Though I was obliged to encounter the oddest and almost insuperable difficulties, I spared neither time, pains, nor money until I had absolutely conquered them," he bragged. This was economical with the truth. The Miner's Friend was notoriously fickle, breaking down as often as it worked because its joints literally melted in the coal fires that it took to heat it. And only the most opulent mines could afford it because it gobbled up so much fuel.

A competitor named Thomas Newcomen made a much better model in 1699 by injecting cold water inside the cylinder to dissipate the steam, and these engines became the gold standard of water removal for six decades. But then came the moment when a Scottish technician named James Watt took a walk around downtown Glasgow on a Sunday in May 1765, a year after he had been assigned to repair one of Newcomen's engines. He reflected on how too much of the energy was leaking away as the cylinder was being reheated. "I was thinking upon the engine at the time," Watt recalled later, "and had gone as far as the Herd's house when the idea came into my mind, that as steam was an elastic body, it would rush into a vacuum, and if a connection were made between the cylinder and an exhausted vessel, it would rush into it. . . . I had not walked further than the Golf house when the whole thing was arranged in my mind."

As soon as the Sabbath was over, Watt threw together a model of an engine with a separate condensing chamber, jerry-rigged with a thimble from the sewing basket of his wife, Margaret. It worked. Watt moved to Birmingham and formed a partnership with the entrepreneur Matthew Boulton, whose iron shop, at a place called Soho, was a premier skunk works of its day. They sold engines all over Britain, and especially in the mining regions.

Watt later said (prefiguring Henry Ford) that he tried to make his engines "cheap as well as good," foreseeing a demand from cotton mills, which could now turn their spindles with something other than a river.

James Watt did not invent the steam engine per se. He had only made a slight modification to an idea that had been percolating in Western civilization for more than eighteen hundred years. The basic ingredients—fire, iron and water—had been in the hands of black-smiths for centuries, but it took the coal-drunk economy of seventeenth-century Britain to bring steam roaring into the world. "Nature can be conquered if we can but find her weak side," said Watt.

The train arrived at the Newcastle station just after 9:00 P.M., and I checked in to a backpackers' hotel before taking a night walk around the neoclassical streets, which were tangled and town-housed and full of statues. This city was like the Silicon Valley of the early nineteenth century, in what must have been an exhilarating time to be young and idealistic. A small group of brilliant men had been gathered with one of the great secrets of nature now at their disposal—namely, that the sudden expansion of vaporous water can tear down a mountain when used properly. And the best way to create steam was by burning coal, which was lying all over the river Tyne and its tributaries.

A 1787 map of the region shows a crazy-quilt pattern of rutted tracks leading from the coal mines to the Tyne. These were called wagonways, and some of them were simple dirt paths for the convenience of an endless procession of draft horses pulling wagons laden with coal chunks. The most efficient of them, however, were on wooden sets of rails. Teamsters had known for centuries that easing the friction between the cart wheels and the ground made the load go a lot smoother.

The flagstones of ancient cities in Greece and Egypt had been scarred with cart paths, worn deep by generations of laborers pushing wagons. These depressed "rails"—the antecedents of the railroad—were typically spaced about five feet apart, the width of the natural outstretch

of a man's arms when he was at labor, as well as the width of his livestock. One of the most ambitious of these early railways was the route
across the neck of land near Corinth in Greece, a route called the
Diolkos, where warships could be wheeled across tracks, saving their
captains a trip around the Peloponnese.

Late-medieval miners had also known that running a cart along a
smooth path was far easier than trying to push it over open turf. The
Bohemian physician Georgius Agricola worked in the silver camps near
St. Joachimsthal in the sixteenth century and described open carts
linked together with iron pins* to keep the procession steady. These
primitive trains made their way to England, where they were used only
by those aristocratic pit owners who could afford it.

One of the most heavily traveled of these cart paths ran alongside
the river Tyne, and a baby named George Stephenson was born alongside it on June 9, 1781. As the son of a mine fireman, he would sit
outside the house and watch the passing horses drag cars full of coal,
knowing it was his imminent fate to drag that coal himself. By fifteen
he was tinkering with James Watt's new engines and had taught himself to read by firelight, an act that would enchant many of his later
biographers.

In 1805 Stephenson met a brilliant but unstable inventor from Cornwall named Richard Trevithick, who had been conducting experiments
with high-pressure steam inside chambers so tight that they could kill a
man if they burst apart. These ventures were considered hazardous
enough that not even James Watt would touch them. The man from
Cornwall had recently mounted one on top of a wheeled carriage and
made it climb a hill at ten miles per hour. There is almost no documen-
tation of what was said at this meeting, but within a decade George

---

* These early railcars were known as *hundt*, or "dogs." The squeak of wood upon wood
  was apparently reminiscent of a bark. In St. Joachimsthal, they often hauled chunks
  of uranium oxide mingled with the silver; the resulting radiation poisoning that
  afflicted the miners was a mystery to everyone, including Agricola.

Stephenson was building the individual parts of a locomotive within a blacksmith's forge. Trevithick meanwhile was on his way into obscurity.

I took a commuter train down the river Tyne to see the cottage where George Stephenson had grown up. In the newspaper that morning was a brief little squib that noted the nineteenth anniversary of the closure of the very last operating coal mine in the region. The bulk of them had died when Prime Minister Margaret Thatcher broke the dominance of the National Union of Miners in a failed 1984 strike. She called the agitating miners "the enemy within," and the pits were sold off and closed in rapid succession. What happened? "Maggie shut them all!" a man had roared to me in a pub the previous night. It was hard for me to tell from his accent if he'd said "shut" or "shot," but the effect was the same: the British now import their power-plant coal from Russia, Indonesia and Colombia.

The 13:54 to Hexham was yet another set of boxy DMUs that sounded like lawn mowers. We sputtered over a bridge that crossed the river, and it afforded a fine view of Newcastle, which has undergone a Pittsburgh-like reinvention from a grimy industrial hive to a smart and fashionable city. But the suburbs still retain a joyless character, with militaristic rows of Georgian terraced houses marching up the valley slopes. They suggested a clock-ordered way of existence that must have colored the daily routines of all the families who had lived here and were fed by the engine and the wheel.

The village of Wylam has turned the old coal path down to the Stephenson cottage into a public walkway, and a few ladies were out walking their dogs along a lane fringed with birch and chestnut trees, their branches lightly frosted over. After a half mile, I came to a lone cottage that had been painted white and is managed as a tearoom by the National Trust. The house was locked up tight. There was a plaque on the side bearing Stephenson's name and a crude rendering of an engine. Beyond it was a hay field with patches of iced-over water trapped in its furrows. Children on a recess from a school up the hill shouted from far away.

I stood outside the garden gate for a few minutes, thinking about peering through a window, but then heard the gathering, rushing sound of a train. It was the 14:54 to Hexham coming through on the other side of the river. Coal has been a dead letter in George Stephenson's hometown for at least a quarter of a century, but the village has been remade into a commuter burg for young families with jobs in Newcastle. I stepped out to the edge of the Tyne—a perfect wintertime tableau of frosted trees and a placid river—to watch the DMUs rattle by on their hourly transit. From here they looked like a toy railroad running through an imagined landscape.

Stephenson's invention quickly became an indispensable part of British life, and just as quickly it brought about a great social embarrassment: people were suddenly forced to talk with strangers. The earliest train carriages were built like stagecoaches with benches facing one another, which might mean the horror of prolonged eye contact. The silences could be excruciating. And so the habit of reading a book while traveling—as an escape from boredom and awkwardness—led to a literacy explosion among the bourgeois classes as low-cost books became widely available within the railway stations.

A young man named W. H. Smith earned the license to sell newspapers and books along the Birmingham Railway and later opened a stall in London's Euston station; the chain now blankets the nation. In France, Louis Hachette copied Smith's success and opened a "railway library" in 1852. Romance novels, detective thrillers, travel essays, children's fables—all could be picked up for pennies in the fleeting minutes before departure. In 1936 a publishing executive named Allen Lane took a train to visit his superstar author Agatha Christie and became dismayed at the lowbrow selection in the station kiosk. Lane was convinced there was a market among train riders for quality fiction and prose, and he went on to found the publishing house Penguin in a church basement in London.

Reading while on the train is an enduring custom in Britain and throughout the world. In fact, that long-ago woman in the Pennsylvania snowstorm was reading when I first spotted her: a nameless woman absorbed in a nameless book. When they aren't nose-deep in their reading, British rail travelers typically put on their moodiest expressions, looking as though they've just received a baptism in vinegar. But I discovered they would brighten if I plopped down beside them with a map and looked confused. This is a nation not just of shopkeepers but of champion direction givers, which is how I started talking to a retired butcher named Bob MacKenzie. I asked him how to get to Stockton, and that was all it took.

"This is me day out," he said, slightly beaming. He patted the breast pocket of his leather jacket. Underneath it was a carefully knotted purple tie and a package of Christmas cards for his sister to mail. "Me brother-in-law will pick me up at the station."

Bob told me he had worked for thirty years in a Newcastle butcher shop, chopping up joints and steaks, "but I never was a slaughterman."

The DMUs were loud and clanky, but they were warm, and a proper lady next to me set her paper cup of tea down on the vented heater at our feet. The train passed over a baluster bridge above the Tyne and then into a region of low hills before settling onto a coastal shelf with an unobstructed view of the North Sea. Sailing ships full of Newcastle coal had once traveled down this coast before the railroad killed the business. The sea looked tranquil, though rain was brewing to the west.

I had fallen silent, and Bob started narrating the landscape in one- and two-word bursts to keep the conversation going. "New estates," he said as we passed by a construction crew putting up row houses. "Shallies," he said, pointing to a bunch of metal trailers down by the water. "Rain," he said, pointing to the clouds. "Rugby stadium." "Cows." "Dunes." "Ships." This was a railway he had been traveling for more than sixty years—he was born in Hartlepool—and he was happy to show it off for a visitor. "Picture show," he said, pointing to a cinema named Vue as we came close to the Hartlepool station. What turned out to be the last of the day's sunshine was filtering through a set of powerful-looking cranes on the docks.

"I must be leaving you now," he said, standing up and offering me his hand. I shook it and wished him a merry Christmas.

As soon as we departed Hartlepool for Middlesbrough, a strange fog settled in and the visibility dropped to about thirty feet. At the same time, it appeared as though a light snow had come in the night before and had failed to melt. The grass blades seemed coated in an angel-food topping, and the trackside trees grew indistinct, a J. R. R. Tolkien vision come to life. Sunlight seemed to come from everywhere and nowhere at the same time.

The DMU crawled through this eldritch scene for another half hour before alighting at Stockton, a depressed, coal-haunted town whose streets were mostly deserted and bereft of Christmas lights and where a pawnshop's poster urged the reader to USE THE TREASURES YOU OWN TO SECURE A HANDY CASH LOAN. But there was access here to the Wear River, which had once made it a vital coal port in the 1820s.

So vital, in fact, that it was chosen as the termination point for the world's first true railroad: the Stockton & Darlington, a brainchild of George Stephenson, who had convinced a local Quaker merchant named Edward Pease to invest his fortune not into a canal but in this untested new machine and the tracks that it required.

This had been an expensive proposition, which Stephenson never could have paid for himself. Ridges had to be blasted away, embankments had to be laid, an arched bridge had to be erected over the Skerne River, and—most challenging of all—the rail bed had to traverse a swamp known as Myers Flat Bog that seemed to devour all the dirt that Stephenson's laborers could shovel into it. A farmer named John Potts took great delight in taunting the crews: he told them fairies were eating the gravel at night and would come back in the day to eat the men themselves, and their relatives after them. In those days public-works projects required the approval of Parliament, and Pease had to use his political clout to silence the Duke of Cleveland, who feared losing his favorite fox-hunting fields.

Stephenson treated the opening day of September 27, 1825, as a gigantic social event with an extravagant luncheon at the end, and he invited every person of note within a hundred miles. Correspondents from the big newspapers had been persuaded to attend, and the man from the *Newcastle Courant* reported "an immense concourse of spectators" lined up to see the new device, with "the fields on each side of the railway being literally covered with ladies and gentlemen on horseback and pedestrians of all kinds." There were five wagons full of coal, another full of flour sacks, an open carriage for the surveyors, a bespangled coach named *Experiment Locomotion* with padded seats for the financiers, another fourteen cars for the workmen—who all stood—and six more coal cars bringing up the rear, each of them draped with flags and banners. Heading up this strange parade: a wheezing locomotive belching coal smoke and bearing a nameplate that read LOCOMOTION. Every railway* employee wore a blue sash over his right shoulder. The colored procession was accompanied by a man on horseback carrying a banner that proclaimed PERICULUM PRIVATUM UTILITAS PUBLICA, which meant "Private Risk for Public Benefit."

Mounting a steam engine on a track took more than just technical skill. The creator also had to find a suitably dramatic way to sell this strange-looking golem on wheels to the public. And that was the historical role played by George Stephenson, who was quickly lionized by journalists charmed by his up-from-coal-dust story and called him the "Father of the Railway," even though his contribution was more that of a promoter and a project manager than an actual inventor. "In science,"

---

* As local systems sprang up in Britain in the 1820s, journalists called them "railroads," but the popular term morphed within two decades to "railways," which is the preferred term in Britain today. The term "railroad" remains the vernacular in the United States.

noted Charles Darwin, "credit goes to the man who convinces the world, not the man to whom the idea first occurs."

The rail bed once traveled by the Stockton & Darlington is still used today—with almost no pomp whatsoever—as a dead-end branch for a set of hardy old DMUs run by Northern Rail. I had taken this line a few years before in the company of Richard Wimbury, a sixty-six-year-old former schoolteacher with a hawk nose and salted hair.

"Now, over there," said Wimbury, pointing out the window to a junction called Heighington, "is where they unloaded *Locomotion*. They took her down from Newcastle on a horse and cart." I could see nothing but a lonely pub, a line of trees and a crossing bar dutifully bowed over a lane. But this was holy ground indeed: the spot where the first locomotive on a scheduled railway had been fired into life. *Locomotion* was a strange-looking, elephantine device on wheels, and there was a minor problem getting the coal aflame that day.

An elderly laborer named Robert Metcalf, who sometimes used a magnifying glass to light his pipe on sunny days, came forward and trained the sun's beam on the kindling, called oakum. Metcalf later wrote down his recollections without punctuation.

"I took me pipe glass and let me pipe I thought to myself I would try to put fire to Jimmy oakum it blaze away well the fire going rapidly lantern and candle was to no use so No. 1 fire was put to her by the pour of the sun." Kindled by the sun's rays, a curl of smoke rose and grew from the coal pile; the chamber warmed, the fire spreading; water bubbled in the iron belly, rose to full boil, and steam gathered in the top dome. *Locomotion* began to sputter and hiss.

Some of those who came to watch had cowered at the sight of the machine puffing with what might have seemed agony and menace, as if its keg-shaped belly were about to rupture. Travel by a machine was an entirely new idea in the human consciousness in 1825, and it seems that many of those watching the first run of the Stockton & Darlington could not quite fathom what they were seeing. The engine might as well have been a creature from another planet. It chugged over the Skerne River on a huge stone bridge with white Romanesque arches, and the smoke pouring out of the stack came laced with embers that fell into the crowd and burned little holes in some of the women's parasols.

"Those people must have wondered what those locomotives bellowing steam were going to do," Wimbury said. "There was a sense that people were not *meant* to go faster than horses. Fire and steam were seen as destructive. And yet, steam locomotives had all the aura and frisson of atomic power or the space shuttle." Our velocity on this poorly used branch was somewhere near twenty-five miles per hour, which was not very much faster than the top velocity of *Locomotion.*

Wimbury wore black-framed glasses perched on that aquiline nose and was chatty and enthusiastic about the importance of the Stockton & Darlington, even if others in town were not as concerned, and he viewed this indifference with bemused exasperation. He drew a detailed map in my notebook, complete with numbered legend, showing me how I could find the house where George Stephenson first hatched the plan with his great Quaker benefactor Edward Pease. *"Now pizza take-aways!!"* he scrawled indignantly in the margins.

When the conductor that morning had come by to collect our fare, Wimbury asked him if he knew the significance of the short line we were traveling.

"I can't say I've thought of it much, really," the conductor replied. "Five pound fifteen, please." Wimbury drew his lips tight and shook his head.

I rode the line back to Darlington and walked back through the core of the old Quaker merchant town, which had been the victim of a bad concrete makeover. At the height of the railway age in the late nineteenth century, this had been a hub for the construction of locomotives, iron bridges, rails and, of course, the mining of coal to power it all. But that economy was gone. A former Lutheran church near the main rail station is covered with signs that advertise an appliance dealership called Bathroom World; toilets are now sold where worshippers used to kneel. And sure enough, when I went to visit the decrepit old row house where Edward Pease used to live, there was a brightly lit joint called Best Kebab at street level. The upstairs windows disclosed a room full of junk, a refrigerator tipped on its side.

The 16:56 to York was punctual and sleek: a high-speed electric train manufactured by a French multinational company named Alstom that zipped away through the darkened fields at the speed of 110 miles an hour. I found a seat near an older man in a green sweater nodding off in front of a book of crossword puzzles. Across the aisle a beautiful young woman in a stylish coat and high boots was texting a message: . . . AND THEN I WILL BE HOOOOOOME. A light rain had begun to fall. At York the floors were slick with it, and the staff had put out signs warning people not to slip.

This was one of the most graceful railway stations in England, the tracks curving past the platforms and out of sight at a pleasing elliptical sweep. The structure had been bombed into smithereens by the Luftwaffe on April 29, 1942—Hitler had used a Baedecker railway travel guide to pick his targets and chose York because it earned more than three stars as a cultural site. The British rebuilt the station completely after the war. Inside the foyer were a group of eight well-dressed and shivering children singing "O Come, All Ye Faithful." A man ringing a bell next to a pot explained that they were raising money for a local charity. "Yes, we'll sub these kids out for another choir here in a few minutes," he said.

The next day I went to keep an appointment with a man named Jonathan Tyler. His office was on the top floor of a sixteenth-century building with a staircase kinked at odd angles from hundreds of years of water damage but with a dazzling skylight view of the York Minster cathedral spires. The screen saver on his computer is a photo of the Ribblehead Viaduct, a colossal train bridge of stone arches across the Yorkshire Dales. He proposed to his wife under the twenty-fourth arch.

Tyler is a nattily dressed man with a white beard and the slight air of an elf. He now works as a highly paid transportation consultant, but he got his start at British Rail in the early 1960s, working as a junior economist under a director who would come to be called "the most hated man in Britain" and the personification of all that was heartless and wrongheaded with the modern railroads.

This man was Richard Beeching, a former metallurgist who produced a 1963 fiat called *The Reshaping of British Railways*, which concentrated traffic into four major trunk lines emanating from London like bicycle spokes. At the same time, it eliminated half of the passenger network and shuttered about four thousand country depots. Within the decade peaceful little crofts with names like Chilsworthy, Wadebridge, Nanstallion and Bridestone lost their trains forever, along with Sandplace, Downton, Templecombe, Whimple, Fishponds and Pill.

A certain way of life seemed to disappear along with the trains. The mass amputation—which has since become known as the "Beeching Axe"—was resented by those who didn't own a car as well as those many Britons who simply loved trains for aesthetic reasons. "I suppose I'll always be looked on as the axeman," Beeching wrote later, "but it was surgery, not mad chopping."

Tyler also thinks history will view his old boss more kindly, as he was only bowing to economic reality. But he isn't so sure about this current state of British rails, which he sees as the shabby residue of a great heritage.

"As you will have no doubt noticed, the franchise system is in total disarray," he said as we sat for coffee. "We've recently seen reports detailing unbelievable incompetence on the part of the Ministry of Transportation. In many ways we've got the best railway we've ever had, and it is being gutted at the same time."

Almost every problem is rooted, said Tyler, in a decision made for free-market ideological reasons in 1993 in the last days of the premiership of John Major.* The railroads had been state property since the end of World War II and were run by a doddering national corporation called British Rail, which was perceived as a prime candidate for a sale. The government kept ownership of the tracks but let companies bid for the rights to run regional monopolies. "It was a scheme," wrote journalist Andrew Murray, "only a lawyer could love." The Labour Party protested the deal but did nothing to reverse it when they won power under Tony Blair the following year.

More than twenty companies now have their own piece of the British mainland—with one giant called FirstGroup as the king among them—but without a coordinated vision and with taxpayers funding most of the repair and improvements. Britain's rails are now routinely more expensive than plane flights, and government subsidies have doubled since the privatization, leaving many to wonder what was ever "private" about the idea.

"There is no sense of a national network anymore," said Tyler. "This diminishes the appeal to people who don't think of traveling by rail and whose mentality is that of the bus. The rail share of the market between the large cities is in the single digits. The focus on the marketing is 'Here's a cheap ticket, wouldn't you like to go to Edinburgh?' instead of a sustained campaign to make it an everyday experience."

And yet despite all this, he acknowledged, the railroads are still an important part of the British collective unconscious. "There's no doubt a majority of the population wants to keep it," he said. "They may complain about it. But they would never tolerate the abandonment of the rails." Britons will stomach the trouble as they always have, just as they muddled quite effectively through the Luftwaffe bombings and unemployment doldrums and cold water baths. "Mustn't grumble," goes the

---

* His predecessor as Tory prime minister, Margaret Thatcher, did not support privatizing the rails even though she had a personal distaste for train travel. Only once in her eleven years as prime minister did she ride on a train.

old saying, but that's a lie. Everyone whines here—quite professionally—but serious reform happens rarely. Communism never stood a chance here, as Bill Bryson has observed, because while the British have a genius for ridiculing those in authority, they never get outraged enough to mount a true revolt. Hitler thought he would have an easy surrender because Britain was a nation shot through with moldy class resentments, unhealthy boozing and economic inequality, but the people rallied for their island with Shakespearean ferocity. Deep in their sarcastic hearts, the British crave order and hierarchy. Maybe that's why they love railroad timetables so much.

After saying good-bye to Tyler and making my way down his crazily warped staircase, I went over to the York Minster to hear a Christmas concert. The nave was jammed with holiday tourists clutching shopping bags. I leaned my green backpack against a side wall and listened while a woman in front of me in a red sweater and duck boots got up and paced around near the transept as the uniformed band played and the choir sang "God Rest Ye Merry, Gentlemen." I was getting restless myself and envied her freedom of motion but didn't want to draw attention to myself.

About an hour later, I saw the same woman pacing back and forth on a platform at the York railway station. A balding man carrying some sort of musical case came up to her a few seconds later: it looked as though we were waiting for the same 21:23 train to Leeds.

I asked them if they had been at the concert, and they acknowledged that this was so. "My back hurts," she said, a little sheepishly. "I can't remain sitting for long."

Her husband's name was Simon, and he had been a trombonist in the band, and though he was an agnostic, he always found himself inside multiple churches in the winter due to the concert schedule. Agricultural fairs were the big thing in the summer. Simon was a music tutor who had mustered out of a career in the Royal Navy after managing to miss every British overseas conflict since the Falklands War. He lived with his wife, Philomena—she of the restless pacing—near the small town of Ganforth, twenty-six miles away, and always took the train because both hated to drive, especially in York's twisting medieval streets.

"Oh, this railway is going to rot, don't worry," said Simon as we settled into seats.

"Don't get him started," said Philomena.

"Too late already," he said. "If there's no leaves on the tracks, if there's no rain, no snow, no congestion, no landslides—oh, and if the driver's there and not late from the 13:45 from Peterborough or something daft like that—*then* maybe it'll be on time." He went on for a while before Philomena interrupted him.

"Isn't this the town with the funny name?" she asked, pointing out the windows.

"Lower Poppleton, yes." They both giggled. It was clear they had been married a long time.

"We'll be back to the old British Rail before long," Simon predicted as the two of them prepared to get off. "But even *they* didn't know how to run it."

I rode into Leeds and then Manchester by myself, the northern Midlands passing by in darkness. I could see brick walls and gunmetal rails shining under high lamps, but there were dead coal mines out in the hills, their drowned innards honeycombing several fathoms under the grass. The black fuel pulled out of them had built up the swarming cities with their looms and stamp presses and all the rails that connected them with the harbors.

This belt of England was a heartland of industrial misery in the nineteenth century because of the wonders of Watt's steam engine and Stephenson's railroad. Mark Twain once said he would like to live here because the difference between death and Manchester would be barely noticeable. The son of a sewing-thread manufacturer, Friedrich Engels was so dismayed by the "filth, ruin, and uninhabitableness" he saw here in the slums that he wrote a block-by-block survey called *The Condition of the Working Class in England* and later formed a long partnership with a journalist named Karl Marx.

Manchester is now the home of an enormously wealthy football team and a relentless party culture, as if today's residents were trying to absorb the pleasures denied those who came before, a penance of hedonistic duties—satanic wages exchanged for Dionysus's comforts.

I never saw the city in daylight because I stayed just twelve hours, and what I remember comes back to me in fragments: shadowy rectangles of former warehouses near the train station, a short alley called Mangle Street, water in the shipping quay that looked like obsidian sludge, fiftyish men dancing together in a huddle inside an Irish bar and chanting "We got soul, we got soul" to one another as if trying to be convincing, a woman in black patterned tights and a bandage dress standing on a corner and eating greasy chips from a Styrofoam box, a couple making out in a bar with the delicacy and tenderness of hummingbirds at a feeder, a smiling woman presenting herself in a bouncer-filled doorway with a *Please oh please*, a transvestite in a ball gown blowing me a kiss from an alley in the morning light as I went to catch the 7:47 to Liverpool inside the sleepy Picadilly station.

I told the woman behind the glass that I wanted to take "the middle route" through a place called Newton-le-Willows, and she answered through her microphone, "Now, why would you want to do that?" I just did, I told her, and she shrugged.

While it may have been the slower way, this was the local commuter route that exactly followed the path of the Liverpool & Manchester, which was the next railroad that George Stephenson and his son were contracted to build after the splash of the Stockton & Darlington. The L&M used a crude system of signaling that used colored disks and crossbars. Red warned of danger, green was for caution and white told the engineer it was safe to proceed. In time these would evolve into the familiar streetlight signals of red, yellow and green.

The vivacious actress Fanny Kemble had been invited up to the

engine by George Stephenson, who supplied her with running com-
mentary as they drove along the tracks a few days before the ceremonial
opening. In a letter to her friend Harriet St. Leger, she offers a vivid
account of what it felt like to ride an iron horse for the first time.

> You can't imagine how strange it seemed to be journeying on thus,
> without any visible cause of progress other than the magical
> machine, with its flying white breath and rhythmical, unvarying
> pace, between these rocky walls, which are already clothed with
> moss and ferns and grasses; and when I reflected that these great
> masses of stone had been cut asunder to allow our passage thus far
> below the surface of the earth, I felt as if no fairy tale was ever half
> so wonderful as what I saw. Bridges were thrown from side to side
> across the top of these cliffs, and the people looking down upon
> us from them seemed like pigmies standing in the sky. . . . You
> cannot conceive what that sensation of cutting the air was; the
> motion is as smooth as possible, too. I could either have read or
> written; and as it was, I stood up, and with my bonnet off "drank
> the air before me." . . . When I closed my eyes this sensation of
> flying was quite delightful, and strange beyond description; yet,
> strange as it was, I had a perfect sense of security, and not the
> slightest fear.

Kemble's sense of traveling ecstasy soon turned to the man who had
made it possible for her. The ancient link between vehicles and sex, at
this very moment, entered the modern age.

> Now for a word or two about the master of all these marvels, with
> whom I am most horribly in love. He is a man of from fifty to
> fifty-five years of age; his face is fine, though careworn, and bears
> an expression of deep thoughtfulness; his mode of explaining his
> ideas is peculiar and very original, striking, and forcible; and

although his accent indicates strongly his north-country birth, his language has not the slightest touch of vulgarity or coarseness. He has certainly turned my head.

The Duke of Wellington, however, was not enchanted—not with the bluff workingmen who were running the rails, nor with their invention. The railways initially struck him as "a premium to the lower classes to go uselessly wandering around the country." He personally disliked the coal smoke and the rocking motion inherent in rail travel. He was also an eyewitness to one of history's first fatal railroad accidents on the opening day of the Liverpool & Manchester, where, as the prime minister, he was a guest of honor. The bizarre accident happened right in front of him. An acquaintance from Parliament, William Huskisson, got out of his carriage during a stop and came over to talk with the duke. At that moment an engine—as it happened, the *Rocket* that had so delighted Fanny Kemble—rolled by on a side track and clipped his leg. "I have met my death. God forgive me!" yelled Huskisson. He bled to death later in the day.

Another disaster soon unfolded: the crowds at Manchester began to riot when the duke's train pulled in to the station. Though he was still remembered as the man who had humiliated Napoleon a quarter century before, he opposed voting rights for millworkers, which made him a hated figure in Manchester. Fanny Kemble reported that the crowd of "grim and grimy" protesters greeted the duke with "groans and hisses," and the slow-moving locomotive had to push them out of the way. The crowd then hurled bricks and vegetables at the duke's railcar and forced him to miss the refreshments served in the train shed. Newspapers from the United States and India gleefully reported the scene.

But the rails would soon have a far more important royal friend. The young Queen Victoria took her first trip in 1842, from Windsor to London, and, unlike the duke, was thrilled by the speed and the rocking of the carriages. "I am quite charmed by it," she confided in a letter to her uncle, King Leopold of Belgium. The royal family then bought an estate at Balmoral in Scotland, a distance that would have made horse travel unfeasible. Her periodic trips around the country in a procession of iron and steam—with scheduled visits in country towns—helped give the train the prestige it desperately needed to win over investors. Victoria became a real face to her subjects outside London: more than just a line in an anthem or a portrait on the wall.

The 1830 opening of the Liverpool & Manchester would be the event that inspired the first railway constructions in France and the United States. And it touched off a seven-year period of euphoric financial speculation known as "Railway Mania." Within twenty years there were more than six thousand miles of track in Britain, with urban tracks laid across one another at haphazard angles in the shape of diamonds. At least seventy entirely new towns sprang up as service centers for the iron horse, including a city called Middlesbrough that seemed to an observer "like some enchanted spectacle, some Arabian Nights' vision."

The 8:49 to Liverpool was—naturally—a half-full set of outdated DMUs, and it rumbled out of Manchester on schedule, through the part of town called Spinningfields, once a grimy wasteland of textile mills and now a semi-posh enclave of government and finance. Above it is Beetham Tower, which is a Hilton hotel on the bottom and a nest of condos on the top. We passed wire spools and oil tanks and paralleled the culvert of the M602 motorway before emerging into a rural horizon: wide downs flanked by birch trees and rugby fields with a light layer of mist over them. A dingy series of garden allotments with a lonely sniffing dog wandering around outside and no owner in sight. A few used diapers hung from tree limbs.

I tried to imagine what it might have been like for Fanny Kemble to ride shotgun with George Stephenson and see this same countryside from the prow of a chuffing locomotive, swaying along at what must have seemed the impossible speed of twenty-five miles an hour.

Just before we got to Kenyon Junction, the conductor told me to look out the window for the small and neglected memorial to Huskisson among the hedges, near the spot where he had been fatally clipped by the *Rocket*.

As we neared Liverpool's Lime Street station, we passed through a culvert with walls that appeared to rise up at least thirty feet, high enough to block out the sun. They were as smooth as Navajo sandstone. This had been bored out in 1836 and had been in continuous use ever since, the conductor told me. "All the more impressive," he said, "when you consider it was all done by Irish navvies working with wheelbarrows and picks." I couldn't place his accent and asked if he himself was Irish, but he gave me a disapproving look and told me he was a native of Liverpool.

He had been talking about the ragged class of nineteenth-century laborers, usually illiterate farmhands, known as "navvies"—hard-drinking and risk-taking men who were hired in gangs to smash the right-of-way in a direct line from station to station. Many of them had experienced digging canals and were known by the euphemism "navi-gators." They wore the diminutive "navvy" as a term of pride. Polite society shunned them, but these magnificent railways would have been impossible without their contributions of sweat and blood.

Their primary task was cleaving the hillsides so that tracks could be laid on a level plain for the weak locomotive engines of the day. Teams of navvies known as "butty gangs" blasted a route with gunpowder and then hauled the dirt out with the same kind of harness that so many children were then using in the coal mines: a man at the back of a full wheelbarrow would buckle a thick belt around his waist, then attach that to a rope dangling from the top of the slope and allow himself to be pulled up by a horse. This was how the Lime Street approach had been dug out, and it was dangerous. One 1827 fatality happened as "the poor fellow was in the act of undermining a heavy head of clay, fourteen or fifteen feet high, when the mass fell upon him and literally crushed his bowels out of his body," as a Liverpool paper told it.

The navvies wrecked old England along with themselves, erecting a bizarre new kingdom of tracks. In a passage from his 1848 novel *Dombey and Son*, Charles Dickens gives a snapshot of the scene outside London:

> Everywhere were bridges that led nowhere; thoroughfares that were wholly impassable; Babel towers of chimneys, wanting half their height; temporary wooden houses and enclosures, in the most unlikely situations; carcasses of ragged tenements, and fragments of unfinished walls and arches, and piles of scaffolding, and wildernesses of bricks, and giant forms of cranes, and tripods straddling above nothing. There were a hundred thousand shapes and substances of incompleteness, wildly mingled out of their places, upside down, burrowing in the earth, aspiring in the air, mouldering in the water and unintelligible as any dream.

Many drank whiskey during their shifts to offset the misery. In one incident three were killed in succession when they dared one another to leap over an open shaft and each failed in turn. But they took pride in their work and depended on one another. Nicknames were promiscuously bestowed: Mountainpecker, Fighting Jack, Cat's Meat, Gipsy Joe. The customary uniform was moleskin trousers, velveteen coat, a white felt hat with the brim turned up and hobnail boots. They demanded rations of two pounds of beef and a gallon of beer per day. Whenever they lived in one place for long, it was usually in a house built of sod bricks and usually with a rotating cast of girlfriends.

Their morals were alarming to the staid places into which they swarmed, and violence against locals was not uncommon. In Hereford in October of 1855, seven drunken navvies burst into a house on Bowsey Lane in "an indecent and uncivilized manner, pulled an unnamed girl out of bed and thrashed her with their fists, blackening her eye, scattering her teeth and swelling her jaw," noted the *Morning Chronicle* with the leering morality of the penny press. "Death terminated the woman's suffering at six o'clock," the paper also noted, low in the story.

Embarrassed by the bad behavior, the railways hired chaplains to rouse a sense of piety within the ranks, and some of these missionaries preached better than others. The Reverend William St. George Sargent, resident parson to the Lancaster and Carlisle, took a hostile view of his flock. "Their infidel opinions lead them to doubt the authority of the word of God and very often to deny the existence of a First Cause," he complained. Another pastor observed with despair that most of the workers believed that people had no souls and were only "machines of flesh and blood."

They must have seen a potent symbol in the strange-looking machine for which they were clearing the way, the "five-hundred-ton bolt" of the locomotive, as the journalist Stephen Crane called it. In the cab of such a fearsome vehicle, a man seemed almost an afterthought, a disposable gear. Drivers had to stand astride the keg of the boiler, blanketed by red heat rising from the firebox and peering out a narrow window into a haze of gas lamps and floating cinders. Trust had to be placed in the system rather than in one's own eyes.

I had barely four hours to wander around the Liverpool waterfront before getting on the express train to London. This was a Virgin Train operated by Richard Branson's company, and it had the pinched feel of an aircraft as well as modular blue lights in the vestibules that made it look like a lunar rover in a movie. It was also completely full. A bronze-haired woman with a small child asked me pointedly if I'd move my backpack out of the way for her, and I complied, sitting across from her as she began to read to her child from a book called *The Magic Porridge Pot.* We started rolling with the silence of a ghost—the train was electric—and we were soon making a graceful sweep around the southern edge of Liverpool Bay on a viaduct with numerous arches, the opening vista of the two-hour trip to London. The woman caught my eye and smiled at me.

"Home for the holidays?" I asked.

"We're going home. To London. We spent the day in Liverpool visiting my parents."

"This train is quick."

"Most certainly. It used to take four and a half hours. This is always a big trip for us."

A good many of the passengers had cleared out at John Lennon Airport, and the woman took her daughter—Marianne was her name—over to an empty seat where she could stretch out. A couple across the aisle broke out a lunch of oily chicken from Morrison's, and its stench quickly filled the compartment.

Across the table from me was a man with a delicate face reading a golf magazine. He told me he sold bathroom sets and was on his way south for a weekend conference. "I hate London traffic. That's why I'm on this train."

"Are you from anywhere near there?"

"Nae, man, I'm from Liverpool, I'm a Scouser."

"Sorry. I'm not too good with accents."

"I noticed."

The train was an Italian-made Class 390 Pendolino designed to tilt gently on the curves and capable of a top speed of 140 miles an hour, though its velocity on this route was limited to 125 because of track restrictions. It was still nearly twice that of what an American passenger train was allowed to travel, and the landscape blurred by impressively. Out the windows I saw a plain as flat as central Ohio, though with an occasional volcanic knob on which the ruins of a fortress might be standing and one where the occupants had almost certainly sucked all the wealth from the surrounding fields and converted it into magnificent furniture and swords. It was not uncommon during the Middle Ages for a person to be born, grow up, marry, labor and die of old age without ever venturing more than five or ten miles in any one direction. I was covering that distance in less than two minutes without lifting a foot, and this made me feel lazy and undeserving of the modernity into which I'd been born. And I was also ruing all the brocaded spots on the map that I was ignorantly hurtling past: Birmingham, Coventry, Stratford-upon-Avon, Oxford. This was the price of getting to London in two hours. The train giveth, the train taketh away.

Going from Liverpool to London on horse used to take four saddle-sore days, and a trip by stagecoach cost the year's wages of a serf. But steam trains could complete the same journey in an afternoon, and they could also haul more than sixty tons of minerals or factory goods with them. This guaranteed a future for industrial capitalism and big commodities and helped spell doom for most local artisan economies.

Before the rails English towns had to be self-sufficient or die. The traveling range for a particular good or service—oats, locksmithing, surgery, apples—was about twenty-five miles. The railways expanded that sphere ninefold, meaning that economies and human relationships could thrive over great distances. As the celebrity preacher Sydney Smith put it, in a statement that might as well have been made today about the Internet, "Everything is near, everything is immediate—time, distance and delay are abolished."

A favorite cliché of the journalists who had written about the seeming magic of the early railroad was that it "annihilated space and time." Karl Marx later picked up the phrase, and it is sometimes attributed to him, but its real source is a poem by Alexander Pope.

> *Ye Gods! Annihilate but space and time,*
> *And make two lovers happy.*

As we annihilated the Oxfordshire countryside and drew closer to London, the human settlements thickened. We passed smart little estate clusters with smart little hybrid cars parked outside. No doubt the families inside would soon be watching a BBC *Newsnight* report about a rambunctious price-control debate within the European Union. A garish football stadium passed by on the east. The sky promised rain, and I said as much to the bathroom salesman across from me. "What's new?" he responded. "This is like a soomer's day to us, mate." From the next seat, little Marianne was brushing the blond hair of her dolly and making a shushing sound—*sh-sh-sh-sh*—that echoed the clicking of the tracks beneath us as we drew into Euston station, one of seven major stations that cling to the edges of the city like earmuffs.

Euston used to be a gem among stations, with a giant classical arch out front, but it was demolished in 1962 and replaced by the current graceless cube that was meant to symbolize "the electric age." It had green flagstone floors and the same inescapable chain stores present in every large British depot: Boots, Marks & Spencer, Burger King, WHSmith. I wanted to get out of it as soon as I arrived. My next train was at Paddington station in any case, and so I crossed the street to get into the London Underground.

Bolted to the tiled wall was the classic multicolored map of the Tube with the stations marked as ticks on a line and their names in a friendly font called Johnston, in which the letter O is represented with a perfect circle. The map had been designed in 1931 by an electrical engineer named Harry Beck, who understood that passengers didn't really care about where the aboveground stations were located in the real physical world. They just wanted to know what order they appeared in and where they were supposed to change trains.

Sure enough, the map was useless for aboveground pedestrians because it had no scale. But Harry Beck understood the "annihilation" of space and time better than almost anybody and how a machine on wheels creates its own alien geography. I had just traversed 211 miles of impossibly rich English countryside, and there had been only three chances to step off, just three crystallized points of interest, three miss-it-or-else stations that had to stand for every other village and farm that lay in between. And all in the merciless service of time.

I sat on the underground train to Paddington station on a springy seat and stared at the cheerful Tube map that existed in a universe of its own devising. And it occurred to me that it was one of the totems of Britain that I quite liked. Now, there were aspects of the nation and the people that were genuinely annoying: the disgusting sausages and fried toast at breakfast, the way the high streets locked up tight at six o'clock, the meaningless tabloid stories, the occasional bursts of xenophobia ("The Arabs, you deal with them with the back of your hand," one man told me in Newcastle), the way they stood at shop tills and repeatedly said "Thank *yew*, thank *yew*" to one another as if they had nothing else to say. I could never be a real Anglophile; monarchy feels to me like a lacy remnant of barbarism.

But I appreciated so much else: the boxy Anglican church tops that looked like sky fortresses against unbelief, the rambling hotels with bizarre half staircases, the overstuffed pub furniture, the zinc sandwich of the pound coin and the thumping seigniorage—*pound!*—that the word itself implied, the red and green boats on the canals, the way young and old people mingled amiably together in pubs as they really wouldn't in age-conscious America, the street signs bolted high onto the walls, the funny Shavian names of the streets they advertised (Cromptons Lane, Threadneedle Street, Wilmslow Road), the electric tea beakers that worked at the speed of nuclear plants, the little biscuits placed next to the instant coffee as if in apology, the overriding sense that this was, after all, *the mother country*—the fussy, dotty progenitor of much that was familiar and refined in America. Most of all: I liked their trains. This was the motherland of trains. I loved these British trains, even if the British wouldn't stop complaining about them, and even if they were invariably portrayed as steaming toward the chalky cliffs of apocalypse. (Truth be told, I even liked the complaining.)

A bolt of lightning—unusual for wintertime London—made a fortissimo crash as I rode the escalator up from the Tube, and a few travelers around me jumped and giggled. I stepped through a side entrance to the railway station, checked the electronic boards overhead and saw there was time for a quick dinner before the night train to Exeter. But I was reluctant to leave the station.

Great arcs of glazed glass yawned high above. Holiday shoppers were walking all around me with a purposeful tread. A few children clung to a statue of the children's-book character Paddington Bear, who wore a floppy hat and a perpetual iron stare. A female voice over the loudspeaker called the train numbers, which echoed all around and became indistinct.

This place was built in 1854 as the terminal of the Great Western Railway, inspired by an airy structure called the Crystal Palace, a magnificent oyster shell of iron and glass that debuted at the Great Exhibition in Hyde Park three years prior. Rows and rows of trains had come chuffing in triumphant entry to their platforms at Paddington under a brilliant dome flooded with sunlight and coal smoke, meant to be viewed "not as a railway station but a spectacle," as one observer put it.

The *Times* estimated that not one rural citizen in a hundred had seen London before the coming of the railways. By the time Paddington station was built, it was a rare British subject who had not yet visited his capital, and his first look was usually at rail alcazars like this. The builders meant them to be structural climaxes of a sort—neoclassical temples to the technology that had made the journey possible.

Some people came just to watch the streams of travelers rush by and listen to the shouts for boarding, and the station loafer became a distinct kind of character all over the globe. "The only way of catching a train I have ever discovered is to miss the train before," wrote the mystery novelist and philosopher G. K. Chesterton. "Do this and you will find in a railway station much of the quietude and consolation of a cathedral. It has many of the same characteristics of a great ecclesiastical building; it has vast arches, void spaces, colored lights, and above all, it has a recurrence of ritual." In a fascinating book called *The Railway Station: A Social History*, Jeffrey Richards and John M. MacKenzie suggest a conscious appropriation of the mysteria of churches: there was engine steam that was like incense, the liturgical chanting of boarding announcements, the gentle press of crowds and the everlasting promise of a journey far out of the range of human sight.

I let the holiday crowds stream around me and listened to the numbers being called in the calm female voice, and it occurred to me that these were patterns that constantly rearranged themselves and have been rearranging themselves daily on these floors for more than a hundred fifty years—the rushing to steam trains that have long since gone to red rust in the earth and the people who rode them now dust themselves—and the faces today are only another rearrangement of a world in ceaseless motion.

Then the rainstorm arrived. I became aware of it only because of the indistinct washing sound on the framed arcs of glass above the train shed, an elongated note of *ahhhhh* that intensified as the evening cloudburst dumped stronger waves of water. Drips began falling on the floor from unseen leaks above. And although this was not my native country and I was hungry and I didn't know where I would be sleeping tonight and was surrounded by total strangers, I felt obscurely and completely at home.

The Great Western Railway was sometimes called "God's Wonderful Railway," and it has a place in the British imagination like that of the Mississippi steamboat or the Oregon Trail in the United States—a stupendous nineteenth-century innovation that helped unify a nation and delighted millions in the process.

Part of it was the mythology that surrounded a pint-size insomniac and cigar addict named Isambard Kingdom Brunel, the chief engineer who put up bridges he designed himself over gorges that seemed impossibly wide and cruel. The Box Tunnel he built near Bath was the longest tunnel in the world at that time and was oriented in such a way that the sun shines completely through it on April 9 of each year—which happens to have been Brunel's birthday.*

---

* Whether this was indeed deliberate is one of the great argument starters of British rail lore.

When riding on the bumpy Liverpool & Manchester, he wrote in his diary with a shaking hand, "The time is not far off when we shall be able to take our coffee and write while going noiselessly and smoothly at 45 miles per hour. Let me try." And so Brunel dared to place his rails seven feet apart to give the passengers a more comfortable ride, disparaging George Stephenson's standard width as a "coal-wagon gauge." (The wide tracks had to be ripped out later, at enormous expense, to conform to the standard gauge in use throughout the nation.)

The GWR helped pioneer the concept of seaside vacations for even those of modest income, and the railway's stylish Art Deco posters advertised dowdy places like Bristol as if they were Bermuda and ran special chocolate-painted trains up to what it called "Shakespeare Land," urging customers to "See Your Own Country First!" Another flagship was the *Cornish Riviera Express*, designed to excite the imagination of beachgoers about the railway's farthest extension to a town called Penzance on the southwesternmost leg of the mainland. It was there that I was heading tonight.

Though best known as the setting of a Gilbert and Sullivan operetta, Penzance had been more of a salvage yard than a pirate hideout. Westbound clipper ships would occasionally wreck against seaside boulders, and the locals were known to swoop in and claim the washed-up cargo whether or not there were any survivors. The line to Penzance—the ne plus ultra of the whole British system—is now operated by FirstGroup, a multinational company that grew to prominence in the mid-1980s by acquiring bus systems on the cheap from beleaguered city councils. It also happens to own Greyhound Lines as well as thousands of yellow school buses in America.

The night train was full, and I wound up with my back against a carriage bulkhead, sitting on the floor next to an architect who had just come back to England from six months in China with his girlfriend, and he was therefore seeing his own country with the eyes of a newcomer for a few fresh hours. England looked old, he told me. Old and made of gray stones and lazily horizontal compared to the aggressive porcupine that was Beijing. The train was diesel, but it was capable of 110 miles an hour, and I felt the wheels turning with blistering speed underneath me while the lights of Berkshire and Wiltshire smeared past on the windows above me. All that British oldness he was describing was an obscurity I had to take on faith.

I stayed that night in the pleasantly worn-out Great Western Hotel—a trackside creation that has evaded demolition since 1860— and had a few pints in the downstairs pub, which happened to be a railwayman's hangout. A few conductors from FirstGroup were gathered in a corner and telling stories. They bade me to join them, and I heard a series of yarns like this: "So the 15:10 to Penzance is delayed and they tell the passengers that the train is delayed for mechanical difficulties, but that's bloody rubbish. The driver never showed up, did he? They pinched him for the earlier train!"

One old gentleman there, Mike Bowker, had been a mechanic on steam engines before they were phased out for diesel in the 1960s. "Oh, they were filthy things," he said. "The real pleasure was the camaraderie. The trains you worked with . . . they were only tools." Another of them took out his phone and played for me a few minutes of a 1936 documentary about the London, Midland and Scottish Railway's overnight delivery service, called *Night Mail*. It opens with a W. H. Auden poem that is read with the urgency and the rhythm of the piston on a steam engine. It sounds like proto-rap.

> *This is the Night Mail crossing the border,*
> *Bringing the cheque and the postal order,*
> *Letters for the rich, letters for the poor,*
> *The shop at the corner and the girl next door.*

This kind of verse is like Holy Scripture to British rail enthusiasts, some of whom document the movements of individual trains by their serial numbers, skulking about the tracks with camera and notepad, knowing the innards of the engines often better than the mechanics do. Public-health professionals have suggested that the "trainspotting" habit usually comes with a dose of Asperger syndrome. I am not one to say. They are a lot of fun to drink with, however.

Before shuffling off to sleep, I had been given advice to sit on the left side of the train out of Exeter the following morning, and I was intensely glad for it. The tracks clung to the west side of the river Exe and opened to a view of the widening water. The rains of the night before that had caused the cloudburst over Paddington had yielded to an early afternoon of breeze and scattered showers (the semipermanent climate of all of England), and there was enough sunlight to create a full rainbow over on the other side of the river, its footings seeming to move with the speed of the train.

We passed little boats in the harbor at Exmouth and a series of condominiums painted yellow, red and blue, then banked in a gentle curve to the west, and there in an abrupt unveiling was the moody void of the English Channel, lined with low cliffs, which the railroad passed on a shelf that hugged the sea. We went through a short tunnel at Dawlish and cruised next to the waves for several miles. An older couple walked hand in hand on one of the beaches under red cliffs. Then we turned north at the estuary of the Teign, a river so wide that Brunel could not bridge its mouth,* and past gabled estates dotting the low hills.

This was near the heart of County Devon, which must be one of the most physically attractive regions in the Northern Hemisphere. It is the England of England. If you gave a talented five-year-old child a box of crayons and asked him or her to draw a picture of the countryside, you

---

* He loved the area, though, and used one of the estates to recover from an accident in 1843: while performing a magic trick to amuse his children, he had inhaled a half-sovereign coin that stuck in his sinuses. His attempts to build a machine to remove it were a failure, but his father suggested he lie facedown on a board and cough until it came out. That worked.

would get back a picture that looks very much like Devon: white pillowy clouds, green knolls, stone walls, tidy farmhouses. The perfect image of bucolic peace seems to have been grown here in a hay field during the Late Middle Ages and exported to every corner of the planet.

The train cut through roadless terrain that looked much as it had when the navvies of Brunel's South Devon Railway Company had blasted and chopped their way through here in 1844. I saw a fox sniffing at some grass and turning to look curiously at the railcars. We stopped at Plymouth, and I walked around the main thoroughfare, which had been rebuilt from Luftwaffe raids in a frigid style called Heroic Modernism. The train to Penzance left the next hour—not enough time to go visit the ersatz Plymouth Steps, where the Mayflower sailors almost certainly did not disembark—and we wound through mountainous darkness all the way to a small town called Camborne, a mining outpost that was the home for one of the truly tragic figures in railroad history.

The temperamental mechanic Richard Trevithick, the son of a mine engineer, had made a critical adjustment to James Watt's steam engine, and it was his idea to mount the contraption on wheels and run it down a set of metal rails. All three of the necessary parts of the railroad, joined at last. But he was almost certainly a victim of what we now know of as manic depression and he failed to cultivate the kinds of powerful friends who could have hooked him up with money. His habit of quitting early didn't help either. If he had been a more thoughtful businessman, or even a good showman, Britain would have had railways twenty years earlier than it did. Trevithick deserved to be world famous for his insights, but instead he is the answer to a trivia question.

He didn't put a lot down on paper, and when he did, it was an absolute mess. A page from his workshop notes shows columns of figures stacked across the page, slanting diagonally, apparently meant to add up, but there is no discernible addition or multiplication. Restless sentences describe a machine that only he could see: "The blow with a 80 inch cylinder 7.9 stroke, 14 strokes per minute, blown through 3.6 ft long of 20 inch diameter pipe of 3 inch thick 14 inch diameter inside through 3/8 inch tube. . . ."

School had bored him—the local teacher called him "disobedient, slow, obstinate, [a] spoiled boy, frequently absent and very inattentive"—but he loved tinkering with Watt's steam engines, and as a young man he helped the local copper miners figure out ways to alter their pumping machines so as to dodge the oppressive patent laws. It was in this culture of piracy that Trevithick hit on his key insight: locating the piston as a direct recipient of steam. Trevithick used self-contained boilers that could withstand pressure of up to fifty pounds per square inch without risk of blowing apart the whole contraption. The spent steam was expelled up the stack instead of being condensed, which had the effect of "drawing the fire," an effect like blowing oxygen on coals to make them hotter. In 1804 he mounted the device on wheels and—on an impulsive wager—ran it up a set of wagon rails at a Welsh mine called Penydarren. The engine chewed up the wooden rails but ran perfectly and demonstrated an astonishing capability for hauling weights.

Yet there would be no follow-up. He got distracted and traveled up to the Newcastle coal region in 1805 to confer with some potential partners. At some point during that trip, he apparently spent time with an ambitious inventor named George Stephenson. This visit is probably when the inadvertent cross-pollination of the railroad idea took place: brought up from the copper country of Cornwall to the coal mines of the northeast, where it found a willing audience. The Stockton & Darlington made its first run twenty years later.

All that was left for Trevithick was a strange epilogue. At the age of forty-two, he accepted the invitation of a Swiss silver impresario to travel to Peru in an attempt to drain the mines there. A contract with the royal mint in Spain made it seem like a sure bet, and Trevithick was told there would soon be a statue of him made of pure silver. Newspapers in Lima noted the arrival of the mechanic "Don Ricardo," and he and his engines traveled via pack mule up canyon trails to Cerro de

Pasco to see what they could do. He grew frustrated at his inability to earn a mining concession for himself and—as he had so many times before—quit. The revolutionary leader Simón Bolívar met him and then forced him to design a rifle that fired a bullet that shattered on impact. Trevithick obliged but slipped away after Bolívar tried to draft him into the army.

Broke and frustrated, Trevithick found his way to a dingy hotel at the Colombian port of Cartagena after he had flipped over his canoe and injured his leg. While he lay there suffering in the tropical heat, a chance meeting took place. There was another Englishman staying at the inn, and he made no special effort to befriend the ailing Trevithick until a companion berated him.

"It is not credible to your father's son that he and you should be here day after day like two strange cats in a garret," said this companion. "It would not sound well at home."

"Who is it?" asked the guest.

"The inventor of the locomotive, your father's friend and fellow-worker," came the answer. "His name is Trevithick, you may have heard it."

Robert Stephenson had indeed heard the name. And so the son of the hugely wealthy man who had scored an incalculable triumph with the famous Stockton & Darlington crossed the hotel lobby to talk with the impulsive patent dodger who had invented the high-pressure steam engine that had made said triumph possible. Stephenson eventually gave him fifty pounds—half of his savings—so the wounded man could make his way back across the ocean to England.

One of the most important people today who keeps Trevithick's name alive is Philip Hosken, a seventy-eight-year-old former Chrysler distributor who wrote a book called *The Oblivion of Trevithick*. Hosken worked for a time in the concrete business in Saudi Arabia, where the sand granules tend to come in an oval shape because of the wind and are therefore unsuitable for concrete, which requires a more angular base. He ran a mill that ground up a mineral called andesite, therefore giving him the ability to say with some truth that he "sold sand to the Arabs."

I met him in a pub near the site of Camborne Hill, where Trevithick had a workshop. Hosken had shaggy gray hair and wore a gray cardigan sweater, white tennis shoes and a permanently quizzical facial expression. He started in on his favorite topic.

"People in this country think that the railroad began on the day that George Stephenson brought out his engine with wet paint on it, and they ignore the whole evolution of it in the mining fields," he said. "Stephenson was just clever enough to change his abilities all along the way. What is forgotten about that generation is they all copied each other."

We took a short walk up the slight rise of the hill, which is where Trevithick made the impulsive choice to test an early prototype engine called *Puffing Devil* on Christmas Day in 1801. The hill today looks like an ordinary bourgeois lane in an English country village—there are town houses on both sides and a rock wall down at the base about a quarter mile away. The road is pitched at a gentle but unmistakable angle.

"How the hell he got up this road, I don't know," murmured Hosken as we walked down Camborne Hill toward the site of Trevithick's vanished workshop. But he managed it nonetheless, at a speed that may have approached ten miles an hour, with at least six joyriders hanging on to the sides. "She went off like a little bird," recalled one of them. A few days later, Trevithick tried to drive it two miles to show it off to a local nobleman. The top-heavy carriage tipped over into a ditch on the way. While waiting for repairs, Trevithick and his friends went to an inn where, according to one observer, "they comforted their hearts with a roast goose and proper drinks" while the engine continued to burn its coal. The water boiled away, and *Puffing Devil* caught fire. The party emerged hours later, reeling and tipsy, to find blackened sticks and metal warped beyond use.

For a two-hundred-year commemoration of the Camborne Hill

run, Hosken got hold of some of the original drawings and rebuilt a coal-fired replica to make a drive up the same hill in front of a cheering crowd. The carriage worked, but the ponderous climb gave Hosken a new appreciation of his subject.

"Transmitting that power through the wheels would have been very difficult—the wheels would spin," he told me. "We know the size of the cylinders and the stroke had to be equivalent to the turn of the wheel. Every chuff and puff equaled a rotation. It's a miracle that it worked at all. To come uphill in the rain, lurching and banging all over the place . . ." The residents of the town tended to have a magical world-view, and at least one thought the instrument was of the devil.

On the walk back up the hill, I asked Hosken why Trevithick's contribution was so important.

"The steam engine itself is an almost-human thing. It's warm. It snorts and farts and dribbles on the floor and does all the things a human being would do. It's a lovable thing. That cylindrical boiler makes it what it is. This technology was a great leap for man—not in the lunar sense but as an acknowledgment that progress works in steps. And so whether you're talking about a coffeemaker or a nuclear submarine or an airplane or a railroad, you're using a high-pressure engine. Which is what Trevithick brought to us."

From this primitive birthplace of the railroad at Camborne, there are only two more scheduled stops to the very end of the line. The train winds through a Cornish mining landscape of low hills and creeks, dotted with the brick spires of the engine houses that once held the steam pumps that everybody had been trying to pirate. They looked like ruined Norman castles.

I was on the lookout for more of them when I met a man going to St. Ives. The little dog with him had his hair chopped into strange tufts. "I had to cut him meself," said the man, whose name was Colin. "I'm on disability. This dog I got from a store. He had brain damage. I called out twenty names to him, but the only one he responded to was Rambo. So that's his name." He caught on that I was from the United States and went on to tell me about his career as an antiques dealer and about a sister of his who had died two weeks before in Mississippi. Shipping her ashes back was going to cost him two thousand pounds.

This seemed an awkward time to interrupt a story, but he had to get off at Hayle, and I stood in the vestibule while he kept talking to me through the sliding window as the train started to move. Rambo sniffed around at his feet. As the train left the platform behind, he was still talking to me, shouting about his sister and the two thousand pounds as I rolled out of sight.

We arrived at Penzance some ten minutes later. The city was an attractive boomerang of houses and shops curled around the bay and terraced up the slope. A warmish breeze was blowing in. Buses out to the promontory at Land's End were infrequent, they told me at the tourist office, and I had just missed one.

"There's nothing out there this time of year," I was told. And why did I want to go *there* when there were many other diverting things to see in Penzance? I shrugged and walked the two miles to the edge of town, stuck out my thumb and watched disinterested faces pass for about an hour until a psychotherapist in a Mercedes stopped for me. He was on his way to supply a rented holiday cottage in a village called Sennen, which had a pub, a church and a few weather-torn houses amid a horizon of treeless grass. The last few hectares of English dirt looked a lot like Iceland.

It was kind of him to pick up a hitcher, I said as he let me out.

"I always do," he replied.

From this last country lane, it was about a half-mile walk to the outer gates of a tacky amusement park that was closed down for the winter. Few things look sorrier than a shuttered carnival. But past the movie theater and the petting zoo and the hotel was a truly magnificent set of cliffs with the ocean crashing below. Almost nobody else was around; I had the spot virtually to myself. I stepped over a rope with a sign that warned DANGEROUS CLIFFS, much as I had trespassed on Dunnet Head in Scotland, and crept carefully out onto the wet grass and down the side of a cliff as far as I could reasonably go—to the outermost tip of the British mainland, an end-to-end journey accomplished entirely by train, except for two motorized stubs at each end and a brief walk across a London street.

There were some lichen-coated boulders and then a lighthouse on an outcropping across a quarter-mile reach of water. And beyond that nothing but the massive Atlantic under gray skies. For about ten happy minutes, I sat there watching the sea slosh in its saucer before growing restless myself. I climbed back up the cliff toward the road—and the railhead.

THE PEOPLE, AND ALL THE PEOPLE

New Delhi to Varanasi

The old gatehouse at the edge of Varanasi is lit by one bare bulb, and its filament has all the wattage of a sick firefly. When sunset comes and it gets too dark for the evening-shift gateman to write in the ledger in front of him, he puts a match to a kerosene lantern.

The smoke rises toward the ceiling, which is a hollow pyramid slicked with grime. The walls of this brick hut are two feet thick, good insulation for the oppressive summers, but the gateman, Sita Ram, does not like sitting in here: too gloomy and airless. And the quiet inside means that sometimes he falls asleep with his head on the desk. But he claims never to have slept through a ringing telephone, which would be a slip that would cost lives.

He prefers to be near the tracks, where he has to stand at least four times every hour to manually close the metal gates that keep all the cars and motorbikes and cows and people on Phulwaria Road from wandering onto the trunk line to New Delhi in front of the trains when they pass.

"I have a running fight with the public," he says. "They don't like being stopped. But duty is duty."

Gatehouse 5CT2 was built by the British in the 1860s, but it still performs its original function. Except for a hand-cranked telephone, it has used much the same technology for the last century and a half. When a train approaches, it is the job of the gateman to shoo people off the tracks, close the gates, note the passing of the train with ink in his bulky ledger and report each safe passage via phone to the stationmaster.

The job is simple and repetitive and occasionally dangerous. By the railroad's count, there are approximately 38,000 points in the nation of India where the tracks intersect a road of some importance, and full-time gatemen are assigned to patrol 16,500 of them around the clock, in shifts of eight hours each. Mechanical crossbars and blinking lights cost money, and gatemen are cheap by comparison. And in a country where a single government job can keep a whole extended family from going hungry, the leadership has every incentive to maintain this antique scheme.

The phone inside the gatehouse rang, and Sita Ram went in to answer. He spoke a few words of Hindi and hung up. A westbound train was on the way. He trotted out to go close the twin sets of white-painted steel gates on either side of the tracks. These gates would not have looked out of place in a Kansas cattle pasture.

The flow of traffic on Phulwaria Road came to a reluctant halt, even though dozens of people on foot ducked around the posts and darted across the tracks on their way down the road. Some of the trespassers looked furtive, others merely careless. They continued leaking around like sweat drops until seconds before the coal train went blaring past, its wheels making a vicious slicing sound. Sita Ram paid no attention to the train, or to the trespassers.

"About two months ago, there was a man on a motorcycle who tried to make it past a train," he told me as the horn subsided. "He was too slow, and he was killed. This was my mistake."

The life of a gateman can be a lonely one, and Ram sometimes gets tired of his job. People can become arrogant when the gates are clanged shut on them, and it is not unheard of for an especially angry motorist to pull a gun on a gateman, demanding passage. Pedestrians can elude a gate—a car cannot. But the fifty-year-old Ram is an easygoing sort, and after five years of this the locals around Phulwaria Road have come to see him as a fixture. Men with nothing better to do come by to gossip and chew tobacco, which he enjoys. He also has a good relationship with the stationmaster, whose commands on the telephone are his lifeline. The crank on the side of the telephone rings a bell in the Varanasi station.

What happens if it should fail? I ask.

Ram points to a second telephone. If that fails, too, he has to dispatch a "runner"—that is, anyone from the neighborhood who happens to be standing nearby—to run or drive like hell the four kilometers into Varanasi and let the stationmaster know of a signal breakdown. This rarely happens. What happens more often is casual death. People die here, and they die at grade crossings every day all over India, but the bodies are removed, the blood seeps into the ballast and seventeen thousand trains a day keep running on schedule. The national system of hand-operated gates is primitive and ponderous, but it all works somehow, and there are no serious plans to modernize it. The army of the gatemen will stay afoot. The arrangement keeps men like Sita Ram earning a good salary (in his case, about three dollars per day) in a nation of chronic unemployment.

The phone warbles—a coal train approaches in the direction of Lucknow. Ram excuses himself politely and steps outside. He has two minutes to secure the crossing.

Indian Railways likes to call itself the biggest employer on the planet. This is not entirely accurate. With a total estimated payroll of 1.5 million people, it is actually the eighth-largest single employer of human beings, behind such other contenders as the People's Liberation Army of China, the U.S. Department of Defense and Walmart.

As with any railroad, a vast array of unseen staff is necessary to keep the cars rolling, but in the state-driven apparatus in India, the effect is hyperexponential. There are drivers, conductors and instructors; mechanics, pipe fitters and technicians; cooks, accountants and clerks; stevedores, porters and gangmen; trackmen, welders, mates and keymen; managers, regional managers, section managers, district regional managers and stationmasters—more than seven hundred job categories in all and, as Bill Aitken has written, "a million grades of hierarchy."

This multiplicity of tasks has been a defining feature of the railroad since its inception, and nothing compares to it except perhaps the movement of an army in wartime. The labor costs are gigantic, though commensurate with the huge revenues rail systems generally reap. There may be no better method of job creation ever invented than a railroad.

Yet India is a special case, as the jobs here consume entire identities as nowhere else on earth. To work for the railroad at any level is to possess a near-lifetime sinecure, especially if the person is made an officer—that is, "gazetted." Few people are ever fired, and few would dream of quitting. Railroad men are railroad men until they die. An in-house magazine in 1947 said this: "It is not a family of blood relatives; it is a family bound together by loyalty and service. Blood relatives quarrel and fall apart, the [railway] family is true to itself."

Most employees of Indian Railways will quickly, even cheerfully, confess that the organization is ridiculously overstuffed. There are patronage hires at every level, deadwood that nobody cares to abate as well as pointless workers kept around to justify a department's size. Automation of any process is suspect. The conventional estimate is that only 20 percent of the staff of Indian Railways does any real work, and most of those are manual laborers doing track maintenance. According to a World Bank study, Indian Railways spends a staggering 53 percent of its budget on its employees—about double the pie wedge of China, the only comparable system by size, which also manages to move about twice the freight as India does.

I shared a commuter seat one afternoon with an accountant in a steel-procurement division who told me one of the cardinal principles in his office was to "always prefer manpower to new equipment." Why equip locomotives with an expensive communication system when it was easier to pay a driver's assistant to hold a walkie-talkie?

"Population is the biggest problem in this country," he said, clutching a sports bag in the third-class carriage section we were sharing with eight others. "There's a huge abundance of labor, and we can hire people for a hundred rupees"—less than two dollars—"a day. So why bother?" He went on to tell me that he frequently had days where there was nothing to do but listen to music on his headphones. These were his favorite days.

There are occasional calls in India's parliament to trim the payroll in the name of cost savings. The calls are generally ignored, or acknowledged with the most cursory of trimming. The deepest proposals to fire employees rarely exceed 1 percent. Managers up and down the line use the phrase "social responsibility" when they talk about the need to keep paying ten clerks to do the job of two, or paying fifty thousand men like Sita Ram to keep opening and closing cattle gates all night long.

"I know it doesn't make any business sense," said Rakesh Chopra, a member of the board that governs the system. "But the frontline workers, they need those jobs."

He said this to me while we sat on wicker chairs on the lawn of the house in which he was staying: a beautiful 1950s villa of squares and ovals and mullioned white windows. The house was inside a guarded "Railway Colony" for top officers in the Chanakyapuri section of New Delhi, near most of the foreign legations.

Colonies like these are nestled in every major town in India— islands of bourgeois comfort in the midst of garbage-strewn streets and the labyrinths of slums. The lawn was shaded by mango and asoka trees. A statue of the Virgin Mary stood under an arch of white stones over an artificial stream that didn't flow. A few feet away was a cinder etching of the god Shiva with snakes on his shoulders.

Chopra had invited me to have breakfast with him the day before the minister of railways, Mamata Banerjee, was scheduled to present the next year's budget to parliament. This is always a big theatrical event for the department, a time to publicly reward allies with pork and allow critics to vent frustrations with the ministry and the railways in general. Her speech was interrupted several times by hecklers and hooters who complained she was steering too many projects toward her home state of West Bengal. The minister, who can be brittle when pushed, snapped back at one interjector, "If you don't listen, I will *cut!*"

Nobody mistook her threat: she was talking about the new railway line through his district. Laughter and applause followed this rejoinder. Banerjee's budget included more than a hundred new commuter trains in Mumbai, the construction of hospitals and schools on railway land, 1,021 kilometers of new track and no layoffs of any significance.

This came as a surprise to no one. Chopra had told me that the firing of unnecessary staff is avoided as a matter of policy, because it "would lead to all kinds of traumatic family situations" across the nation, as well as create a general depressant effect on the economy. Stripping people of their paychecks is anathema to the giant Keynesian jobs juggernaut that Indian Railways has always represented. "If you're not below the poverty line," said Chopra, "you will spend money. And that helps the economy."

So Indian Railways propelled itself into the future as a kind of rolling tautology. It had to keep all those cars moving because the jobs were needed to keep the cars moving. India's twenty-first-century capitalist aims are rooted in software and calling centers and biotechnology, but the foundation belongs to an older place: the post–World War II socialist-leaning India of big nationalized industries, high tariffs and strangling gobs of permissions and regulations for anyone who tries to buck the system.

The head of the New Delhi office of the All India Railwayman's Association—a powerful trade union—summed it up for me in one cryptic formula. His name is Shiva Gopal Mishra, and he wore a gray tunic buttoned up to the neck in the style of Chairman Mao.

"The railways are yours," he told me with a smile. "But they belong to us."

In addition to larding its employees, the management of Indian Railways always obeys another directive: keeping third-class passenger fares not just affordable but vanishingly cheap. In a nation of more than a billion people, it is still possible to cross the entire country for about ten dollars. Most daily commutes cost the equivalent of a nickel. The carriages are filthy and the crowds are smothering, but the fare is what keeps destitute people showing up for work and able to feed their families.

Mamata Banerjee's predecessor as minister, a slab-haired man named Lalu Prasad Yadav, elevated this principle into high doctrine. Gifted with a stage presence and a taste for folksy speech, he enjoyed a cultish following among his constituency in the state of Bihar. Dolls, cosmetics, tobacco and a brand of cattle feed were named after him; barbers began offering haircuts in his distinctive Mr. Spock comb-forward.

He kept a herd of cows in the garden of his government house, and his allusions tended toward the bovine. His management formula was expressed as "If you don't milk your cow fully, it falls sick, and if the cow falls sick, the farmer goes sick." In another instance he questioned why the railways had spent money on high-powered locomotives that could pull twenty-four cars when most of the station platforms on that particular line were long enough for only fourteen. "Indian Railways purchased a Jersey cow but forgot to milk it," he said. Jail terms for corruption in his past only seemed to heighten his populist charm, as did his often-expressed wish to be prime minister someday.

Lalu inherited a railway close to bankruptcy and immediately boosted revenue by introducing around-the-clock freight loading. Instead of laying off staff (almost impossible in India), he curtailed hiring quotas. He introduced computerized reservations, made it easier to book first-class seats without having to pay a bribe and took out ads in major newspapers featuring his own face and that of Bholu, the cartoon elephant mascot of Indian Railways who wears a conductor's cap and holds a lantern. AVAIL THE SCHEME OF AUTOMATIC UPGRADATION OF CLASS, said the legend. The elephant is smiling. Lalu is not.

He kept fares at rock-bottom prices for India's poor and made a huge show of his generosity. Bashing the employees within his own ministry—the same ones he refused to fire—certainly didn't hurt him with voters. "Those who reside in air-conditioned offices do not realize what a rupee means to a poor milkmaid," he liked to say.

The economist Shagun Mehrotra recounted the evangelical atmosphere at one of his rallies in 2008. (This following version translates Indian currencies to U.S.)

Lalu took the microphone and asked the crowd, "Do you know in the last four years the railways earned six billion dollars in profits?"

A voice from the crowd responds, "No, sir."

"Four years ago what was the passenger fee from Hathua to Siwan?"

"Sir, fifteen cents."

"How much is the fare now?"

"Sir, nine cents."

"Did the railway minister ever reduce passenger fares in the past?"

"No, sir."

"Every year I reduced the passenger fares, yet the railways made a profit of six billion dollars over the last four years. What do you think?"

The audience screams its approval. "Congratulations, sir, this is great!"

Lalu was only framing in theatrical terms what most Indians believe about their railways, as instinctively as though it were a part of the national unconscious: that the rails exist because of the people and for the benefit of all the people and that without their bracing power as an internal steel frame, as well as a source of employment, India might have never risen to status as a twenty-first-century power and would have fallen into postcolonial victimhood, like a Congo or a Cambodia. This may not be far from wrong.

Traveling illegally is a breeze. Conductors aren't diligent about collecting tickets, and enough humanity is usually packed into third class to make paying a needless bother. Mahatma Gandhi, no friend of the previous British management, used to preach against it, with little effect. Yet the majority of "ticketless travel" is done more out of necessity than dishonesty. The lines at the windows are theaters of chaos, the people behind the windows are surly, the scheduling boards sometimes broken or wrong. In most cases you can just get on the train without paying.

Riding lawfully takes a lot more patience. I showed up at New Delhi Station on a Monday morning to get on board the *Guwahati Express* for the city of Varanasi, and determined to do it the right way. The station itself, even on its best days, is a sweatbox of passengers and soldiers. The late arrival of various inbound trains is announced by a female voice over the loudspeaker, followed by a lament: *We deeply regret the inconvenience.* Then two triumphant musical notes that sound like a score on a football video game.

I had bought a ticket on a *rajdhani*, meaning that it was an express train originating from New Delhi and therefore considered worthy of special security. A conductor directed me to the wrong compartment, so I hunted down the chief conductor, a harried middle-aged man who inspected my ticket and pointed me to a bottom seat in a carriage stuffed with baggage. *This* was the right place, he assured me, though the numbers did not line up. I looked out the cracked and duct-taped window at the good-bye scenes on the platform until the same chief conductor came by to tell me I was once again not in the right place. He examined my ticket once more.

"But this is where you told me to go," I said.

He shook his head. Again something was wrong, and furthermore it was not his error. "This is a station administration problem," he said vaguely. Then he disappeared down the corridor on another errand. I waited for him to come back, but he never reappeared. A steward came by instead, carrying a rose and a box of warm mango juice with a thin straw poking out the top. I decided not to press the issue and just stayed in place.

A sign in the passageway at the end of a car: ANY UNIDENTIFIED ARTICLE MAY BE A BOMB. KEEP AWAY AND INFORM RAILWAY POLICE. Planting luggage bombs on capital express trains is a past tactic of the Karachi Project—the loose syndicate of domestic terrorists trained by Pakistan to harass India over the possession of the Kashmir province. They killed ten people with a bomb smuggled onto the Patna–New Delhi train in 2005, and everyone knows how easy it would be to slip one aboard again within the squall of luggage and passengers that crashes against the train at every major stop.

The security was visible, though mostly theatrical. A squad of soldiers with rifles and green uniforms sat in a booth by themselves near the kitchen; several of them were dozing, even as we rolled east out of the capital's tangled center and over the wide Yamuna River and past the innumerable slum clusters that flank it for its entire course.

The kitchen car itself was a wonderful thing—a long, greasy cage of blue-flame burners and steel vats full of aloo mutter and cooks with sweat on their faces, puffing up roti in hot pans and all on display from a narrow passageway that ran the length of the car.

I lurched through it eastward with the train, tossed by the sea motion, walking with my hands pressed against the outer wall, and found the chief steward making notations in a book with a blue felt marker. There were also notes inscribed on the palm of his hand, which he offered to me in greeting. Amit Kumar said he had been on the job less than three months and was still getting the hang of the schedule. He would be up until midnight tonight, he said, and then be up again by 5:00 A.M. It would count as a relatively good night's rest.

"This is a top government train," he told me. "The heart of Indian Railways." The prestige of the train was why he often felt nervous, like an attendant on a third-rate airline who must fly every day. The soldiers sitting nearby were no guarantors of safety. "Our lives are not safe here. This is a train on the fringe. They don't have the security for it." But Amit liked his job, even with its embedded paradox: a lifetime sinecure in exchange for constant risk. He was the one who had delivered the roses to the first-class sleeping cars. The best part was meeting people from across the nation, countrymen he would never speak with otherwise.

"You see what's going on all over India," he said. "All the stations and all the people. You see what they're doing with their lives, what civilizes them. The color of their saris."

A young man from the kitchen came into the compartment. There was a huge, ugly burn on his lower arm, a wound from the splash of something excruciatingly hot. But he didn't seem to be in pain. He wore a sheepish smile. Amit looked at the red blotch without expression. Then he excused himself to dig the burn cream from the first-aid kit under the bench, and I watched him spread the placebo gently on his new employee's hurt arm.

Outside the bars of the window, the countryside rolled backward. We stopped at Murdabad to take on more passengers, and I watched stray monkeys climb the spindle legs of the catwalk over the tracks. Then, without a whistle, we were running again, and the platform salesmen and their oranges scrolled away, and we were out in the mustard plain once more. Stacks of drying cow pies were piled on a roadside berm, as perfectly shaped as Frisbees and as geometrical as a target. These pyramids of cow poop were all over Uttar Pradesh. The disks were burned for household fuel and had most likely been patted into shape by the hands of children.

I remembered reading an old *Bradshaw's* railway guide for wealthy British leisure travelers to India: the nineteenth-century equivalent to a *Fodor's* or a *Lonely Planet*. After providing the reader a list of bizarre commands to be uttered to Hindi-speaking peons ("Bring me cold meat in the twinkling of an eye!"), the author tried to diminish the hopes of first-time travelers, who might have been expecting a visual feast from the windows. "The country consists of extensive plains and hot monotonous jungle, fertilized by numerous rivers and interspersed with a few ranges and hills and occasional bursts of fine scenery, but India in general is not so beautiful or so rich as the new-comer expects to find it."

We had crossed into Uttar Pradesh, the wide breadbasket at the heart of northern India where fields of mustard greens and sugarcane were broken up by the occasional radio tower or small mud-brick village or pool of opaque fetid water. The *Guwahati Express* hurtled at approximately seventy miles an hour past all of it. The colors grew deeper in the afternoon light, which was a constant indirect haze; the brothy light of India, a unique trick of the day's temperature and the burning leftovers from the basmati harvest. In the cities the carbonaceous filth made you blow black from your nose each night, yet out here, clacking through still fields, the diaphanous murk seemed gentle. A climate scientist later explained to me that the superheated air of the daytime cooled down in the afternoons and highlighted the suspended aerosol, bouncing the dying daylight around a billion little floating mirrors. The Mexican poet Octavio Paz had worked here as a diplomat, and he had titled his essay-memoir *In Light of India*. It may be the softest glow in the world, this Indian light, making the horizon smudgy with obscure whites and grays, but nearby objects seemed numinous, almost radiating from the inside.

"Life would be weak without witness," Amit had told me while tending to his friend's wounded arm. "Lots of people wouldn't be able to go anywhere without this railway."

But the railways in India weren't originally about jobs—or even people at all.

In fact, they were originally conceived as little more than a conveyor belt to move riches to the ports and troops toward the trouble. The British merchant autocrats who colonized India and built the railways for their own enrichment were never aware they were creating the single greatest rearranging force in the lives of the masses they ruled, fashioning a modern nation out of a mélange of tongues, beliefs and cultures; they nudged India's class-obsessed citizens into thinking of themselves as one people. The rails were an astonishing legacy of India's colonial era. Some call it the only good one.

The British had been forcing themselves into India—first as traders, then as rulers—for more than two hundred years before the invention of the railroads. They had started with a small silk factory in the town of Surat* in the year 1608 and branched out from there along the east and west coasts as merchant rivals to the Portuguese, making deals with local princes in exchange for nutmeg and the woven textiles that were becoming fashionable in London.

The British East India Company found it easy to make these deals because "India" was not yet a coherent nation; it was a dizzying kaleidoscope of fiefdoms divided by a multiplicity of languages—at least three hundred—spoken across the subcontinent. These tiny nations frequently skirmished over gemstones and territory. The most powerful among them was in an Ottoman-like state of decay. The Moghuls were an Islamic dynasty who had invaded from the central steppes of Asia and whose grieving Shah Jahan had built the glowing white Taj Mahal for his dead wife. The British clerk-conqueror Robert Clive sealed their fate in the Battle of Plassey in 1757 by buying off the soldiers of the opposition, who were already reluctant to fight.

Clive governed his new territory through a blend of what he called "tricks, chicanery, intrigues, politics and Lord knows what," which might have stood as an emblem for the first century of British rule in India, venal and corrupt even by eighteenth-century standards. The East India Company found abundant riches in the spice and opium trades, operated its own private army and built a marbled seat of gov-

---

* The name means "face." It is today the diamond-polishing capital of the world.

ernment on the Hooghly River at Calcutta, where young men from Britain could come to accept a minor post and become fabulously rich through questionable means.

When "railway mania" swept Britain in the 1840s, it was inevitable that the technology would soon be exported to the richest colony in the empire. But the work of building the Indian lines was left to private individuals like Rowland Macdonald Stephenson, an engineering student and the son of a bankrupt bon vivant. The younger Stephenson resolved to live a more honorable life than his wastrel father had and took a job with a steamship line in Calcutta. Then he read the news about the iron tentacles spreading over Britain.

A railway would be perfect in the tropics, he thought, and he took his case to the newspapers, writing calm and deliberate articles about his pet cause, which, he said, could "raise long-prostrate India from the dust" and "transmute the pestilential marsh into a healthy garden, teeming with fertility and verdure."

He was initially dismissed as a crank, but within five years he had approval to build the first line from Calcutta to New Delhi with the help of the most powerful man in India: James Andrew Broun-Ramsay, also known as Lord Dalhousie, who was appointed governor-general in 1848. Known for his fanatical work ethic and accustomed to sixteen-hour stretches at his desk, Dalhousie immediately saw how much cotton could be moved and how the hill men in the tribal areas of present-day Waziristan might be tamed* by a show of the white man's technology. He saw railways as "public monuments vastly surpassing in real grandeur the aqueducts of Rome, the pyramids of Egypt, the Great Wall of China, the temples, palaces and mausoleums of the great Moghul monuments." The railways would be private but under tight state watch and obsequious to its aims: essentially a fascist economic model.

---

* No railway line in India would be built, it was said, that could not bear the weight of an Armstrong gun.

Construction on the East Indian Railway began in 1850. The carriages and locomotives had to be tucked inside clipper ships and sailed around the Cape of Good Hope. Within thirteen years at least 3 million tons of railway equipment would be moved this way. Each mile of track required an entire ship's load of iron. And that was the easiest part of the job. The tropical rainfall in India made the ground soggy, and millions of cubic feet of dirt had to be shoveled to lay a rail bed. Hundreds of streams had to be filled in, and if they were too wide, they had to be crossed with a metal bridge that had been forged in Manchester or Newcastle and sent over in prepackaged sections. And on the other side of the country, the Great India Peninsular Railway began to wind out of the port of Bombay and toward a slab of mountains called the Bhor Ghats that lie to the east of Bombay. The words mean "landing stairs," which was an apt description for their rough inclines, shot through with steep drop-offs and angular protrusions smothered in trees and green moss. They are only two thousand feet high but posed a formidable barrier and always had. Clouds of mist enshroud the rough peaks for most of the year.

The Bhor Ghats became the deadliest stretch of railway construction in Asia. Thousands of natives were recruited to shovel the dirt, cut the trees, pound the spikes, light the gunpowder and shoulder the rails. The British companies promised to pay hard cash (even in meager amounts this was always welcome), and there was never any shortage of fresh laborers when the first battalions either walked off the job, disgusted with the work, or got killed. The word "coolie"—from the Urdu *quli*, meaning slave—came into wide circulation during this period, and the regard for their lives was low. They harnessed themselves with shaky ropes to chip away at the hard granite on the cliffs and spent twelve-hour days inside dank tunnels prone to collapse. The death rate was close to one-third due to gunpowder blasts, falls from the cliffs, crushing by machinery and, especially, the cholera that ran unchecked through the miserable, sweating camps. And when it was finished in

1860, the line was one of the marvels of the world, a stupendous feat of earthmoving and zigzagging.

Most impressive was the novel Z-shaped turnaround where a train had to be backed up down a spur and fitted with another engine before it could continue the ascent. "It is a vast series of viaducts and tunnels," said the *Illustrated London News*. It was said of this line, as of many others in India, that under every sleeper tie a dead worker might as well have been buried.

Miserable and wasteful at it may have been, the Bhor Ghat construction succeeded in developing a new class of skilled laborers among Indians—the first seeds of a middle class. Thousands of coolies were taught how to be blacksmiths and masons and carpenters, and this pioneering group passed these skills on to their sons and cousins. It especially helped if the recruit was "Anglo-Indian," the offspring of a British father and an Indian mother. Such employees were fully welcome in neither culture and belonged only to the railway. They were especially useful as strikebreakers.

The better paid among them were invited to live in special "railway colonies" near the steam workshops, which became like dynastic enclaves. They took on the aspect of country villages in Nottingham, "laid out with military precision, to each house its just share of garden, its red brick path, its growth of tree and its neat little wicker gate," wrote Rudyard Kipling. The houses had high ceilings and wraparound verandas for drinking gin and tonics in the evenings.

The staff swelled as the railways grew, and the uppermost ranks still remained barred to Indian applicants. A committee would later describe Indian Railways' management as "like a thin film of oil on the top of a glass of water resting upon but hardly mixing with the seven hundred thousand below." The system was carrying 13 million Indian passengers a year by 1870, the vast majority in the dank and cagelike third-class cars. The entire network across the nation envisioned by the onetime fantasist Rowland Stephenson was more or less complete by 1890—

almost fifty-seven thousand miles of track, including the Darjeeling Himalayan Railway, which switchbacked up nearly seven thousand feet into the hills.

The crown of this empire-within-the-empire was Victoria Terminus at the heart of Bombay, built on the site of a shrine to Mumba Devi, who had given her name to the city, present-day Mumbai. Nearby had been a gallows used by the Portuguese to execute local criminals. The symbolism was lost on nobody—*this* was the new symbol of foreign might. The station was a gray-granite fortress with wings stretching out like muscular arms, carved gargoyles from Hindu mythos leering down off its towers and a sixteen-foot statue named *Progress* crowning the top of the dome. The architecture was a hypnotic combination of Venetian, Gothic and Indo-Islamic, and its eclecticism was copied in hundreds of lesser stations and gatehouses all over the country. The British bankroll it took to erect the railway system and all its stations, according to economist Daniel Thorner, "formed the single largest unit of international investment in the nineteenth century."

For cheerleaders of the British Empire, steam transportation was bringing not just a sense of nationhood to a grab-bag confederacy of lowborn but also imbuing the passengers with an appreciation for the religion of progress. The railways would help turn them into "Englishmen" and pull them into a new era. And much romantic hyperbole often accompanied this notion.

The Indophile scholar Edwin Arnold predicted that the "fire cow" in the subcontinent "would be the most persuasive missionary that ever preached in the east." Sir John Kaye believed that the railroad had "taught Indians the great truth that Time is Money," and he expressed some pleasure that the rationality of the train was begun to subvert classical Hindu notions of the circularity of time. "The fire carriage and the iron road was a heavy blow to the Brahminical Priesthood," he noted approvingly.

Indeed, one of the deepest changes to India hinged on this subtle yet all-pervasive point. Railways needed timetables if they were to operate safely, and that required a uniform time measured to the second by a mechanical clock. This was an alien idea to a culture that had passed the seasons by the phases of the moon and the sun. So the British grabbed hold of the cosmos and forever glued time upon the land in the name of order and safety on the tracks. By 1871 most railroads were setting all their clocks according to the time in Madras.

"Railway time" gradually became encrusted into the consciousness of every city and village along the lines, at least for anyone who wanted to take a train or ship his crops. Crowds mobbed the stations for hours or even days before their train was scheduled to depart, for fear of missing it, and the British Indian Association had to ask the government to build shelters for them. "It cannot be expected from them that they should come in only at the proper time," noted the petition, because "most of them have an indefinite idea of time."

The time fabric of the universe had never been parceled and divided in this way before, and distances had never seen such telescoping. The shock was bound to cause some cognitive disruption, such as it was with one classically educated man whose first experience with the railway was documented in an 1854 edition of the *Bengal Hurkaru* and later related by the journalist Ajit Dayal. The scholar was a religious man, and he took numerous precautions before leaving on his journey: he checked his astrological chart, repeated the name of his patron deity and bathed three times in a river. But when he got on the train and started to move faster than walking speed, a horrific revelation came to him.

"He went as far as Hooghly, but declined to undertake the return journey, because, said he, too much traveling in the car of fire is calculated to shorten life, for seeing that it annihilates time and space and curtails the length of every other journey, shall it not also shorten the journey of human life?"

If there was one citizen who embodied this schizophrenia about Indian railways, it was the independence leader and philosopher Mohandas K. Gandhi. He detested them and what they had done to rural life in his country. He considered them profane, even evil. Complaining about them was a lifelong hobby. But Gandhi could never stop himself from using them. Gandhi was an enthusiastic traveler and a frequent railway passenger until the day he died.

One of the most formative moments of his life had taken place on a train. He grew up in the coastal state of Gujarat and received a legal education in London before, at the age of twenty-four, accepting a post as a barrister in Natal, South Africa, which was also part of the British Empire. While traveling to litigate a case in 1893, Gandhi was asked by a white passenger to leave his first-class compartment and travel in third class with the rest of the "coloreds." He refused, and the conductor showed up to enforce the segregation rule, which had somehow been overlooked when the nattily dressed Gandhi had boarded.

"I tell you, I was permitted to travel in this compartment at Durban, and I insist on going in it," Gandhi told the conductor.

"No you won't," was the reply. "You will either leave this compartment or I will call a police constable to push you out."

"Yes, you may. I refuse to get out voluntarily."

Gandhi was ejected at the next stop, the high, cold town of Maritzburg, where his luggage was put under lock and key. It was late at night. He sat there on a bench, shivering and waiting until morning, afraid to ask the stationmaster for permission to retrieve his overcoat from the storage locker because he feared arousing the ire of yet another white official. He later described the experience as a moral awakening.

"The hardship to which I was subjected was superficial—only a symptom of the deep disease of color prejudice," he wrote in 1909. "I should try, if possible, to root out the disease and suffer hardships in the process." Gandhi said he considered abandoning his journey and skipping the case he was supposed to work on in Pretoria. But he resolved to repress his anger and pride, and when the window opened the next morning, he bought a first-class ticket and got on board the next train. More abuse followed on that journey, which he did not document in specifics. One week after arriving in the capital, he delivered his first political speech to a group of Indian residents, many of whom had come to Africa specifically to be laborers on the railroads.

Gandhi developed his philosophies of nonviolent resistance while helping fight for the civil rights of the Indian rail worker diaspora in South Africa. He took those principles back to India with him in 1915 and among his first targets was the railway system, which he accused of aggravating caste and class distinctions with its different qualities of service, as well as destroying the harmony of village life. British governors-general liked to point out that the trains had brought grain shipments to starving pockets of people between the years of 1860 and 1908, but Gandhi made the point in his 1910 classic *Hind Swaraj* that the railways had *caused* the famines in the first place by creating incentives for small farmers to ship their harvests to distant cities.

The railways, said Gandhi, were only applying salve to wounds they themselves had gouged. They were the tools of British rule and were now the chains of Indian dependence; he called them "the true badge of slavery," among other names, and implied that they had taken on a suprahuman importance in the way India was governed. "It is not the British people who are ruling India," he said, "but it is modern civilization, through its railways, telegraphs, telephone and almost every invention which has claimed to be the triumph of civilization."

His criticisms grew sharper as he traveled more and as he began to shed every personal attachment to Western ways of life. "I hope you will not make the mistake of thinking that if the railway line was brought nearer to every village in India the problem of distress would be solved," he wrote in 1927. "If you study the history of railways, you will find that this railway system of ours is simply sucking the village and leaving it absolutely dry." The real beneficiaries of the expansion had been British steel mills and ironworks, not the Indian people, who in Gandhi's view were left with low-wage jobs and crumbs.

This recalled a mistaken prediction of Karl Marx, who had written approvingly (in a freelanced article for the *New-York Daily Tribune* in 1853, during his newspapering days) that the coming of the railway to India would inevitably create a homegrown cluster of industry and dissolve the "hereditary divisions of labor" in that country, eliminating the caste system for good measure. This never happened, at least in the way that Marx envisioned. The railways brought a flood of manufactured goods to the countryside—clothes, lanterns, forks, machetes—but almost none of the factories that created them. Those, of course, were back in Britain.

Economics were not Gandhi's only problem with railed life. Technophobia also helped shape his disgust. He saw something pernicious in a mechanism that transported people faster than a horse could trot or a ship could sail, and this put him on the same rough plane as Thoreau and the unnamed Bengali scholar who thought the journey shortened life. "God set a limit to man's locomotive ambition in the constitution of his body," wrote Gandhi. "Man immediately proceeded to discover means of overcoming the limit. . . . According to this reasoning, it must be apparent to you that railways are a most dangerous institution. Owing to them, man has gone further away from his Maker."

Travel on the rails was like anesthesia compared with the full-bodied experience of life that Gandhi preferred, and he also found much to dislike about the physical upkeep of the carriages. The amenities in third class were only "sheep comforts"; the overcrowding and dirt were offensive to him, as were the "pushers" employed by the railways to pack more bodies into the sweltering carriages. There was a man of his acquaintance who always fasted before a rail journey so he wouldn't face the horror of having to use the filthy third-class toilet. Gandhi made a hobby out of writing acidic letters of complaint to the administration, saying their trains brought ruffians to holy pilgrimage sites as well as spread plague into rural towns. "Evil," he wrote, "has wings." By contrast, good travels like a snail.

Yet, for all his complaints, Gandhi *loved* the railways. He traveled them incessantly, all over India, and he drew many of his conclusions about the lives of ordinary citizens from the people with whom he shared a carriage seat or the floor. When choosing a place for his ashram, and therefore a pulpit to spread his ideas, he chose Sevagram, which was an easy walk to a massive rail junction. He deplored the attacks on the trains during the Quit India Movement: the carriages that were burned and overturned, the tracks that were ripped up, the employees who were beaten.

This angry outpouring was only a natural extension of anti-British fervor—the railways were the most obvious manifestation and tool of the Union Jack, even if they ultimately did more to help speed the day when Britain would make her exit. The railways spread the idea of independence and allowed revolutionaries to find one another. Moreover, the nineteenth-century prophets of steam were not wrong about the creation of "one India" linked by steel. Wrote the BBC correspondent and historian Mark Tully, "It is arguable that without the railways, the united India whose independence the Mahatma fought for would not have existed."

Gandhi is a revered figure in India today, and his criticisms of the railway are sometimes quoted with mordant wit when Indian passengers are confronted by the same tactile unpleasantness that he experienced: the filthy cars, the clogged toilets, the revolting food. Less appreciated is his sentiment that the railways demeaned India and were tools of subjugation. Perhaps it is a reflection of the new ownership.

"If his dream was realized," one high-ranking railway official told me, "people might not be moving at all. I believe when the farmer in Kashmir is allowed to get his goods into Jamir, that is *connection*. That man is going to talk about that melon that he ate. This man has become a teacher. That taste, the smell of that melon. All this is communication. This is the significance of being in touch with others. . . . Gandhi realized this mode of transport allowed him to be in touch."

A correspondent once questioned him on this apparent contradiction: why did he give so much business to an institution he loathed? Gandhi answered by comparing the railway system of India to his own body. It had odors and needs that were a nuisance. But while he would have preferred to be incorporeal, he was compelled to tolerate them and even, to some extent, enjoy them. The railways were like that, too.

"There are certain things," Gandhi said, "which you can't escape."

The necessities of the body to which Gandhi referred have had one singularly troubling effect on Indian Railways.

Ask any section engineer in New Delhi about his biggest maintenance headache and he will give an unembarrassed answer, though tiredly and without any laughter. If he smiles, it will only be because of the futility of bringing a permanent solution to a problem that sounds like a bad joke but costs Indian Railways hundreds of millions of dollars in man-hours and equipment each year. The steel rails in India, particularly those nearest to urban stations, must be frequently replaced because poor people have a habit of defecating on them.

Aesthetics are not the issue. Nor is health. The problem is purely mechanical. The uric acid in human feces gradually eats through the steel fasteners known as dog spikes, or, less colloquially, elastic rail clips, that hold the rails on to their ties. When the metal in them breaks down because of acid deterioration, the rails inch themselves out of alignment and the track buckles. In advanced cases the rails themselves begin to corrode. Derailments may follow.

"The shit will jam these clips," line supervisor Rajesh Vaidya told me. He spoke in a calm and dispassionate tone, meaning not to be profane but exact. "The metal will be compromised from six millimeters down to one, or less." Insects attracted by the mess then go on to eat and erode the wooden sleepers, which has always been a problem in India.*

The modern problem with feces is made worse because the toilets on the trains do not have holding tanks. The waste falls directly onto the tracks, as if the train itself were defecating. You can stand over the hole of the commode and watch the ties whiz by underneath as you accomplish your business. Doors are never locked when a train is parked in a station, which makes things foul on a hot day. And makes those rails, in particular, all the more warped.

Yet there is almost nothing Indian Railways can do except keep replacing the rails, at a faster rate of turnover than virtually any other system in the world. Retrofitting cars with toilet tanks would be unthinkably expensive. And that is a bare fraction of the problem.

"Open defecation," as the social scientists call it, is a fact of life in the limitless slum warrens of India, where the small houses of bricks and tarp can conceal immaculate interiors but no toilets. Almost half of India's 205 million households don't have one that flushes. The custom is to use a metal pot in the corner and then empty it outside. Or simply go outside. For rural peasants the fields are the usual place, and the fertilizer goes to good use. The cities create a tougher choice for the impoverished. Barely 10 percent of these cities even have a formal sewage system, let alone a useful option for those who sleep in shacks or out in the open. A significant portion of India's estimated daily load of one hundred thousand tons of feces voided in public ends up on the nation's railroad tracks. The Hindi word for this universal human output happens to be almost as universal: *goo*.

Four powerful social factors contribute to the goo on the tracks. The first is a widespread (and partly accurate) perception among the poor that the tracks are a cleaner place to defecate than ordinary ground

* In 1910 a Boston visitor reported that the white ant was "the greatest enemy" of the railroad. "This insect eats the ties, the telegraph poles and everything wooden."

because the waste seeps and washes down among the rocks instead of just drying out in the sun. The second is that railroad right-of-way is seen as a gray zone between public and private space, where a highly personal act can be executed with as much solitude as one can find in urban India. Only railway employees are technically allowed to walk there, but the rule is widely flouted and almost never enforced.

Thirdly is the polite tradition of avoidance that surrounds the issue. The topic is naturally embarrassing and is—even subconsciously—near the roots of India's pervasive caste system, whose contours first appeared with rigidity in the third century B.C. and whose lowest members were the *dalits*, whose jobs included collecting garbage from the streets and scraping feces from latrines, jobs euphemistically described as sweeping. Their very name—which famously means "untouchables"—is a window into the Freudian dread embedded in the Indian social structure and the way it mimics the innate human tendency to deny and compartmentalize the mortal effluent of the body.

Mahatma Gandhi, a great crusader against the caste system, also fulminated against the sanitary conditions of the cities and urged his countrymen—in a rare bit of admiration for Western ways—to adopt more "English" toilet practices. "The cause of many of our diseases is the condition of our lavatories and our bad habit of disposing of excreta anywhere and everywhere," he wrote in the newspaper *Navajivan* in 1925. He was broaching a subject that was at once taboo and yet all-pervasive.

The fourth and possibly most intractable reason for the goo problem has to do with a simple fact of railroad geography. One truism from the earliest days of railway mania in Britain—that remains robust today—is that urban land within strolling distance of the stations tends to be prized for its commercial value, but land adjacent to the tracks farther than about a half mile of a stop generally declines in price and often becomes derelict because of the noise, blight and permanent bisecting effect of the steel line. Shantytowns have sprung up along railway lines in India like insulation wrapped around an electric wire. These settlements are often of questionable legality, as there is no political will or incentive to evict a cluster of poor people who have nowhere else to go. Some of them have existed by the tracks since the nineteenth century and have taken on characteristics of fully mature communities, with leadership councils, day care, social service organizations and sturdy and tidy brick homes with satellite TV dishes and pirated electricity.

I walked along one of these jerry-built neighborhoods that hugged a trunk line near Vivekananda Road at the very heart of commercial New Delhi, yet hidden from general view. The line supervisor, Rajesh Vaidya, showed me just how narrow the margin was between the slipstream of a train and the front doors of the brick huts. Locomotives passed within two feet of cots where people were sleeping at midday and about eighteen inches from utility cables doubling as clotheslines, sagging heavy with laundry.

Sitting in a chair in the sunlight was a sixty-year-old man named Lalloo Ram, who told me he has made his home next to these tracks more than half his life and that he ceased to hear the trains years ago. They pass with their horns afire at the rate of about one every two minutes; they are part of the background. Why does he live here? "We don't have any other option," Ram told me.

Vaidya spoke a few phrases into his walkie-talkie, and we were soon joined by a team of four men in turbans and jumpsuits pushing a strange contraption along one of the rails. It looked like a polished cherrywood couch on top of a hand-powered rail cart, which is exactly what it happened to be. The official term is "trolley," and they are widely used by Indian Railways track inspectors who ride them to scrutinize the metal paths in front of them while being pushed by a team of lower-ranking colleagues. A more colonial relic could not be envisioned, and it was in fact a mid-nineteenth-century contrivance of the British. It was not hard to see a white overseer from Dorset wearing a pith helmet, jolly good, spurring his Hindoo coolies to propel him through the jungle and have him back to the villa for gin and tonics with the colonel by four.

I was bidden to sit on the wicker-framed couch with Rajesh and a labor contractor named Shiv Kumar while the four pushing men guided us south, away from the slum. The tracks in front of us, I am sorry to say, were liberally covered in crap. Turds were on the sleepers, the ballast and the dog spikes. When we got off for Vaidya to inspect some earth-works, I stepped in a fresh pile.

Vaidya shrugged and smiled in solidarity. Nobody worked on Indian Railways for very long without that experience. "In some parts of New Delhi," he said, "it is up to here." With the toe of a sneaker, he pointed at the top of a rail four inches off the ground.

People live, people eat, people have to move their bowels. This was the iron law of the maintenance agenda at Indian Railways. The flow of excreta on the tracks is as regular and unstoppable as rains in the summer. Periodic efforts to turn back the flood have succeeded like King Canute. Threats to prosecute trespassers with two-dollar fines are ignored. Government programs to erect more "community toilets" for the poor have made incremental progress here and there, but it cannot yet be measured by the only quotient that matters: the stuff that lies on the tracks, which keeps coming.

I talked with Bhagat Ram, one of the hundreds of thousands of line workers across India who has to wipe it away and pry up the bilirubin-warped rails in the endless cycle of digestion, elimination and replace-ment.

"I feel like people are shitting on my work," he complained. "I'm angry, but what can I do? Just wrap a cloth around my nose and go back to work."

The *Guwahati Express* streamed on into the late afternoon through Uttar Pradesh, which looked as flat and fertile as the Mississippi Delta, the evening sun warm against the spider-cracked glass of the carriage. Fields of yellow-tipped mustard grass and shimmering trees made a lazy, checkered blur from beyond them. There were smokestacks with broad round bottoms that looked like freakishly large anthills; they were village kilns for baking bricks from clay.

We were threading the Indo-Gangetic Plain, a broad crescent that stretches from Pakistan to Myanmar end to end and supports about one-sixth of the world's population. The Himalayas at the northeast boundary are the ice gates to China. A necklace of antique cities sprawls from the rivers, but this is also the rural breadbasket where crops have grown in the same irrigated plots for four thousand years. The ground was a flat basin of solid loess and good brick-making clay, which also made it a surveyor's dream. In 1848 a British pamphleteer named W. P. Andrew had touted it as "the best portion of country, perhaps in the globe," through which to run a line.

The view made this hyperbole entirely believable. We rolled like a marble over a glass tabletop. The only obstacles seemed to be the occasional south-flowing rivers, threads of slow, gray liquid arched with maroon bridges that have borne trains on their backs since Queen Victoria put "Empress of India" on her list of titles.

"They did really marvelous work," a bridge engineer named K. B. Lal would tell me. "What they did then is totally structurally secure. Of course, they thought they would *be* here today, never thought they would leave this early. Now all we have to do is grease the bearings."

After suppers of lentils and bread were eaten off the metal food trays called *thali* and the boxes of apple juice sucked dry, the majority of travelers in second class pulled back the nappy curtains of their benches and drifted off or lay staring at the swaying ivory ceiling as we rocked along to Varanasi.

In an upper berth, a Ph.D. student named Freddie Basan was watching a DVD of *The Devil Wears Prada* on his laptop computer, but he took out his earbuds to talk with me. He wore a green T-shirt, jeans and small glasses, and he looked a bit different ethnically from his fellow passengers. Freddie explained he was from the Indian state of Nagaland, a sliver of isolated hills in the far northeastern appendage of the nation, hard by Myanmar, which had never been truly connected to the rest of India. Christian missionaries from the United States had enormous proselytizing success there in the late nineteenth century, and as a result Nagaland is today nearly three-quarters Baptist—a percentage that exceeds even Mississippi. Freddie himself is Catholic; his name is short for Ferdinand.

There have been periodic bursts of secessionist fervor in Nagaland, occasionally culminating in violence. The equation was about to change forever, though: the government announced in 2006 it would build a railway line from the biggest city of Dimapur to the provincial capital at Kohima, spending $190 million to achieve a policy—slowly realized—of forging a physical link to New Delhi in every regional seat of power.

Nagaland's indigenous people were torn on the issue, said Freddie, and there was enough confusion about it to prevent any organized resistance. "They think India will come in and dilute their way of life," he said. But the prospects of easier traveling and being able to ship farm products to market were also seductive. The train will pass through twenty-four villages on its way to the capital, and land prices will surely rise in all of them. Nagaland was in some sense a microcosm of India: a not entirely willing recipient of the railroad, which would see its cultural distinctions sanded down but see its income rise, too. Freddie was trying to find the best way to write about all this in a chapter for his dissertation at Jawaharlal Nehru University, which he has provisionally titled *Ethnic Conflict and the Rights of Minorities*.

Freddie, too, feels torn. He is a member of the Khasi ethnic group, but he feels guilty because he does not know his ancestral language. There is no script for it; it is only spoken, and within his family it will likely die with his parents. He distinguished himself by going off to New Delhi for a graduate degree, but there he picked up a taste for movies and video games. The coming of the railway will surely do the same thing for Nagaland on a grand scale.

"We are slowly dying because we want the good life," he told me. "There will be anger, of course. There will be intermingling of people. There will be intermarriage, and we won't be able to classify the offspring. . . . There is a calculated risk involved. But this is the way we became a nation. It is all very contradictory."

He took the train himself because he didn't have any choice—the road journey to Nagaland was excruciatingly long—but he had come to enjoy these trips. "You meet different people. And even if we have differences, I learn from them. If there's one way to togetherness in India, this is it."

We were by then passing Lucknow, the capital of Uttar Pradesh, whose boosters liked to call it the "Constantinople of India" because its former rulers, the Nawabs of Awadh, put a premium on graceful architecture and racial tolerance. The British made it a railway hub for northern India in the 1860s and proceeded to turn it into a place that reminded them of Paddington station, destroying rows of muddy markets and cottages to make it right-angled and orderly.

"Lucknow has been improved off the face of the earth," complained W. H. Russell in 1875. "Swarded parks, vistas, rides and drives, far prettier than those of the Bois de Boulogne, spread out where once there were narrow streets, teeming bazaars, palaces. They are like oceans beneath which thousands of wrecks lie buried." We called there for ten minutes, took on new passengers and bags of cotton and were off again.

Death and the railroad have been intertwined from the beginning, and the link is borne out daily on the operations side. Especially for those who replace the rails.

Those who do this work in India are at substantially greater risk than most of their counterparts on the earth, thanks to the antique equipment, loose precautions and general lack of a safety culture. But the men of Indian Railways pull up steel every single day, as though the shadow of nonexistence were a distant smudge to be ignored, even though it could leap at them without warning each time they set foot onto the ballast. Those workers who go out to repair the track, known in India as "gangmen," are risking themselves daily as a sacrifice to the nature-defying power of the railway, which threatens to kill for a moment's distraction.

"He was lying right there," said the gangman, pointing to a space between the platform and the fence at Tilak Bridge where the dead man was found. His name was Rajaram Darbari, a track worker, and his skull had been cracked the week before by a moving freight locomotive. Members of his gang were hard at work nearby, prying up and replacing corroded rails—exactly what they had been doing when their colleague was killed.

"The man doing the inspection cried out a train was coming," said the gangman. "But he didn't hear. We went down here and saw the dead man lying next to the track. The police came and said they weren't sure he was dead. They took him to the hospital." There was no blood on him; all the trauma was internal. But nothing could be done. He was a father of seven.

The gangman telling me this story was Bhagwati Prasad. He cradled two signaling flags in his hand, one red and one green, and he had seen many incidents just like this. I asked him what the mistake had been. "It was a matter of chance," he said, offhandedly. "He was a little less alert. He thought the train was slower than it actually was. And it was difficult for him to get off the track."

The spot to which Darbari was thrown and presumably died was littered with the customary banquet of trash that speckles New Delhi: juice boxes, potato-chip bags, cardboard, brown weeds, maroon saliva sprays of tobacco juice. Darbari's replacement was at work just down the line, and trains were rushing beside him every three minutes or so. He didn't bother to look up.

The rail this gang replacing was supposed to have been good for a decade, but a year of sun and feces had warped the steel to the point where the junction was no longer stable. It was now a safety hazard. Darbari's death was regrettable but it would not change the schedule. The stationmaster blocked traffic to that section for an hour, and the crew went to it with practiced haste. Ten gangmen in orange reflective vests, most of them wearing turbans, used man-high crowbars and stiff wire brushes to pry and shovel the stone ballast out of the way; ten more used their crowbars to roll another seventeen-hundred-pound rail into position.

"Pull the rail!" hollered the crew chief in Hindi. "All of it! Roll it!" Two men in a crouch pushed and pulled a hacksaw between them to bite through the defective rail. This is a difficult thing to do during the summer, when rails become like superheated panhandles and thick gloves are needed to touch them. But in February they were cool. When only a stem of a connection remained and the blacksmith gave the order, Maikoo Lal stepped up with a sledgehammer and delivered a round-house blow to clink it apart. To me it looked like the swing of a circus strongman. Lal told me later that it was a light tap by his standards—a baby's kiss.

The gangmen shimmed and levered the new rail into its place, and a few crouched down to the junction, packing red graphite clay in a vise block. A crucible full of metal shavings (it looked like an ice-cream cone on stilts) was placed over the gap, and everyone stood back while it was lit with a potassium nitrate charge. There was not a safety goggle in sight. A tremendous green-orange fire began to burn inside; sparks showered upward, and I felt a few of them land in my hair and bite into my scalp. The temperature in the cauldron reached approximately 2,220 degrees Fahrenheit. A ferocious red salve of iron oxide and aluminum soon dribbled onto the joint in a trickle and then a pour, bathing everything under the funnel in a bluish glaze.

This is a rudimentary but effective technique called "thermite welding," invented in Germany in 1895 and still used to seal rails together in India. The men waited for the cake of iron to cool into gray before they whacked it rhythmically with mallets and axes, splitting it open like a pineapple and trimming it down to the proportion of the rails. The ballast was poked back into place and the rail snapped to the concrete with a pretzel-like clip. The entire operation had taken less than half an hour. If seriously pressed for time, I was told, this gang could have done it in five minutes.

When the iron chopping was nearing its end, I wandered away and, while looking down at the sleepers, heard someone shouting at me. Then the air was torn open by the outraged scream of a horn coming from a place I couldn't see.

I looked up and around, dizzy and jarred, and then felt a hand on my arm, yanking me off to one side with an urgency that left no room for dissent. Only as I got off the track did I see, with amazement, the diesel locomotive advancing at a menacing rate toward the place where I had just been standing. The horn had shaken my senses. It had confused me more than warned me. The locomotive passed, and the driver gave me a reproachful glance from the cab as he went by.

"You stay with me!" ordered Rajesh Vaidya, the section engineer who had just rescued me. "Anything can happen out here."

Just a brief reverie and a moment's confusion—this was exactly what had thrown Rajaram Darbari into the garbage with a crushed skull the month before. New Delhi is a famously anarchic city on the roadways—barreling rickshaws and razor-thin passes and millimeter margins are the scenery of an everyday journey—but no geography quite supplies the constant opportunities for meaningless death more than these tracks. This is inhuman terrain; there are no neutral places to stand.

Rakesh Chopra, who is now on the railway board, told me that he ordered an investigation into fatalities when he worked as a district regional manager in Mumbai. He and his staff interviewed wounded accident survivors and asked detailed questions about what they were experiencing in the seconds before the train struck them. Chopra was initially frustrated at the lack of coherent recall. "Our people were so simple that they wouldn't tell us what they were thinking," he said. "We realized this was the point. When the train is approaching and the horn is sounding, you are actually mentally unstable in that moment. You are unaware of how far you are from the train. It is a state I can only describe as *giddiness*."

A new directive came from his office, which some considered bizarre but did have a noticeable effect on reducing casualties. If a gangman saw a train approaching him, he was to immediately sit down. And when he heard the whistle, he was to stare down at the ground instead of looking for the source of the sound. Slow-moving locomotives could brake faster than a giddy man could blunder his way out of danger. Track repair was switched to the nighttime when possible, as trains with their headlamps blazing in the dark turned out to be easier to avoid than trains emerging from a sunny horizon. Depth perception, oddly, worked better in the dark.

Giddiness. It recalled the world's first recorded train fatality, the unfortunate William Huskisson, who was crushed to death during the demonstration run of the Liverpool & Manchester in 1830. A witness, the actress Fanny Kemble, wrote about the scene in a letter, and it is apparent that his mental state in the seconds before his accident was just as that noticed by Rakesh Chopra almost two centuries later:

> Poor Mr. Huskisson . . . bewildered by the frantic cries of "Stop the engine! Clear the track!" that resounded on all sides, completely lost his head, looked helplessly to the right and left and was instantly prostrated by the fatal machine, which dashed down like a thunderbolt upon him.

The number of people crushed by trains every year is a matter of dispute. Fatality statistics are duly compiled by Indian Railways, but they are understood to be a bad joke, as people are found dead next to the tracks and buried by their families without any investigation or police response. The deaths of gangmen can be quickly forgotten and never enter the logbooks. One trade-union estimate put the death toll at about one hundred for the New Delhi section alone, when the nationwide tally was said to be just ten. But the pride of the managers is on the line, and they are loath to report these grisly mistakes.

Railway board member C. M. Khosla has identified what he calls a "pernicious practice of doctoring accident statistics" throughout Indian Railways. The result of the bad information is a culture where workers' lives are considered expendable. "Statistical manipulation has bred complacency," Khosla has written, "and poor standards of safety persist, wittingly or unwittingly."

The official fatality numbers are expressed as a lump sum. In the most recent time frame available, from 2010 to 2011, a total of 381 people were said to have been killed in accidents. This number is an aggregate of dead passengers, railway staff and "others" (usually meaning trespassers or gate jumpers). But the real number is probably ten or fifteen times as large.

When speaking on the record, railway officials claim that many of these fatalities are not their fault. An unknown number were suicides. One common method of self-dispatch is to lay one's neck on the rail after a curve and await the coming of the guillotine. Adding to the murk,* some of the "passenger" fatalities may have not been railroad-related at all. Scam artists have been known to stuff a valid train ticket into the pockets

---

* Another hazard, somewhat unique to India, is the wild elephants struck and killed when they wander onto the tracks. This happens at least three times a year, and most often when herds are migrating in search of food.

of a dead person and drag the corpse out to the tracks. The family then pretends their relative fell out of a moving train and files a claim under the notorious Section 124 of the Railway Act, which forces Indian Railways to pay compensation for anyone killed while riding the rails. The exact payoffs are set by a tribunal, which is sometimes able to detect fraud and sometimes not. The ticket-bearing corpses can be either left in the garbage at the side of the right-of-way or tossed under the wheels, which helps mangle the evidence but increases the chance of getting caught.

Only rarely does a locomotive driver finish a career without killing at least one person. Consider the mobs of children on bicycles, limping old men, motorcyclists, delivery boys and tottering mothers who mass up impatiently behind the hand-cranked gates and sometimes dart across, bewildered into fatal giddiness when the horn screams.

A driver named Sanjay Mishra, twenty-eight years old and not yet a decade into his career, told me that he has lost count of the number of people who have died under his wheels. The range is somewhere between five and ten. "I used to get angry about it," he said. "Now I just accept it. It could be avoided if they had been alert."

Mishra had originally wanted to be a teacher, but he couldn't find a job and didn't want to explain the alphabet to children. He scored high on the railway exam and won a coveted job as a driver. He is now paid $780 a month, more than double the salary of his assistant. But he earns it. The hours typically go longer than the allotted time, the cabs are uncooled, the driving is eye-crossingly tiring, especially in the morning mist, and his hearing is already damaged from the blasts of the air horn he is compelled to sound more than twenty times an hour; the railway does not allow him to wear earplugs. His arm was once cut by broken glass when somebody, irritated at the late arrival of the train, hurled a rock at the windshield. "This is life in India," he says.

The Indian Railway Loco Runningmen Organisation has complained that its drivers are often working sixteen-hour days without a break. And thanks to Lalu's hiring freezes, the driver staff is 40 percent short and everyone has to pick up the slack, which means everyone is usually exhausted. "We are cut off from society," a driver named Shailendra Agarwal told me. He wore a black turtleneck sweater under his standard-issue blue shirt. "We can celebrate weddings and holidays only if we don't happen to be scheduled."

When I asked him if he liked his job, I expected to hear an extended complaint, but instead I got a puzzled stare. This was a ridiculous question within Indian Railways. *Nobody* ever quit, and it was extraordinarily hard to be fired. Of course he liked his job—almost nothing else better could be conceived for a young man in India. It was the equivalent of being in a royal retinue. The fatigue and the chills and the accidental manslaughters were obstacles to be overcome.

"We fight like warriors in this job," Agarwal said. "Warriors are dedicated to their nation, and so are we to ours." No psychological leave is granted for a driver who runs down a pedestrian, and a gang crew who loses a colleague is expected to go back to work within the hour. Official time cannot be set aside for mourning, at least not on this level. The rails must be kept welded in the ceaseless struggle against shit and sun and tardiness.

Bhagat Ram, a hardy fifty-four-year-old, one of the two hundred thousand gangmen who keep the rails intact, rolled up his pant leg and showed me the scar left from a mishap with a concrete sleeper. He was helping unload a heaped pile of them from a flatcar when one got stuck, dangling from the edge by its foot. Ram went over to help loosen it at the same time a man on top of the car gave it a tremendous shove. The bar of concrete landed on Ram's left leg, snapping the bone. He had to be carried for two excruciating kilometers on the shoulders of his coworkers. The injury put him out for seven months.

Ram never attended a day of school and has worked for the railroads most of his life. He now earns a salary of about three dollars a day. The work is long and boring. "At the end of the day, I feel like fainting. This is hard-earned money. But what else am I going to do in life?"

What he meant was that no other jobs would be available to a man of his age and talents. His family, a wife and three boys and a father now approaching a hundred years old, lives in a state called Himachal, and he can see them only once every few months. The railroad gives him free passage. Most of his saved-up salary comes with him.

"In my village I have a lot of respect," he said. "My family gets respect. They are illiterate, but they get prestige." He wears a green sweater and tennis shoes and a cap with the legend USA.

When the men (they are always men) in Ram's gang are hauling a rail together, they sometimes sing a chant of two lines. The leader makes a call, and the men answer as a chorus. The lyrics are both coarse and creative, in the style of the U.S. Army's beloved "Sound Off." The Hindi word for this work song is *boli*. One of the best known, roughly translated, is:

> *You pull that rail with all your fire*
> *Or else you'll get rammed in the ass later on!*

Another *boli* addresses a fictional woman passerby:

> *What's that inside your blouse?*
> *There are red pigeons hiding inside!*

A cleaner one extols the company's party line, with an acknowledgment that most of the men are migrants who will be remitting their wages to home villages, far from where they're camping:

> *If you don't work hard*
> *You are sending stolen money back home!*

Like the locomotive drivers, the gangmen in India are worked extremely hard. The job of tearing up corroded rails is never finished.

Indian Railways carries 2 million tons of freight every day over a network long enough to wrap itself around the earth three times.

The flamboyant railway minister Lalu Prasad took a public interest in the lives of the gangmen. When he observed some of them walking barefoot on the sharp ballast stones, he made sure that shoes were available for them. But the same methods he used for boosting the revenue of Indian Railways from negative cash to $6 billion were also contributing to the dismal safety record. Volume tripled in five years, and he accomplished this by stuffing wagons beyond their intended limits. When the rules got in his way, he rewrote them. A key safety benchmark, for example, is "axle load," which is the maximum weight of a train on any given section of track. It had been 20.3 tons per wagon. Lalu raised it to 28.3. This meant his trains could carry more coal, mineral oil and steel, but at a crushing price to the rails that had to bear the weight and to the gangmen who had to go out and replace them even faster.

"Overloading of wagons beyond designed capacity was the mechanism for earning more revenue," concluded the *Indian Express* newspaper. "The issues of long-term impact on the safety of bridges and axles and track were brushed aside, enabling Indian Railways to earn what others would take away."

Rakesh Chopra compared the system to a reanimated corpse. "If the bones are okay and the muscles still work, we'll just replace the head and the eyes and go on using the body."

What was keeping the Indian railroads at work and dispensing salaries, in other words, was the same thing that made them so deadly.

"To see a mail express train getting smashed is a horror," said Vikas Arya. "It keeps you up for about a week."

He is a district regional engineer for power locomotives, a man of importance in his field who was selected to be an officer when he was a teenager. He favors V-necked tennis sweaters and smokes cigarettes double-inhaled through his nose. There is a plastic electric map of the Northern Division on the wall of his office, inside the colonnaded division headquarters whose first stone was laid by Lady Russell in 1936.

Vikas smoked and stared at the ceiling while he told me a story from early in his career.

"I was assigned to a city called Jabalpur somewhat south of here. There was a young assistant pilot under my watch, a bright young man named Ajay. Twenty-three years old. He came to me one day and gave me a box of sweets, asking for a favor. He wanted to be transferred to another run because he was about to be married and wanted to be closer to his wife. I said okay. We shook hands on it. And three to four days later, he picks up a train that's headed down a slope that goes from the town of Manikpur down to a station at Ohan. This was one of the steepest gradients in the district. The vertical drop is one meter for every hundred traveled. And their brakes failed.

"That train was soon traveling at a speed of sixty or seventy miles an hour on a line with a speed restriction of twenty-five miles an hour. They panicked. Now, down at Ohan there were only two tracks, and both of them were occupied with stationary trains: a passenger train and a goods train full of cement bags. A collision was about three minutes away, and the stationmaster had a choice of which track to attempt to clear.

"Well, you can't evacuate a passenger train in three minutes, so he orders the goods train out as fast as it can go. At the back of that train was a guard who stepped on, and he was waving a red flag and waving his arms at the approaching train. He knew that train was traveling at a very high speed right towards him. They had managed to travel about three kilometers away from the station, and just before the impact the guard dove for his life. He tumbled away down an embankment. But the two men on board the runaway train did not jump, even though they could have. They had what I would call a certain dedication to their duties.

"The force of the impact ripped the engine block loose and sent it cutting through the front of the cab like a knife blade. Twelve cars in the cement train were derailed. There were bags and bags of the gray powder everywhere. We found the driver's body very quickly. He looked fine, but his skull was caved in. The young assistant, we couldn't find him. His body was missing. There were bags and bags of powdered cement everywhere—they had broken open, and there were gray piles of dust.

"Now we had to restore the line, and I was receiving pressure to clear the wreckage immediately. And I told them, 'Are you mad? We can't just leave a guy who performed so valiantly. We cannot just haul away his parts with the wreckage.' So I ordered half my team to start repairing track and the other half to start digging through the cement with their bare hands. There must have been five hundred bags that had broken open. Finally we found him. There was a hand sticking out of the gray pile. He came out of it looking like a statue of blood and concrete.

"Five to six hours later, the track was repaired, the wreckage was hauled away and the line was running as normal. It did not make the newspapers. So many things like this happen in India."

I asked, "The two men had the opportunity to jump and they didn't?"

"They did not."

"Why not?"

"I remember another accident similar to this where, again, four men were involved. The two who jumped before the collision were reprimanded and demoted. But the two who were killed were commended posthumously. They had the opportunity to save their lives but did not take the option."

"What was going through their minds?" I asked.

"You don't abandon ship and run away. You will never find this in our rule books. But it is a strong value."

PLEASE DO NOT ACCEPT FOOD DRINKS ETC. FROM UNKNOWN PERSONS OR CO-PASSENGERS, said the sign. THEY MAY BE ANTISOCIAL ELEMENTS OUT TO DRUG YOU AND THEN ROB YOU OF YOUR BELONGINGS.

I stood in the vestibule next to this sign with some restless men who were smoking. A twenty-nine-year-old man named Deep wore a New York Yankees baseball cap and a T-shirt that said CLUBS VS. FIGHTS covering an ample belly. He passed me a brand of cigarette called Flake. It tasted earthy and burned. We watched as two younger men stood in the jamb of the wide-open portal (these are almost never locked on Indian Railways) and stuck their heads far out into the dark, poles whipping by at seventy miles an hour. A slip or a jolt would have sent them flying. Deep only laughed at them. "This is what passes for adventure," he told me.

He then pointed out a mouse scrambling across the vestibule, and this got him going on a favorite national subject: the dingy atmosphere of the trains. The problem was not with the management, he felt, but with the passengers.

"You should treat this as public property," he said. "You should take care of this place like your own house." This didn't stop him from throwing his Flake cigarette onto the floor after he had smoked it down.

We were an hour away from a midnight arrival at Varanasi, not the terminus of the *Guwahati Express* but a major junction where this train would call for barely ten minutes. Like Lucknow, it had become a transport hub in the 1870s, following a famine that had laid waste to the barge traffic on the Ganges. Varanasi generously accommodated the iron horse, just as it has absorbed pilgrims into its elastic fibers since its hazy founding three thousand years ago.

Also called Benares, it is considered by most Hindus to be the holiest place on earth, having been visited by the Lord Shiva five thousand years ago. A folk belief, not found in the Vedic scriptures, says that dying here guarantees a deliverance from the cycle of birth and death and an instant pass to eternal relief. A cluster of hospices and retirement villas along the banks makes a tidy business out of this belief, charging premium rack rates as guests wait to die, which can take months or years. Elderly beggars who don't have such means lie on flagstones instead and subsist on alms from the other pilgrims, who clog the twist of streets near the river. Bathing in the river is said to wash away sins, and pyramid-like stone steps called "ghats" lead a pilgrim down to Mother Ganga. There are several spots alongside the ghats where corpses are burned on log fires; the ashes are tossed into the slow-moving water.

Hinduism is the most flexible and absorbent of the world's big religions, bringing into its main body a ceaseless multitude of deities. Any village or family is welcome to attach its own local god to the pantheon without fear of being accused of heresy. There those gods can join the hierarchy of Shiva and Ganesh and Hanuman and a thousand others. A kaleidoscope of rituals and practices operates underneath just a few basic points of theology: the unity of matter in one absolute being, the cycles of birth and rebirth, the yearning to join with eternity, the ultimate nonlinearity of time that was so contrary to the ethos of the railway. And this, too: the physical world is nothing but a dream of separation from the inexpressible reality of the universe, the cosmic spirit called Brahman.

But for a faith that considers the material world to be an illusion, Hinduism puts a huge premium on sacred geography. One of the primary reasons that Indians welcomed long-distance rail was for the pilgrimage to sacred spots, and Varanasi benefited more than almost any other place. Temples jammed the road crossings; holy men sold themselves for counsel; sweetmeat vendors harangued the supplicants; the colonial viceroys were forced to install hydrants and stone curbs to handle the crush of worshippers the railways unloaded each day. "The people are using the trains to go to the shrines, and our pilgrimage traffic is enormous," a British administrator told the journalist Frank Carpenter in 1910. "It used to take weeks or months for the average pilgrim to go to Benares or some other distant sacred locality. The man now finds that he can get there by rail in hours or days." *Pilgrims, sir, they're worse than horses*, had been the complaint of old-time colonial conductors, and the sour feeling was reciprocated: Gandhi had complained that railways made the holy places unholy and turned worship into a commercial enterprise. He was correct about the economics at least, for Varanasi became a great twentieth-century railroad boomtown—an improbable mingling of low and high purpose—and it remains so today.

There are approximately a million religious visitors to the city each year, most of whom arrive on the train, but I didn't meet any of them on the *Guwahati Express*. I instead got to talking with an official on a government board of textiles who was riding second class on his way to Varanasi for a manufacturers' conference. Silk had been woven there since Gautama Buddha came through as a traveling preacher in the fifth century B.C., and it was still a big-money industry. Pankaj Sharma could have taken a discount flight to Varanasi on his agency's tab, but he told me that he liked the ease and the conversation that the train afforded. He ranted to me for an hour about American foreign policy, smiling ironically in the right places, and I gave it back to him with equally good-natured rancor, and by the time we both detrained at the candy-orange castle of the Varanasi train station, we were friends.

The flagstones were crowded with sleepers lying in geometrical rows, all under pastel-colorful and spangled blankets, waiting for a train that might be tomorrow or days in the future. A few of them had what looked like the entirety of their belongings with them, bundles wrapped in giant sheets of cloth bound together with rubber belts designed for automobile engines or stuffed into the parcels called "holdalls."

The economist John Kenneth Galbraith, who served as JFK's ambassador to India, had described the country—not without some admiration—as "a functioning anarchy." And there is no better place to see it than the average big-city railway station, with all its buzzing crowds and hucksters and bodily stench, the trains chuffing into their platforms on time or not, the slop in the toilets, the flies, the square bales of cotton and bags of lentils stacked ten feet high, the frenzy of rickshaw wallahs outside waiting to set upon the lone traveler. But they were all here, this moving citizenry, on their way to a wedding, a pilgrimage or a job. They were going to get where they were going, on board an unwitting gift of the British. This magnificent machine had not been built for them, but it had become their inheritance.

Mounted above the station was a statue—not of an anthropomorphic god but of the Ashoka Chakra, the wheel that adorns the center of India's national flag. The spokes on this wheel represent the transient material aspects of life, the ones that are forever tumbling in motion. The center hub is what never changes. The wheel occupied the tower face where a giant clock might otherwise be displayed.

As I walked outside the train station with Pankaj and we turned and made our ways to our respective hotels, it seemed to me that for all its inefficiencies and dangers—the antique equipment and acid-warped steel, the overstuffed office blocks and grimy carriages, its history of colonial greed—that for all its myriad subhuman qualities, Indian Railways was actually the most human institution in the whole nation.

I climbed over a concrete barrier and threaded my way through the postmidnight traffic toward Patel Road. Past the belt of grilling onions and soot and motors, the streets took on a lime-colored and melancholic aspect, full of blank windows. Almost nobody was about in these residential blocks, except a cow feeding on a pile of straw. The night was mild, and the air smelled dark and suffused with mildew. I didn't feel like going to sleep quite yet, so I hailed a bicycle rickshaw and paid the driver a hundred rupees to pedal me down to the river.

BOUND FOR GLORY

New York to Los Angeles

George Gershwin was on a train to Boston in 1924 when he began to daydream. The *ca-tunk ca-tunk* of the wheels was having a strange effect on him.

He thought of an offer he'd received to write an experimental concerto for an exhibition. Gershwin wasn't convinced he could write anything memorable in a short period of time, but he changed his mind somewhere between New York and Boston. "It was on the train, with its steely rhythms, its rattle-ty bang, that is so often so stimulating to a composer—I frequently hear music in the very heart of the noise," he later told a biographer. "I heard it as a sort of musical kaleidoscope of America, of our vast melting pot, of our unduplicated national pep, of our metropolitan madness."

A musical figuration came together in his mind, and by the time he reached South Station, the outlines of *Rhapsody in Blue* were plain. Back in his apartment on 110th Street in Manhattan, he wrote it in a state of what he called "subconscious composing," where the notes "oozed out of [his] fingers." The piece debuted five weeks later, winning almost universal praise for its expansive and flowing texture.

Rhapsody in Blue is often portrayed as a love poem to the cities of the United States, especially New York City, but a deeper subject lurks within: the America connected by steel rails and locomotives, the empire of railroads that America had once been, the astonishing steam-powered device that could carom from New York to Chicago in eighteen hours and that had transformed a seaboard republic of small farmers and merchants into a continental power of speed and industrial might. The American train in Gershwin's time was at its high-water mark. On any given day, there were twenty thousand passenger trains making journeys on over a quarter million miles of track.

And even though America remains a country of living railroads, they occupy a much lower profile today. Freight rail is still reasonably healthy: there are now six dominant North American carriers—CSX, BNSF, Norfolk Southern, Union Pacific, Canadian Pacific and Canadian National—and together they haul about 40 percent of the nation's goods when measured by distance and weight.

There is also a healthy set of commuter rails that spoke outward from big-city downtowns. All of these are heavily subsidized by local and federal taxes, and they carry about a half million regular riders each day on lines like San Francisco's Caltrain, Los Angeles' Metrolink, Chicago's Metra, Philadelphia's SEPTA, New Jersey Transit and New York City's Long Island Rail Road. But the vast majority of American citizens have never once been on board a passenger train, except perhaps the toy steam railroad that circles the edges of Disneyland and Disney World. For most, the train is a figure of romance or childhood poetry rather than a tool of modernity.

Yet that old identity—American Train Sublime—still dwells in the collective unconscious of who we are: our prodigious growth, our faith in business, our love of velocity, our confidence in technology, our capacity for seeing beauty in the newcomer. "Paint me a small railroad station then, ten minutes before dark," wrote John Cheever at the beginning of his novel *Bullet Park*.

We travel by plane, oftener than not, and yet the spirit of our country seems to have remained a country of railroads. You wake in a pullman bedroom at three a.m. in a city the name of which you do not know and may never discover. A man stands on the platform with a child on his shoulders. They are waving goodbye to some traveler, but what is the child doing up so late and why is the man crying? On a siding beyond the platform there is a lighted dining car where a waiter sits alone at a table, adding up his accounts. Beyond this is a water tower and beyond this a well-lighted and empty street. Then you think happily that this is your country—unique, mysterious and vast.

I went to New York City for the purpose of getting on board a train to Washington and then making my way to the opposite coast via Amtrak without stopping. I wanted to see what remained of this old country of railroads and who was still riding them. The logical place to start was Penn Station.

Though I have lived in Manhattan off and on throughout the years, I gawked with a newcomer's eyes at the raw display of oddballery on Sixth Avenue that the city takes for granted. A woman with her hair dyed red swayed on the corner of Thirty-fourth Street and chanted verses from the Book of Amos, mixed with admonitions of her own devising. Another woman wearing a T-shirt that said GIVE THESE A CHANCE over voluptuous middle-aged breasts strolled past. A man in a saggy, oil-stained coat folded a pizza slice in half and speared it into his mouth. Dank air blew up from a double subway grate, in front of a pair of Sikh brothers frying hot dogs at their cart; an electric zipper sign scrolled a message in red dot matrix over their heads: I LOVE NY. BIRMILA RAM. Orthodox Jews with prayer shawls sidestepped through the knots of people waiting for taxis in front of Penn Station, which is barely discernible as a train station at all but rather as an ugly plinth of offices defending the puck-shaped sports arena of Madison Square Garden.

A traveler enters this dismal underground station by taking an escalator that feeds into a shopping concourse, where there is a chain drugstore, a men's tie store called Tiecoon, a women's stocking emporium called Elegance, a TGIFriday's restaurant where two bald men were drinking happy-hour beers and watching a women's soccer game.

Directly beneath the basketball court where the New York Knicks play home games is the subterranean waiting room for the trains, which has all the charm of a county jail. A banner hangs from the walls: an Amtrak house ad featuring silhouettes of chatty patrons clustered in a bar car. OUR TRAINS STILL LET OFF PLENTY OF STEAM, it insists. An electronic console affixed to the ceiling boasts of the trains that are now boarding; the Northeast Regionals going to towns for the responsible souls who married early and bought sensible homes in New Rochelle, Stamford, Bridgeport, New Haven, Wallingford and Meriden. Amtrak's only real revenue base is centered in this corridor; everything else loses money.

In the crowd of people gazing upward was one who reminded me of a woman I once loved in California. She was tall as a crane in her striped skirt and boots. For all I knew, she might even have been that college girl I spotted years ago blinking away tears in a snowstorm, now fully grown up. I yearned to go up to talk with her. Perhaps she was heading home to one of those bedroom suburbs or perhaps (too much to hope?) to one of the cities through which I would pass on the way out to California. In any case, she was part of a local tableau: women are more casually and effortlessly beautiful in New York City than in any other place I know.

I fortified my nerve—as I had failed to do on the *Pennsylvanian* twenty years ago—and went up to her.

"Hey." I smiled. "Do you know which of these tracks has the train to Washington, D.C.?" A lame opening and a redundant question, but I've talked to strangers with less of a pretext.

She glanced at me, and the man next to her turned, too, and I saw they were together. Both wore wedding rings.

"They should have it onna board inna minute," she told me, smiling back, and I looked up with her. There was a little brown sparrow trapped in here, which must have entered through an open side door. It fluttered around looking for an exit. "Hey, thanks," I told the couple. "Have a good trip." And I silently wished them well, wherever they were going.

Within two minutes the board numbers whirred, the train to Washington was sorted to Track 13, and I showed the uniformed Amtrak clerk my paper ticket at the gate and descended to the cavern of bolted pillars at track level, the only remnant of the old vanished Pennsylvania Station, which had been an architectural marvel, the crown jewel of the Pennsylvania Railroad.

The "Pennsy" was a pin-striped corporation of the old order. Its executives believed it to be the Tiffany railroad of the world, with the tightest schedules, the fastest locomotives and the top managerial talent. In 1904 its president, Alexander Cassatt, approved a stupendous master plan to drill two rail tubes seventy feet under the Hudson River, four more under the East River, a long arcing bridge over the temperamental narrows that the seventeenth-century Dutch sailors had called Hell Gate and—balanced on the fulcrum of it all—a grand edifice patterned after the Baths of Caracalla in Rome.

The resulting Pennsylvania Station looked like a cross between a palazzo and a football stadium. The front was crowned with eagles and marble maidens; the interior was as high as the basilica at St. Peter's, with circular clocks suspended from the ceiling. Travertine marble—an Italian stone the color of warm honey—was used here for the first time in an American building.

"The color effect of the station against the blue of the sky is one of such beauty that it almost hurts, it is so simple, so pure, so serene," wrote Alfred Hoyt Granger in 1913. A visiting William Faulkner thought that "people appeared as small and intent as ants" under the high skylights.

What was once the most magnificent train station in the world was destroyed sixty years later when the safety and convenience of air travel, as well as the congressional decision to build interstate highways, had been creating a long, inglorious decline in passenger trains. Places like Penn Station were seen as moth-eaten and useless. Historic preservationists had failed to gather enough political support to stop the demolition coming as it did in the Kennedy presidency, when Beaux Arts artifacts were being enthusiastically bulldozed to make room for streamlined cubes that now seem like antiques themselves.

The original Penn Station was not perfect: the tracks were far away from the ticketing windows, and the iron stairs were perennially jammed. Some thought the statuary halls created a chilly feeling; there was just too much space and not enough warmth. But it was beloved for its sense of ambition and grandeur.

What replaced it in 1963 was so hideous that it is one of the monumental embarrassments of New York City. The lighting is sterile white, the ceilings are oppressively low and the air is dank. The trains are shut away in the basement, as unseen as sewerage. "One entered the city like a god; one scuttles in now like a rat," complained Yale architecture professor Vincent Scully, in an insult so widely quoted it might as well have been carved into the new façade, as if there were any marble left to carve.

The Northeast Regional train to Washington lay idling like a silver python. I stepped onto it and immediately smelled the unmistakable fragrance of Amtrak: blue toilet fluid, old socks, a lacing of diesel fuel. The coach seats were reclining, as big as living-room chairs, with far more legroom than airline seats. Over the top of each was a napkin of synthetic white cloth to protect the upholstery from people's oily scalps. The windows were tinted a blue-gray color and permanently sealed. This train was already full of travelers, and I found an aisle seat next to a dark-haired young man wearing a blue T-shirt and absorbed in a magazine. We said nothing to each other.

There are no lurches when American trains start to move. The initial propulsion is gentle and noiseless, almost imperceptible, as though the carriage were simply obeying a natural tug of gravity. The power behind it is stupendous—the General Electric locomotive up front of this train weighed thirteen short tons and possessed the nominal horsepower of a dozen Cadillacs—but it felt as effortless as an ice-skater's glide. I tried and failed to hear anything resembling *Rhapsody in Blue*.

The train threaded through the pillars and emerged into sunlight, at the bottom of a square open pit between Thirty-second and Thirty-fourth streets that hadn't been covered since it was first excavated with steam engines and Irish shovelmen in 1904. Then we were in Alexander Cassatt's hard-won Hudson River tube and four minutes of whizzing darkness before emerging back into the afternoon light in the New Jersey wetlands.

We barreled past highway junctions and through the new three-level Frank Lautenberg Secaucus Junction station, a crossroad for commuter trains, and passed a radio tower planted in the midst of a rectangular swamp. A few of the stone maidens from the old Pennsylvania Station had been dumped here, along with loads of broken marble columns and granite shards in 1963. They had lain here with their faces turned up to the sky surrounded by the rest of the fill dirt.

As we chuffed closer to the stalk of the control tower at Newark Liberty International Airport, I risked saying a few words to the guy sitting next to me in the window seat. Now that we had blown Manhattan, time seemed to flatten out and the train's motion became a lulling drone. "So where are you heading tonight?" I asked.

His name was Jeremy, and he had boarded the Amtrak *Vermonter* that morning at White River Junction. It was the end of a weekend visit with a student at Dartmouth Medical School whom he happened to love. This long-distance romance was a tough one for him, eased somewhat by these periodic visits, and the return train always had a melancholy feeling. This was a ten-and-a-half-hour trip, just as pricey as an air ticket, and his friends thought he was crazy, but he told them the train gave him a feeling of liberty. Planes cramped him. The bus depressed him.

Outside the glued-shut window was a late-summer afternoon receding before us at seventy miles per hour. At New Brunswick we crossed the Raritan River, with slanted light pooled on its surface, cut through a hilly corner of the redbrick Rutgers campus and trundled aside rows of Dutch Colonials dappled with the evening sun and then a golf course—or perhaps a cemetery—with a white fountain geysering in the midst of a big lawn. And Martian tank farms with cylinders holding mystery fluids. New Jersey must be the most strangely zoned state in the country, a freehold of industry mingling without shame with Queen Anne homes, mixed hardwood forests and grave sites from the Revolutionary War. A state prison went by on the right, surrounded by double rows of fences and a double twisting of concertina wire on top.

I wondered if the inmates could hear this Amtrak Northeast Regional rushing past, and I thought inevitably of the old Johnny Cash song "Folsom Prison Blues," in which a criminal who'd "shot a man in Reno just to watch him die" was tormented with the hoot of the nearby train whistle and the liberty it represented. I mentioned the idea to Jeremy.

I bet there's rich folks eatin'
From a fancy dining car.
They're probably drinkin' coffee
And smokin' big cigars.

"Yeah, well," said Jeremy, "that's not exactly what happens on Amtrak. You know what I heard at the snack bar? I went there to get a vegetarian burger, and the person in front of me asked for a sandwich, and he asked the attendant, 'Do you guys have a panini press?' The guy told him, 'Yeah, sure we do. It's called a microwave.'"

We trundled over the Delaware River at Trenton, where letters

mounted on a neighboring bridge proclaimed the extinct civic myth
TRENTON MAKES, THE WORLD TAKES, and were into the warehouse
exurbs of northern Philadelphia. Deserted streets arrowed away, and
apartments shuffled past like a series of Edward Hopper paintings on an
educational filmstrip until we paralleled the Schuylkill River and caught
a bend near the art museum and its *Rocky* steps. There was a boathouse
with a row of crew shells lined up on the ramp like the day's fresh catch.

After a pause underneath the magnificent Thirtieth Street Station—
a building spared the fate of Penn Station—we crept away from the city
through double-tracked veins where garbage cluttered in little piles.
Security lights pooled against walls, revealing sinister-looking hollow
spaces where pallets were once stacked for loading onto boxcars. Here
is our hidden nation: best seen through the windows of trains. In this
oil-stained corridor, trackside factories had stamped out heavy equipment and drew immigrants from all over Europe, making new Americans even as they created new prosperity. The train still came through
here, though it hurried past the disused brick shells as might a frightened pedestrian, or a guilty party.

Baltimore soon presented itself with red neon signs shining next to
Interstate 95; it was from near here that Irish laborers had started digging and blasting away hills toward the Patapsco River, making way for
the first tracks of the Baltimore & Ohio. And not far off, either: the site
of its lost cornerstone.

Jeremy and I talked sporadically through the northern suburbs of
Washington, where tobacco and sheep farms had gone over to arrangements of rambling suburban homes and lighted office cubes. When we
shook hands good-bye, I wondered what would happen with his faraway Dartmouth med student and whether the cord of the train would
get them through the years of apartness they were facing.

The barrel vaults of Washington's Union Station were waiting to
swallow up every passenger on the train. This terminal had been built
a little over a century ago as an add-on to the grand civic design of

Washington envisioned by Pierre L'Enfant in the 1780s—white temples connected with promenades—and as a latecomer it did not disappoint. Daniel Burnham's architectural firm went to work, leveling a slum neighborhood named Swampdoodle and building on its site an arrivals hall that was said to be the biggest room in the world at the time (a bit of hype), which included eight elevated statues of Roman warriors with granite shields strategically positioned to cover* their genitals and a private presidential waiting room mindful of the fact that President James A. Garfield had been shot to death twenty years before by a crazed free-love advocate at the Baltimore and Potomac station.

This old rail temple came very close to being obliterated in the 1980s—the roof was collapsing and mushrooms were sprouting in the corners—but Congress came up with a grant to turn the southern half into a shopping concourse and its basement into an arcade of fast-food dispensaries. It isn't such a bad fate, and certainly better than the claw bucket. Across a wide lawn from the entrance was the eminence of the U.S. Capitol, bathed in lemony light. A few yellow cabs sat waiting for fares. When this station opened, Daniel Burnham had ordered his personal credo carved over a side entrance: MAKE NO LITTLE PLANS, FOR THEY HAVE NO MAGIC TO STIR MEN'S BLOOD.

I sometimes think that if I had nothing better to do with my life that I would buy a stack of Amtrak tickets and sit in the club car and listen to people's stories. I would travel in lazy circuits from Florida to Vermont to Oregon to Texas, making friends for an hour or a day and letting them tell me whatever they wanted. And I would happily listen as the American land rattled by.

A train is the perfect environment for conversation. There is space to get up and walk around. The mechanistic *ka-chunk, ka-chunk, ka-chunk* of the motion has a soothing effect, unlike the sterile, narcotizing

---

* A specific request of Congress.

ahhh of a jetliner in flight, even though you'd think the opposite would be true. Leaving dull conversations is easy: just excuse yourself to go look at the view or get another drink. There are always those travelers who ride the trains as if they are flying commercial, shielded against any possibility of human contact with a book or a stony expression, but they miss the point. For all its faults—and there are many—Amtrak keeps the spirit of railroads breathing in America, as well as the spirit of a country that has a certain native affability written into its character.

In some crucial sense, strangers are *supposed* to be talking to one another in this allegedly casteless nation, founded on the ideas of democratic rule and free markets. These spontaneous meetings are how volunteer fire departments get organized, business ventures cooked up, tools borrowed, love affairs suggested, food exchanged, candidates questioned, ideas tested, stories told. And the train is always a hot herbarium of stories. Perhaps the certainty that you will never see a fellow traveler again makes the atmosphere that much more honest on trains. Leo Tolstoy's novella *The Kreutzer Sonata* tells the story of a man who kills his wife in a jealous rage—and then rides around Russia on trains, confessing everything to strangers and hoping for forgiveness.

On a ride through Mississippi one night, I listened to a man with half a mouth of teeth tell me how he killed his best friend in a car accident—he had been drinking, and they hit a tree trunk at sixty. Another man near Memphis had run away from his wife in Michigan and was appearing in a community-theater production of *A Christmas Carol*, where he played the role of Marley's Ghost. Near Erie, Pennsylvania, on another trip, I listened to an ex–taxi driver with WHISKEY BOB tattooed on his arm tell the story of warding off a robber with a pistol and then doing two years of jail time on a weapons charge as a result. An overbearing rural wife in Texas told me about her twelve-year-old son and how he almost shot a neighbor accidentally with a long-range rifle while hunting antelope. This was a neighbor she happened to despise for being a good-looking closet lesbian and "probably running a sugar ranch up there" with her female partner, an executive with the Applebee's restaurant chain who got to fly on a corporate jet. A man of seventy with a silver cross in his lapel showed me the earnest eight-page handwritten letter that he sent to a college girlfriend after the death of his wife, wondering if "the old Larry spark" still burned within her after all this time. Apparently it did, because they were to be married the next month.

Story upon story. The trip is rarely good enough as a solitary experience. The people you meet along the way give it shape and color, and Amtrak is one place where America converses with itself. It is a vestigial whiff of a commonality among citizens, rich and poor, a mode of collective destiny, "this thing we all do together."

I slept for the night at a friend's apartment in Washington and then got on board Amtrak's *Cardinal* bound for Chicago. This train traces a jagged smile shape across the Virginia Piedmont and Appalachia into the midwestern prairies and takes its name from a bit of trivia: it passes through six states—Virginia, West Virginia, Ohio, Kentucky, Indiana and Illinois—and all of them have the cardinal as the official state bird. In its opening minutes, the train was in darkness. It slid under the U.S. Capitol and the Cannon House Office Building via the First Street Tunnel, which was carefully dug out in 1904 by the Washington Terminal Company and has been in continuous use ever since.

Sunlight poured back on us as we came out near New Jersey Avenue, past the appalling curved façade of the Department of Housing and Urban Development, past NASA's headquarters and the L'Enfant Metro stop, with people in careful suits and key-card leashes emerging for work, and under another tunnel below Virginia Avenue and over the Long Bridge next to clogged-up I-395 into Virginia itself, the Pentagon, its malls and cars and satellite dishes on the fringes and the slow river beyond it and the plaqued memorial for the jetliner that slammed into its side on September 11, 2001.

In the club car, a ginger-haired man was drinking Heineken. It was 10:00 A.M. He smiled up at me blandly, and I decided in that moment to finish my coffee with him. He introduced himself as Wayne, and he was heading to Charleston, West Virginia, and it wasn't ten minutes before the stories started coming out.

He had helped build all kinds of things in New Jersey: tract houses, a terminal at Newark airport, the giant Ferris wheel at Six Flags, which he rode only once. The labor had messed him up in all kinds of interesting orthopedic ways. Once Wayne was helping unload concrete sacks from a truck and broke his back. Riding with the Hells Angels when he was younger had taught him about the sweet rush of methamphetamine, and he grabbed at it for relief. This tendency led him to county jail, where the subchieftain of a gang helped himself to a carton of milk off Wayne's tray in the cafeteria one morning. Wayne waited calmly for about five minutes, then crept up and slammed him with his plastic tray in the delicate spot where the skull met the top of the spine. In keeping with timeless jailhouse logic, nobody bothered Wayne after that. "I can be a very nice guy," he said, "but you have to demonstrate strength under pressure."

We passed through a town whose name I could not glimpse, with redbrick storefronts bearing faded paint advertisements for Coca-Cola. The courthouse clock was frozen at an incorrect hour. Wayne went on with his story. He had recently been cohabitating with a wild twenty-three-year-old girlfriend, but not for much longer. What she didn't know was that Wayne was taking this railroad trip to leave her. He had a son living in Charleston, the unplanned product of a teenage dalliance, whom he hadn't seen for almost the entirety of the life of the boy, who was now in his early forties, and Wayne was unsure how the son would react to the sudden appearance of his father at the depot after all this time. He hoped his boy could help him find work in the coal mines.

He certainly wasn't the first person I'd met on a train who was doing a disappearing act on a job or a family—the old Kansas City checkout—though every explanation was different. Wayne's rationale had to do with his girlfriend's recent drunk-driving arrest and her refusal to show up for a court date, despite his strong encouragement. He had finally had enough of her irresponsible ways, he said, and the intimacy was getting stale.

"I told her, 'I know how this works,' " said Wayne. "But she didn't listen."

"I didn't listen either when I was twenty-three," I said.

"Yeah, me neither."

The college town of Charlottesville crawled by, a dusky oil painting of a Piedmont late summer. There were a series of tin warehouses, the big garrison of the University of Virginia hospital, a short look at an academic lawn as we passed over an old stone bridge, a fake round-topped Monticello McMansion on a hill set in the rolling grassy knobs of horse country as we headed west toward the first real wall of the Blue Ridge Mountains and, beyond them, the carboniferous 500-million-year-old Appalachian range.

These slopes had been an intimidating barrier for the first railroad builders in America—the genuine test of whether the sensational new device from England could become not merely a local trolley for farmers but a tool for radically transforming the economy.

One of the first Americans to see it was a colonel named John Stevens who had a steam ferry service over the Hudson River, and when news of the Stockton & Darlington reached him in 1825, he excitedly cobbled together his own small engine and built a circular track for it on the grounds of an estate in Hoboken, New Jersey.* The moneyed classes all over the country took note. The train, wrote James H. Lanman, via a weirdly erotic metaphor in *Merchant* magazine, would "open the ample bosoms of the soil to the genial beams of the fertilizing sun."

New railroad companies multiplied and divided, capital flying fast toward the solid and the sleazy alike. Cities to be linked were typically hitched together with "and" or with an ampersand, in a seeming frenzy to

---

* Now the site of Stevens Institute of Technology.

mate. The New York, New Haven and Hartford. The Detroit, Toledo and Ironton. Philadelphia and Reading. Nashville, Chattanooga & St. Louis. Frankfort and Kokomo. Most of the naming was a marketing gimmick: the prestige of the namesake city could thereby be claimed by an embryonic railroad scheme, even if it was poorly capitalized and doomed to fail.

Not everyone bought it, of course. A French traveler in the United States, Michel Chevalier, observed that in the spirit of American conversation the railroad was a "perfect mania . . . in the water, in the bowels of the earth and in the air. . . . It is more than a machine. It is almost a living being." A minister in Connecticut started telling his parishioners that the sound of a locomotive could drive a listener to insanity. A farmer nicknamed the new trains "hell in a harness," and in the seclusion of Concord, Massachusetts, Henry David Thoreau complained about the invasion of the Boston & Lowell: "The whistle of the locomotive penetrates my woods, summer and winter, sounding like the scream of a hawk sailing over some farmer's yard. . . . I will not have my eyes put out and my ears spoiled by its smoke and steam and hissing."

But there was no stopping it. By the time of the Civil War, there were already thirty thousand miles of track in America. The telescoping of space meant that people became "neighbors" with those living a hundred miles away and ceased to know those who were living down a cattle path away from the track, though it might be only a six-hour walk. The train had already begun to create a new kind of American society.

I gave in and ordered a Heineken just to drink along with Wayne as we clicked steadily down the old main line of the Chesapeake & Ohio up the eastern knobs of the Appalachians coming to the town of Clifton Forge, Virginia. We passed a bank of electrical transformers, and he told me the story of a construction site he once worked on where a meth-addicted thief had attempted to strip away copper wire from a live transformer for a little extra money.

"You know what happened then?" he asked.

"One crispy critter?"

"Yeah, it was ugly. Had to peel him off the ground."

"You've done a lot of strange work."

"It's been interesting. I've never mined coal before, but there's not too many things I can't learn."

Clifton Forge presented itself, and it was not especially attractive. Set in a broad valley of the Jackson River, it featured a twelve-track marshaling yard that wasn't used much anymore except as a parking spot for rolling stock and a convenient wide spot for a federal brake check. There were hopper cars full of coal chunks sitting idle, but most of the coal trains on this route went to the international docks at Newport News without stopping. We were underneath a grimy sky and forested hills that looked vaguely sinister. Though this valley had been dotted with cottages since British colonial times, Clifton Forge was created in 1857, essentially as a frontier outpost of the Chesapeake & Ohio railroad, which used it as a division point and a repair shop for their steam locomotives, making it one of many hundreds of towns conjured out of nowhere because of the technological needs of the new companies. Locomotives could travel only about fifty miles before needing freshwater and a hundred before running out of coal; thousands of villages grew outward from towers and bins. Peer under the surface of almost any American city that lies away from the eastern seaboard and you are almost certain to find a railroad buried in its nativity story.

I detrained onto the damp concrete and paced around for ten minutes, watching a woman in sunglasses from the coach class embrace a man in scruffy overalls. He held the hand of a small child at his side. I wondered where their families had come from, if they were among those who could claim railroad employment in their ancestry: a great-grandfather who worked as a ticket taker for the C&O perhaps, or an engine driver.

These thrown-up places like Clifton Forge were the home base for firemen, brakemen, engineers, trackmen and mechanics, and these built-in artificial populations also made them ideal places to erect a new shoe factory or a lumber warehouse, as well as a tidy Main Street full of merchants. The Great Northern, like many carriers, had planted its stations—and therefore its towns—every eight miles from each other, in monotonous order, because eight miles was the average length a horse-pulled wagon could travel in one day and the railroad wanted the train to be in easy reach of every farmer. Executives in faraway board-rooms could not resist naming these new hamlets after themselves, their wives, their engineers, their investors, their children—anybody close at hand. And in the frenzied space of about fifty years, the national map filled up with Alexandria, Barstow, Carr, Earling, Florence, Harlowton, Kountze, Lenox, Mattoon, Minot, Nickerson, Pooler, Seligman, Selma, Strong City, Tinsley Park, Vinton, Waldo, Zillah and hundreds more instant towns where new residents would work, live, bear children, age and die. Cities like Denver, Minneapolis, Tulsa and Seattle rocketed to prominence as railroad junctions. In 1847 a group of Georgia investors lured the Pennsylvania engineer J. Edgar Thompson to build a line they called the Western & Atlantic emanating from a spot prosaically named Terminus. He disliked the name and rechristened it Atlanta.

The city fathering became so promiscuous that it prompted H. R. Williams, the vice president of the Milwaukee & St. Paul to draft a memo laying out a more rational method of pinning labels on the land. He demanded:

1. A name that is reasonably short
2. A name that is easily spelled
3. A name that in the Morse alphabet will not sound like any other
4. A name that when written in train orders will not look like that of any other station in the vicinity
5. A name that will not sound like any other name when being called in checking baggage or freight
6. A name that will be satisfactory to the Post Office Department
7. A pleasant sounding name

There was arrogance there. Yet the first railroad surveyors were also humble before the land, in their own pragmatic fashion, and built their lines with a relatively gentle footprint—not because of any concern whatsoever for the environment but for the pocketbook. The construction budgets were always tight, and British managers who came to inspect them were invariably shocked at the abysmal quality of the strap rail (a wooden plank capped with a thin layer of iron), the sharp cut of the curves, the loose pack of the fill dirt, as well as the reluctance to blast through a hill or two when necessary. "Build first and fix it later" was the guiding principle. That meant obeying the natural course of rivers and rising gently over mountain slopes—which happened to give spectacular views to the passengers. For the first time in history, a town needed no river, lake or ocean in order to deal in big commodities. "Pushing boldly out into the wilderness, along its iron track villages, towns and cities spring into existence, and are strung together into a consistent whole by its lines of rails, as beads are upon a silken thread," Horace Greeley observed in the *New-York Tribune*. Thousands of the dried-out husks of towns where only the elderly live today are legacies of this irrational spree.

The *Cardinal* blew its whistle, and we moved on from Clifton Forge and into West Virginia and past the frilly Greenbrier Hotel, which was built by the C&O as a resort. Then through another pocket of mountains before we dipped several hundred feet into the gorge along the New River and a chain of little towns with wet collector streets shiny with the lights of convenience stores and headlamps and RV parks down at the flatlands of the river.

This was an unfamiliar place to me, yet somehow I knew it in my bones, this fully functioning deep America that existed day after day, year after year, without my slightest participation, a whole nation of beautiful, ugly, charismatic, irascible, dull, wistful and utterly unique people whose names I would never know, except perhaps glimpsed by chance in a local paper's obituary page, and whom I would never, ever meet. But they had grown up in a roughly similar way to me, gone to schools that observed the same curricula, read the same essential textbooks, spoken the same language, listened to the same music, voted for candidates who said (with minor variations) the same things, spent the same currency, driven the same cars, shopped for the same consumer products.

I think it must be regarded as a miracle that the entirety of this continent could be held together in one big agreement between human beings whose ocular equipment was designed to work at a maximum range of about three miles and whose feeble brains had room for only about a hundred people they could really know or care for very well. But this mammoth nation hugged itself fiercely all the same.

The old main line of the C&O is nothing if not scenic, though the morning departure schedule out of Washington means that darkness falls on the *Cardinal* in summer while it is still inside the New River Gorge. We passed an Art Deco station at Prince, and I looked at it in gray light from the windows of the club car. Beside me was a jowly conductor named Tim Hensley who liked to collect railroad memorabilia. He was a year away from retirement.

"Most of that is going to China," he said, jerking a thumb at a chain of CSX cars heaped with coal, passing by on the opposite track. "That's the big secret of the coal and railroad business today. But I don't think we're truly capable of taking the other business off the highways. We don't have the know-how." He was describing the paradox of the state of West Virginia. It is rich in coal, rich in timber, rich in chemicals yet still stuck in a neocolonial rut. And also the paradox of today's American railroad: a huge infrastructure that supports an energy-efficient method of motion yet is still stuck in a colonial rut.

The Chesapeake & Ohio, on whose old roadbed we were running, gained a reputation as a mountain powerhouse, with beautiful stone bridges, solid small-town depots and a high-quality roadbed of perfectly milled ballast that would have made even the most punctilious British engineer smile. The dark seams of bituminous coal threaded through the Cumberland Plateau and southern West Virginia were a treasure, and they enticed a strange mini-civilization into the obscure rock-strewn valleys inhabited by Scotch-Irish freeholders who had flooded in before the Revolution and carried with them a fierce sense of personal honor that came from the feuds between their warrior tribes in the hazy dreamscape of Great Britain. They had complicated family trees and a reverence for handmade furniture, fiddle music, corn liquor and memorized passages from the King James Bible—and many of them had been hornswoggled into signing away the mineral rights to their land by advance men from Pittsburgh steel mills.

The coal was never very hard to find; it often gleamed from the mountain slopes immediately after the sandstone was blasted away, and the companies typically threw up instant tar-paper towns immediately after the railroad gangs punched into a fresh area. The more advanced of them might have a Presbyterian church; a tavern; a community hall; a school teeming with children; a small hotel for salesmen and prostitutes; flimsy pine homes for the miners; brick houses on a high-set street for the managers in starched shirts; a derelict quarter for immigrant Finns, Bohemians or blacks; a company-owned store with goods priced at confiscatory rates and the ever-present "tipple," which was a silo next to the tracks designed to dump coal into railcars. "The architecture of the coal camps varied somewhat from town to town, but had one common trait—a deadening, monotonous similarity between the buildings," wrote historian Harry M. Caudill. Their names were eccentric and often picked on a whim by the railroads: Twilight, Stopover, Ashcamp, Matewan, Beefhide, Hi-Hat, Coalwood, Carbon Glow, Happy, Neon. They were linked to the regional courthouse town only by wretchedly bad roads or by the tracks themselves. There was little pretense of creating anything but a conveyor belt to haul away wealth.

Railroads had by then done quite a bit to earn a reputation as predators. America had never known a Big Business before the railroads, and it had never seen corruption on this scale before. But context is also important: the "Social Darwinist" ideas of Herbert Spencer—the Ayn Rand selfish-gospel prophet of his day and, as it happened, a former railroad employee—had become a kind of reigning faith among financiers. Only the fittest would survive, they reasoned, which justified all manner of behavior.

But railroads took matters to the extreme. They owned newspapers that were little more than propaganda sheets, bought off entire legislatures, threatened their enemies, placated critics with offers of free tickets. In 1872 the *New York Sun* broke the story of Crédit Mobilier, one of the worst public-corruption scandals of the century. The Union Pacific had formed it as a shell company to bill Congress for the construction of its transcontinental line. Congressmen were offered discounted shares of stock in exchange for their continued support, and the government wound up paying $74 million for a railroad that should have cost $20 million less. The balance disappeared into the pockets of the ring of financiers who controlled it, including UP president Oliver Ames and his congressman brother Oakes Ames. Ridiculed as "Hoax Ames," the latter was censured and forced to resign.*

By the 1870s, trains were no longer the friendly face of progress but had become the visage of the devil, especially in the view of the new antirailroad societies known as "Grange Halls" popping up all over the prairie states demanding the government step in—a Tea Party in reverse. Farmers told one another stories of burning freshly harvested

---

* Defiant in the face of the scandal, the board of the UP tried to boost the disgraced brothers' reputation in 1875 by commissioning a granite pyramid in their honor astride the tracks to the west of Cheyenne, at the highest spot on the transcontinental. Traffic has since been rerouted, the settlement around it has withered to nothing and the bas-relief faces of Oliver and Oakes look out onto sterile emptiness in every direction. A judge in nearby Laramie once tried to make some quick money by filing a claim on the public land where the monument stands and writing the railroad with a request to "take those rocks the hell off my farm." He got nothing.

corn in the stove because it was cheaper than paying to ship it to Chicago and of the damned railroad scalawags who labeled vast loads of pig iron as "miscellaneous goods" on the bill of lading. One Granger resolution invoked the wrath of a biblical Amos:

> The history of the present railway monopoly is a history of repeated injuries and oppressions, all being in direct object to the establishment of an absolute tyranny of the Old World, and having its only parallel in the history of the medieval ages when the strong hand was the only law and the highways of commerce were taxed by the feudal barons, who from the strong walls surrounded by the armies of their vassals, could lay such tribute upon the travelers as their own wills should dictate.

Feeling besieged, railroad presidents started using military terms with their shareholders, comparing themselves to generals on campaign in "hostile territory," laying tracks across competing lines as an army would conquer a battlefield. "War," noted one British diplomat, "is the natural state of an American railway toward all other authorities and its own fellows, just as war was the natural state of cities toward one another in the ancient world." Their combined operating budgets, after all, were ten times that of the federal government, and their employees were an imperial army. By the 1870s more people were working for the far-flung Pennsylvania Railroad than lived in the state of Pennsylvania, and most of them were engaged in the hard labor of laying track.

Contract labor replaced actual slavery on the Chesapeake & Ohio after the Civil War, and the track layers developed a variety of improvised chants while they were swinging hammers or hauling iron. These were updated versions of the old English sea chanteys, meant to be sung in echt-masculine bass while the singers were rigging sails or pulling up anchors. It was not by accident that these early railroad crews became known as "gandy dancers,"* suggesting a muscular rhythm to the work. And the work was awful. Cliff sides had to be removed and flattened. The strongest among them drove in a steel drill with a nine-pound sledgehammer to a depth of four feet, while an apprentice shook the drill loose after every swing. Fingers were routinely smashed this way. Work songs were a natural unifying force, timed to the rapping of the lining bars. "Them bars made you feel *uplifted*—just to hear them going," recalled Alabama track layer Abraham Parker.

Their lyrics lamented this hard life, yearned for home, made a paean to alcohol and drugs, celebrated sexual release. Went one: *Susie, Susie, don't you know? / I can make your belly grow.* The most famous of them concerned a mountainous crewman named John Henry, who was said to have worked on the Big Bend Tunnel for the C&O in Summers County, West Virginia, between 1870 and 1872 and "died with a hammer in his hands."

Most historians believe that Henry existed, though the manner of his death is apocryphal. Apparently the management decided to test a steam-drilling apparatus. The crew was fearful of being displaced by a machine (though they lived in service of one), and they put up their beloved John Henry and his sheep-nosed hammer in a bet to see which could drill more feet in a day. He pledged to either win or die trying. In varying iterations of the piteous song that celebrates him, John Henry beats the machine, loses to the machine, dies on the spot or goes home and dies of a burst aneurysm that night. But in no version does he survive; his own excruciating labor had stolen his life. His mighty temple of flesh thus becomes a *homo sacer*—sacred to a cause—a crucifixion on the steel rail and an offering to the progress of the new age and the amazing machine that drove it.

The capital city of Charleston, a high-walled bowl of electric light, presented itself well after the last trace of the sun had disappeared. I

---

* A name that probably derives from the Gandy Manufacturing Company of Chicago, which made tools for railroad workers.

was going to stay over and shouldered my pack off the *Cardinal* for the walk to a downtown hotel, which lay across a bridge above the Kanawha River. The depot was an Italianate limestone two-story job built by the C&O in 1906 when the coal economy was aflame and the local boosters wanted a nice front door to the state. But today it was hemmed in by a highway viaduct ramp, and tightly so: it looked like you could stretch an arm out a car window and trace its side with your fingertips as you drove past. An upscale restaurant named Laury's was at the ground floor, and it was still open, soft light emanating from the windows.

I thought of stopping in for a whiskey before the mile-long walk but then spotted Wayne the construction worker pacing in front of the wheelchair ramp smoking a cigarette. His son was apparently late.

I decided to skip the drink and went over to talk with him one last time.

"You doing all right?"

"Yeah."

"He knows you're here?"

"Yeah. We just talked. He'll be here in about ten minutes."

"You were saying he works as a draftsman?"

"Yeah. He's got friends who work in the coal business. I'm ready to try that. I can do any kind of work."

We leaned together on a painted steel rail outside the restaurant. I felt a bit awkward, and Wayne was less talkative than before, but I got the feeling he wanted company. I was also curious to see what would happen next.

A blue sport-utility vehicle pulled up into a handicapped spot, and a stout man in a polo shirt, about my age, got out, looked over toward Wayne leaning on the rail and pointed hesitantly. Wayne went over to him, and they man-hugged roughly, each tapping the other's back with their closed fists. The father and son stepped back and regarded each other. Words were exchanged; I couldn't hear them. Then a bark of embarrassed laughter—a tension release—and they embraced again, warmer this time, still laughing.

I wondered what the next few days would bring—if Wayne would indeed find work as a soft-rock miner in the coalfields and if there would be any confrontations over the events and nonevents of thirty years ago. But this seemed like a good time for me to leave—there was nothing else left to do—and I walked toward the road, raising a hand to Wayne as his son drove him away from the old Chesapeake & Ohio depot.

Two nights later the *Cardinal* chuffed up at the Charleston station an hour behind schedule. I shoveled the last of my pasta dinner at Laury's into a Styrofoam carton, paid the bill in a hurry and scrambled onto the train with about ten seconds to spare—only to get immediately shooed out of the club car by an irritated steward, though it wasn't quite closing time. He just wanted to go to bed.

I tried to feel a little sympathy. Amtrak service employees are lucky if they can catch three solid hours of sleep a night. I retreated into the rear coach and found a window seat next to a thin-lipped man wearing sunglasses, looking a bit like the wanted poster for D. B. Cooper. He gave one-word answers to my questions, though he smiled and shook his head when I offered him one of Amtrak's small pillows, covered in a synthetic-crinoline slip. I rested my head against the glass and watched the old chemical plants of the Kanawha Valley, lit up like war monuments. This acrid region was at its apex in the fifties, but some money was still left here in the business of pesticides, caustics, solvents and plastics.

The smeary red-and-yellow lights of a Quik Mart store hurtled past, and the brief sight made me homesick in a way I couldn't name. I closed my eyes until we got to Huntington, West Virginia, the river city named for Collis P. Huntington, the California entrepreneur who had been a director of the corrupt old Central Pacific and also controlled the C&O in the 1870s when he built a massive division point here and named it for himself.

The *Cardinal* swayed and rocked at about ten miles an hour crossing what seemed like an inland sea of parallel tracks, all glistening in
the light from the high stalks of security lamps. This was a huge classification yard for coal, and nearly deserted. Beyond it was a courthouse
and a radio antenna blinking reassuringly in cherry red. *All is well. All
is well.* Then we were back into a patch of woods, and it felt like a scene
from World War II, a sooty forest in central Europe, where uniformed
guards with Sam Browne belts and vicious dogs were lurking nearby,
waiting to demand passports and drag away the unlucky.

The forest of darkened sycamore trees opened up into a vista of the
plain of the Ohio River, this wide and depressed tar-papered spine of a
younger America. Coal barges were still sending their carbon loads
downriver to utilities that used Mississippi water for coolant. This was
not the border of wartime Germany, it was the border of Ohio, but
going over felt like a significant crossing nonetheless. I watched little
farming towns pass by in the silent night before I gave up, inserted
earplugs and popped a sleeping pill that I'd tucked into the watch
pocket of my jeans.

By the time we got to Cincinnati, I was fast asleep, and when I
awoke, Indiana was showing itself off in a rolling portrait of pin-neat
barns and square fields, the very picture of American probity and cleanliness, as if in direct rebuke to the demonic chemical scenes of the night
before. *Oh, traveler, this is where you want to be,* the farms seemed to
announce, though their fields were all sprayed with nitrogen and potassium. *This is the heart of the country.*

I squinted at the D. B. Cooper look-alike. He was still in his sunglasses and overcoat and staring ahead motionlessly; it was impossible
to tell if he was awake. Woozy and nearly thrown off balance by the sea
motion of the cars, I stepped over him carefully on the way to the club
car for coffee. But I was awake enough to imitate the mariner's walk I'd
seen Amtrak conductors make during rough stretches: extend the feet
slightly outward, spread the legs a little more and walk like a penguin.

In a blue vinyl booth was a young man with a resolute beard and a bare upper lip. A fat pen was clipped to his white shirt, which had sparkly buttons with purple glitter. He was wearing a black coat, the usual garb of the Anabaptists, and his hair was curled in a loose pageboy.

Trains through Pennsylvania or the Midwest are almost always carrying at least a few families from the various sects of Amish, the "Plain People," believers in a renegade form of Protestantism who settled in America in the eighteenth and nineteenth centuries. None of them are left in Europe. They can be courteous to outsiders, though they stay mostly on their guard when in public. I said hello, and he offered it back. His name was Noah, a freelance carpenter, and he was traveling with his wife to see relatives in Nebraska, with a stopover in Chicago.

"I don't like cities," he said with a shy smile. He had a thick voice, accented with some sludgy German.

"Tell me something. I'm honestly curious. I know that the Amish tend to avoid technology. You ride in horse buggies and no phones. But why are trains okay?"

"Oh, trains are okay. We can even ride in cars. We just don't own them."

"Why do you choose the train?"

"It's cheaper than paying someone to take us to Nebraska."

That seemed hard to argue, and he wasn't inclined to offer any elaboration. We sat in companionable silence as morning Indiana gleamed around us. Noah went back to his reading, which was a pulp-stock magazine called *Olden Days* with a mailing sticker on it. He was absorbed in a short story called "Tom Swift and His Electric Rifle."

Across the aisle a man sat with his laptop open, a flash drive plugged into its side. His young son sat on his lap. The browser page was set to an Amtrak route map, in which the father was trying to inspire some interest.

"Chicago," he said, pointing. "See that? Chicago."

"I don't want to go there," said the boy.

We called in for two minutes at Rensselaer with its towering, handsome courthouse, and the agricultural picture slowly melded into the webwork of a great city's perimeters. I switched sides in the club car and began to look on the northwestern horizon for the azure serration I knew was coming up ahead.

The C&O had been exceedingly late tapping a line into Chicago; it didn't arrive there until 1934, when it joined dozens of other American railroads at what amounted to the grandest division point on the continent. Because Chicago is *the* premier railroad city of the world: a dreary lakeside port that never would have become the city it is today without the intervention of the railroad at exactly the right time, just as the advancing frontier of settlements needed a good spot to break down wagonloads of wheat and corn and pile them onto barges.

This mosquito-ridden beach on Lake Michigan had been called Checaqua.* The inhabitants of an American fort here had been slaughtered during the War of 1812, but population didn't really begin to arrive until 1837, when a real-estate promoter named William Ogden got himself elected the first mayor and then, setting a Chicago tradition early, used his political connections to sell shares in the "Galena & Chicago Union Railroad," which made a fortune taking wheat and oats into the city. Those tracks never would reach the lead mines at Galena for which they were aiming, because the local haul was so profitable.

A ganglion of rails quickly spread forth from the market core of Chicago, which offered a matchless location next to the docks and an excellent route into the grassy plains of the interior West. Start-up railroads located themselves in this new village as if sucked there by gravity, and none of these carriers was mightier than the Illinois Central, which had become instantly rich off an 1850 law—pushed through Congress

* An improvised pronunciation of a Tamaroa Indian word that was said variously to refer to a skunk, the disembodied voice of a god or "the place of wild onions" that grew on the sandy banks near the river. Its center would eventually be called the Loop for the circular turnaround of its elevated trolley lines.

by Senator Stephen A. Douglas—to deed more than 2.5 million acres of former "Indian country" to the railroad for the purpose of filling it up with people, towns and farms.

The Illinois Central took out advertisements in British and German newspapers depicting healthy livestock, bumper crops, tidy homes and happy residents, with a merry line of Illinois Central railroad cars chugging away in the medium distance. Bragged one ad, "Nowhere else can the industrious farmer secure such immediate results from his labor as on these deep, rich, loamy soils, cultivated with so much ease." These images were mostly fiction, but it didn't stop the poor tenant farmers of Europe from getting excited about the New World.

Shiploads of immigrants were greeted at the docks after Ellis Island by an agent from the Illinois Central who politely but firmly escorted them to "the right train" so they would not be tempted to flee. Though most of the Swedes were heading to join relatives in Minnesota and Wisconsin, many were persuaded to give the "Garden State of the West" a try, as were the Irish track crews who had laid the lines themselves. The railroad printed up guides for cultivating freshly broken fields, invested in the latest crop sciences and sponsored a large state fair.

The railroads made it easier for a Main Street merchant to display goods that constantly turned over—a more autocratic version of an Oriental bazaar—and metropolitan department stores began to take root in Chicago, led by Marshall Field and closely followed by the partnership of the former Minneapolis & St. Louis Railway station agent Richard Sears* and his watchmaker friend Alvah Roebuck. The colorful assortment of all the handkerchiefs, coffee grinders, hard candy,

---

* Sears got his start in the retail business because of a failed scam. A Chicago wholesaler sent a box of pocket watches to Redwood Falls, Minnesota, as a "mistake" and then offered to sell them at a lower price to avoid paying the shipping costs back. Boxes of random merchandise were constantly being shipped all over the U.S. rails in hopes of finding a taker. When the recipient refused to play along, Sears purchased the discounted box and sold the watches himself. In 1887 he moved the business to Chicago, and its influence spread wide.

bedsheets, ladies' shoes, perfumes, neckties and gloves were a fascinating sight to shoppers of that new era, who were becoming accustomed to silent appraisal from the windows. "The customer was kept in motion; he traveled through the department store as a train passenger traveled through the landscape," wrote Wolfgang Schivelbusch. The mind-expanding panorama of goods was spread into the prairie towns and all the little western farms through mail-order catalogs, especially from Sears Roebuck. Families could peruse the pages at leisure, even while in the outhouse, and place orders at the railroad depots that could be fulfilled within two days.

But meat made the city famous. A chain of slaughterhouses clustered on the banks of the Chicago River, a waterway so choked with blood and gristle that it was made to flow backward just to flush out the filth. In these abattoirs the pigs were shooed into an enclosure and clobbered over the head with a hammer. Another man cut its throat, and a third heaved its carcass into a bath of boiling water to loosen the bristles, which were removed with scrapers, and then the body was sawed into halves, the organs yanked out, the head chopped off and the ham and bacon divided with cleavers and knives. Bristles were saved for brushes, and buttons were made of the bones. Organs went into sausages. Everything was used, "everything but the squeal," as the old saying went. The edible chops were thrown into kegs full of pickling solution, an astringent broth of water, salt, molasses and saltpeter that could make meat edible for years. The kegs went on the rails. "The hogs eat the corn and Europe eats the hog," said one promoter. "Corn thus becomes incarnate, for what is a hog but fifteen or twenty bushels of corn on four legs?"

The packers consolidated at the Union Stock Yard and Transit Company, located just west of Halsted Street. Most of the $1 million in sunk costs came from the railroads. Crews digging the foundations in the 1870s found a dark, gooey soil underneath; it was the decomposing remnants of thousands of pig heads that had been secretly buried there in a mass grave during the Civil War.

An instant suburb sprang up outside the walls of the new stock-yards, composed of Irish veterans of the canal, Poles, Serbs, Croats, Germans and every kind of immigrant looking for work, among the taverns and groceries and union halls and monotonous town-house blocks all clustered like a human fence around the animals. A ten-hour shift in the yards was exhausting; muscle and accuracy were demanded. A fat trimmer in an Armour plant once left his bench for ten minutes and came back to find piles of meat stacking up all around. When his co-workers refused to help him catch up, he attacked them with his freshly sharpened knife.

Just beyond a limestone gate adorned with a bull's head was a six-story hotel for the meat brokers. Standing on the top floor overlooking the big blue lake and the death yards and the maze of tracks leading away to the prairie beyond was said to be an experience like standing above the clouds. "Its polished wood surfaces and plush upholstery offered an odd contrast to the wet muck and noisy, fecund odor in the pens just outside the doors," wrote William Cronon.

Local prostitutes could be buzzed up to service the traveling brokers, and a viaduct was built to accommodate the families and tourists, even newlyweds, who came to see the mind-bending sight, as Rudyard Kipling would observe, of the "township of cattlepens" and "the death factory roaring all around." By 1875 a newspaper editor said a visitor could no sooner leave town without seeing the bawling, screaming marvel as he could go to Egypt and not see the pyramids.

The occasional cow or pig left Chicago still alive, destined for local butcher shops to supply customers who demanded fresh meat. A laconic livestock dealer from Cape Cod named Gustavus Swift hated paying the freight charges "on inedible portions." This was 60 percent of the animal when hooves, bones, gristle and organs were counted. Swift was said to be so cheap that he hunted through office wastebaskets for usable pencil stubs, and he strained the runoff streams from his kill floor for chunks of fat that could be made into soap.

Why, he wondered, would a man burn all that coal in a locomotive to ship a cow a thousand miles? Why not chop it up first, then keep it cool on the journey? His solution to this question would forever change the way America ate.

Meatpackers had been conducting experiments with "iceboxes on wheels" at least since the early 1840s, but the first models were ineffective and even dangerous. Carcasses hung from hooks, and a swaying line of them could swing a boxcar right off its tracks if the curves were sharp. Putting the meat directly on the ice only discolored it and made it sour.

Determined to find a better way, Swift asked Andrew J. Chase to help him design an insulated railcar that could be cooled with slowly melting blocks of ice cut from the winter crust of the ponds that surrounded Chicago. The car was fitted with tubes, ducts and brine boxes to ventilate the car with the chill wafting from the blocks of ice. Later designs featured overhead tanks that could be filled with a mixture of crushed ice and rock salt. Swift wanted these refrigerated cars, known as "reefers," run in every month of the year. He built a chain of ice stations and cold-storage warehouses all the way to New England, made deals with Wisconsin ice harvesters and hired an army of salesmen to get orders from local groceries.

Butchers saw their pocketbooks threatened, especially since they believed (accurately) that the New York Central and the Pennsylvania Railroad were secretly charging favorable prices to the Chicago "Big Four" meat barons of Swift, Philip Armour, George Hammond and Nelson Morris. They began a smear campaign against what they called "embalmed beef" that had been slaughtered a week earlier instead of hours.

But the American market for cheap beef turned out to be insatiable; the sandwich was entering the popular urban diet at about the same time, making lunch a quicker affair. Shipping companies took note and began installing ice-packed refrigerator holds, lined with zinc, on their transatlantic lines. A cow born on the range in Texas and dismembered in Chicago might thereby end up being eaten in London. Chains of icehouses—doughty brick fortresses that stored block ice—cropped up along the Illinois Central, the Santa Fe, the Rock Island, the CB&Q and every line with a connection to Chicago. The houses were windowless and smelled awful in the late summer when the ice had become reduced to clumps amid slimy tufts of hay. A trade journal, the *Butcher's Advocate*, deplored "the commercial genius of the men who can kill cattle in far western points, lay the cattle down at the most remote New England crossroads and sell at prices lower than the bare costs of raising and killing native animals."

This was true. The price of beef tenderloins dropped 40 percent by 1883, and Americans lost their prejudice against what had been disparaged as "Chicago beef," as more than twenty-eight thousand refrigerated railcars were rolling from their nexus at Chicago. Butchers quit slaughtering animals themselves. The supermarket meat-display case was born, as was the continent-length groundwork for agriculture on a massive corporate scale. Dull wintertime meals of salt pork, root vegetables and bread could now be enlivened with oranges, lettuce, oysters, peaches, strawberries and bananas, all running up from southern climates via the empire of icehouses and rail links that the Chicago meat industry had laid.

By 1920 four out of every five cows that were eaten in America were killed in Chicago. A quarter century after that, the Santa Fe Railroad was using a million tons of ice to chill fruit grown on Southern California farms. The Erie Railroad became famous as the "route of the perishables" and made a specialty of shipping oranges, watermelons, sausages and steaks from Chicago to its giant terminal at Jersey City for consumption on the dinner tables of the Northeast. The railroads had broadened the sphere of food production and changed the American appetite along with it.

The *Cardinal* flew through these old cattle corridors and the dingy suburbs of Calumet City and Riverdale, past stacked intermodal containers and shattered factory shells and scarred oaks and then into the diametrical rows of painted three-story tenements that form the core of traditional Chicago home life: portable barbecue grills on the fire escapes of sturdy and no-nonsense wood siding painted dark brown. A conveyor belt jutted from the side of a warehouse bearing white-hot metal ingots, a tiny and miraculous demonstration that heavy goods were still being made in the USA. About 40 percent of the cargo shipped on rail in America must pass through Chicago, and typically at crawling speed because of the bottlenecks. This isn't new: companies a hundred years ago were building special lines like the Peoria and Eastern and the Kankakee Belt Line just to avoid the snarls and in the process creating a reckless prairie of "diamonds" where tracks intersect at an angle. A freight train sometimes needs thirty hours just to cross the city, making this one of the only places in America where Amtrak passengers enjoy a speedier trip than does a boxcar of Chinese-made televisions.

We passed west of the new Comiskey Park, where the White Sox play, and aimed for the heart of the Loop, and in minutes we were creaking forward inside a dark cavern of pillars before easing to a stop. Through a set of concrete beams to the immediate east was the greenish chemical water of the Chicago River. There was a bored mutter from the conductor over the PA reminding us to gather our bags—an anticlimactic whimper after our night journey across the mountains. We queued up like cattle at the Superliner staircases and shuffled out onto the platform.

I spotted Noah and his wife, but their bobbing heads, one in a straw hat and the other in a bonnet, were soon lost to sight in the general throng of people streaming through the sliding doors and into the depot. The *Cardinal* was finished.

Chicago Union Station is an awkward truce between civic romance and suburban pragmatism. A drafty 1925 head house was grafted onto a two-story shopping mall with a Soviet-style ticket hall in the basement. Fifty thousand office commuters crush in twice every weekday. Most of them are not using long-distance Amtrak but Metra, the public authority that runs eleven lines snaking out to the western suburbs and the Wisconsin shore, the second-largest regional transportation authority in the nation, behind only New York City's subway system. Metra loses a dependable $300 million every year, and though only 2 percent of working Chicagoans use it, it is considered politically untouchable.* A baggage carousel sits near the gates of the departing Amtrak trains, and an eerie computerized voice sounds through the departure halls, recordings for the hearing-impaired that ricochet off the floors as a traveler walks past, *Track 21 . . . Track 21 . . . Track 21 . . .*

I went outside and visited the site where an older Chicago railway station had once stood. The corner of Twelfth and Michigan is now a grassy field, and a working Metra track off to the east is the only remaining evidence of the big trunk line into the Deep South that once terminated here at what was the Illinois Central Depot, the signature station of the railroad that had plunged into the former slave states and the rich cotton country.

The Illinois Central called itself the "Main Line of Mid-America," and it carried lumber, bananas, limestone, cheese, peanuts, bees and strawberries up from the South. When it carried $15.5 million of gold bullion for Fort Knox, it made sure the newspapers heard about it. But there was no official press release about the most important thing the Illinois Central would ever carry, for its web of southern connections meant that it would play, if only by accident, a critical role in one of the epochal human movements of American history.

The "Great Migration" was a catchall name for the exodus of blacks between 1916 and 1970 from sharecropper cotton and Jim Crow laws and lynchings. More than 6 million African Americans streamed northward on the railroads to begin a new life. The migration doubtlessly would have happened even without the railroads, but they were a

---

* When a longtime director named Phil Pagano found himself under investigation for financial irregularities in May 2010, he killed himself by walking in front of a speeding Metra train. In his pocket was an operations manual explaining the procedure for how to handle a suicide on the tracks.

tool that made it much simpler for ordinary people to turn their word-less exits into a massive social protest.

However, it started because of money. The cheap immigrant labor from Europe dried up at the beginning of World War I—anti-foreigner paranoia was at a high point—but somebody still needed to shovel the coal, pound the rivets and cut the throats of pigs. The Pennsylvania Railroad created a minor sensation in the summer of 1916 when it offered a free ride to Philadelphia to any southern black man who could prove he had a job offer. A huge crowd of applicants showed up at the depot in Savannah, and labor agents began to operate—quietly—in the rural Georgia backwaters, promising fat wages and dignified treatment in the cities of the North.

The loudest enticement, though, came from a newspaper: the *Chicago Defender*, which launched the "Great Northern Drive" on May 15 in hopes of luring residents out of the prejudice-fevered South up to the "promised land." The editor, Robert Abbott, published exaggerated claims of factories willing to dispense free train tickets to new black workers (this almost never happened) and organized special "club rates" on the Illinois Central for groups of black families who could pool their money. Photos of the new homes and schools available to blacks regularly made the pages, as did news of the $2.50-per-day wages offered by the stockyards.

Sympathetic black porters on the Illinois Central, many of them paid out of Abbott's pocket, helped smuggle stacks of these papers along with the merchandise in the freight cars, sometimes with the tacit approval of their bosses. One issue contained a poem called "They're Leaving Memphis in Droves," which they were.

Some are coming on the passenger,
Some are coming on the freight,
Others will be found walking,
For none have time to wait.

Railroads hadn't always been a happy symbol for southern blacks: they had occasionally been the means of ripping families apart when slavery was legal. "We heard wailing and shrieks from the cars," reported Jacob Stroyer, who watched in South Carolina as a train prepared to take newly purchased slaves to Louisiana. But the more hopeful image of the Underground Railroad of the antebellum era was the better comparison for the migrants. Here was an *actual* railroad that could take captives out of bondage, if they were lucky and courageous enough.

The first obstacle was scraping together enough money to pay the fare, which ranged anywhere from fifteen to twenty dollars. For a family whose annual income might hover around two hundred dollars, this was a huge amount. White station clerks were known to refuse sales of long-distance tickets to blacks, and one common trick was to buy a ticket on a short journey in hopes of finding a more sympathetic or indifferent face behind the window at the next station. A canny traveler could also walk down the tracks away from the station and jump on board as a hobo until Memphis, where, as the *Commercial Appeal* reported in 1922, "two hundred Negros on an average . . . leave on every evening Illinois Central northbound train."

Women would dress themselves as men and hope not to be recognized. Stories circulated of families tossing away their furniture and clothing at the railroad depot when they found they could not check it as baggage. Heirlooms were sold for pennies on the dollar. "You could see hundreds of houses where mattresses, beds, wash bowls and pans were thrown around the back yard after people got through picking out what they wanted to take along," said an observer in Decatur, Alabama. One escapee told his boss he was going to see a circus. Some who walked into town to see off a relative or an acquaintance made the decision themselves to leave on the spot, deserting fields full of the owner's crops that wouldn't be harvested. The New Orleans jazz crooner Louis Armstrong watched as his family and friends "crammed everything into their baskets but the kitchen stove." Yet the frenzy to leave was pulsing with hope. A rail passenger car heading north from the Delta was seen with the name of a popular song chalked on the side: FAREWELL, WE'RE GOOD AND GONE. A young Langston Hughes, who grew up in a series of midwestern towns, recalled going down to the depot to stare at the tracks that led to Chicago, "and Chicago was the biggest town in the world for me."

The journey was often a migrant's very first experience of riding a train and of moving any faster than walking speed, which was unnerving, as was the mingling of whites and blacks in the railcars once the train crossed into Illinois.* Families could eat in the dining car among the whites if they could afford it, and some ventured the splurge. Some of the gutsier young men made a point of finding an empty seat next to a white man once the train had crossed the Ohio River—the traditional line of demarcation that the *Defender* routinely called "the Styx."

Charles Denby from Lowndes County, Alabama, recalled years later being "very uncomfortable for the first hour" of sitting next to a white fellow traveler, who at first maintained a cryptic silence. Then came a small courtesy that changed everything. "He was reading a paper," wrote Denby, "and when he finished half, he pushed it to me and asked if I wanted to read. He wanted to know where I was going, and said 'Detroit is a nice place.' This was the most relaxing time I had."

Other travelers sang hymns or prayed or stopped their pocket watches as the sooty crown of Chicago drew closer. The blast furnaces and phalanxes of brick cold-storage warehouses, the acrid stench of the stockyards, the chillier air, the grimy streets, the steel-framed skyscrap-

---

* The 1896 Supreme Court decision *Plessy v. Ferguson*, which enshrined the doctrine of "separate but equal" on southern railroads and in other places of public access, had been triggered by railroad seating arrangements: Homer Plessy, a New Orleans man considered an "octoroon" because he was one-eighth black, made a point in 1892 of trying to ride in a whites-only car of the East Louisiana Railroad. It was a publicity stunt and deliberate lawsuit bait that anticipated Rosa Parks by more than a half a century, but it backfired. The verdict only helped strengthen the practice of setting aside supposedly equal "colored" cars, which were invariably shabby and often placed directly behind the coal tender, meaning that the occupants breathed the worst of the smoke and the cinders.

ers floating on the horizon, the crowds of Poles and Irish workmen in overalls, the women in frocks at the suburban stations and the mind-bending and dazzling scale of the lusty metropolis seemed both wonderful and awful. "To those arriving at night," wrote historian James Grossman, "the sight must have been particularly impressive and disorienting, as the fiery smokestacks never rested, denying the natural rhythms of night and day that ruled agricultural labor."

They disembarked at the Illinois Central Depot, a proud nine-story edifice with a bell tower and an electric DRINK COCA-COLA sign and what was then the largest train shed in the world, an arc of coal-smoked glass and riveted steel. The waters of Lake Michigan stretched out to the vanishing point from the eastern edge of the rail yard, and out the entrance the city roared. "I never seen a city that big," recalled Louis Armstrong, who arrived in 1922. "All those tall buildings. I thought they were universities. I said, no, this is the wrong city. I was fixing to take the next train back home." They were to find Chicago a difficult home in its own way and hardly a paradise—street crime, corrupt politics, segregated neighborhoods, a marginalized power base—but the black experience in America would be profoundly shaped by this railroad hegira.

On a train through Mississippi one night, I met a veteran of the late migration. He was a sad-eyed man named Larry Wilkerson who had been working on a cotton farm near Evergreen, Louisiana, in 1963. On September 19 of that year—he still remembers the date—his sister phoned him from Chicago and told him she knew of a job that paid exponentially more than he was making in the fields. "I dropped that hoe," said Wilkerson, "and caught the train north."

He worked in a restaurant before finding better work with Chicago Public Schools as a substitute teacher and then with Amtrak as a conductor. He was going home to Louisiana to see family but hadn't been feeling right since the day a car had hit him as he was crossing State Street. It put him in a coma for a month, and he'd been unable to speak or move, though he was awake and knew what was happening. They performed several operations on him—"butchered me like a hog"—before he found his voice and recovered, though he walks and speaks slowly.

"Sometimes," he said quietly in the club car, "you feel like you're just going around in circles. If you're just looking around all the places you've been, you think to yourself, Was I good enough? Did I touch enough people? But for now I'm happy to be here. Do what I can do. Say what I can say."

I wandered back into Union Station with its computerized female voice calling out the track numbers and picked up my ticket for a two-day ride out to California on Amtrak's *Southwest Chief*.

Sleeping compartments aren't cheap on this train—I ponied up about nine hundred dollars—and was therefore permitted to sit in the "lounge," which was not the pinnacle of travel luxury. This room features a few padded chairs, a fireplace with a fake log juiced with propane and a soda dispenser stocked with red fruit punch and Sprite. Outside the sliding doors was another waiting room that looked more like an airport gate. The southbound *City of New Orleans* left from there at eight o'clock every night.

Amtrak had tried its best to hype up this particular route over the years, the ghost of the old Illinois Central route that had done so much to draw African Americans up from the debt bondage of sharecropping. That concept wasn't easily salable for tourists, however.

The best marketing gimmick had been a total accident, a premature obituary in the form of the folk song "The City of New Orleans," written by a Chicago musician named Steve Goodman. He and his wife, Nancy, had taken this route to see her grandmother in the twilight days of its ownership by the Illinois Central in 1970. Heavy on the guitar, and with a manic *clickety-clack* beat, the song is a lament told in the voice of the train itself:

Good morning,
America, how are you?

Say, don't you know me?
I'm your native son.
I'm the train they call the
City of New Orleans.
I'll be gone five hundred miles
when the day is done.

Goodman played a short version at a bar called the Earl of Old Town. "That's nice, Steve," said a friend of his upon hearing it, "but you didn't tell us anything that happened on the train." Goodman went back and wrote more lyrics describing card games in the club car and mothers rocking their babies to the rhythm of the rails. Goodman then approached Arlo Guthrie—at that time riding a huge wave of success— and bought him a beer on the condition that he listen to just this one song. Guthrie drank his beer in three minutes, acquired the song on the spot and recorded a radio version with a melancholy rhythm and an accordian accompaniment. For a country in the midst of a Vietnam hangover, the song had just the right blend of jauntiness and sorrow, and it became a hit. Listeners heard what they wanted to hear in that Talmudic question *Say, don't you know me? I'm your native son.* Perhaps another reason for its popularity was the enduring American love for a train song, which had an immense debt to pay to the sociological effect of the *City of New Orleans* and other northbound trains like it.

For when the African Americans came to Chicago and other industrial cities, they brought with them a unique musical style—one of the finest contributions of American culture to the world—which was born and refined in the service areas of the Illinois Central and whose tones and rhythms bore the indelible imprint of the train.

W. C. Handy, who would grow up to be a bandleader in Memphis, recalled a transformational moment in his life that took place on a warm night in Mississippi in 1903: "One night at Tutweiler, as I nodded in the railroad station while waiting for a train that had been delayed nine hours, life suddenly took me by the shoulder and wakened me with a start. As a ragged, lean guitarist played, he pressed a knife on the strings of the guitar in a manner popularized by Hawaiian guitarists who used steel bars. The effect was unforgettable. His song, too, struck me instantly. *Goin' where the Southern cross' the Dog.* The singer repeated the line three times, accompanying himself on the guitar with the weirdest music I had ever heard."

The strange lyric referred to the spot where the Southern Railroad tracks crossed with the Yazoo & Mississippi Valley Railroad, known colloquially as the "Yellow Dog," a tributary to the mighty Illinois Central. The slide guitar had added a second voice to the creation, as mechanical and unearthly—and yet as uncannily human—as the train itself. Handy left the depot without ever finding out the stranger's name, but he never forgot his guttural welcome to the improvisational art form called the blues.

It came from a special kind of wail that had been exchanged between black field workers in the Old South. Plantation managers knew that rhythmic group movements, rather than scattered individual efforts, were the best way to squeeze maximum picking and planting out of their slaves, and they encouraged the same kind of simplistic work chants, regulated by a "leader," that would come to inspire a later generation of railroad workers to keep swinging hammers under the broiling sun, in the wheel-like motions that the bosses encouraged.

These songs were often a cry of misery, welling up and pouring out, and then capped off with a second line that put the first into a new perspective, sometimes ironic. The pattern was AAB, and strongly derivative of the call-and-response of the work chant. Repetition. Repetition. Twist. They channeled the African folk holler, the drums and communal shouts from an atavistic time in the Senegambia that all but the most elderly of the freed slaves had forgotten and knew only from legend.

I've never seen such real hard times before,
I've never seen such real hard times before,
The wolf keeps walking all 'round my door.

The blues used a twelve-bar scale, with flattened third and seventh notes, which sounded "off" compared with European-style harmonies. And they were meant to be played loose-limbed and improvised among groups of friends in a shack or a juke joint, rather than the sheet-music recitals of the white ruling class, which was more at home in a drawing room or at a barn dance.

Most important of all, this was happening in the Mississippi Delta, where the train was the most powerful and intriguing machine around. A symbol of white dominance, true, but also a means to speed away from trouble: a leviathan offering freedom. And its sound—that magnificent, holy sound—was arresting and could be easily imitated. A bluesman could wail like a locomotive, and the guitar made an excellent device for imitating the sound of wheels rolling across iron. A rolling train spoke the four "voices" of music: the soprano of the whistle, the alto of the signal bell, the bass of the locomotive and the baritone drone of the steel wheels hitting on Bessemer steel rails. It was perhaps inevitable that blues "quoted" the train, as Franz Schubert had quoted galloping horses in his "Erlkönig" a hundred years prior. Those African Americans fleeing the South via the Illinois Central would take their music into the clubs of Chicago and turn it into something hotter and faster, more dependent upon horns, electric guitar and the peerless train-imitating tool of the harmonica.

These became the "city blues" played by performers like Muddy Waters and Jimmy Reed and promoted on radio stations WVON and WGES, making the Delta wails available to the opulent North Side and across the prim prairies. The greatest of the Mississippi bluesmen, Charley Patton, made some of his best recordings about trains, including "Peavine Blues," about the same Yellow Dog line whose refrain first bewitched W. C. Handy in 1903, and it hammered home one of the most durable ideas of the blues: getting on the train and riding away from an inconstant lady.

> *I think I heard the Pea Vine when it blowed,*
> *I think I heard the Pea Vine when it blowed,*
> *It blow just like my rider gettin' on board.*

The presence of the train—as either a tempo or a subject—in American popular music is hardly universal in the modern age, but it now shows up so frequently as to be unremarkable, even barely noticeable. In the hollow age of Amtrak, its musical vocabulary is still as comfortable as that of love. Barely a day goes by on an American pop station when trains are not referenced at least twenty times; the count flies to fifty on country stations. Kenny Rogers met his dying gambler on a "train bound to nowhere." Berlin sings of a woman sleeping next to a soldier while "Riding on the Metro," to the electronic insistence of passing signals. The Doobie Brothers pay tribute to the Illinois Central and the Southern Central Freight amid the unmistakable *click-clicking* beat and whistling wail of *looooove* that signifies the railroad on cold steel rails in "Long Train Running."

When Gladys Knight set out to record a song about disappointment in Hollywood, her producers changed the name of a song called "Midnight Plane to Houston" to "Midnight Train to Georgia" because it sounded more romantic and melancholy. The renegade country star Mickey Newbury reminded his listeners that when you're on foot there's nothing faster than a train. Sheena Easton is a lonely housewife whose life is deprived of meaning when her man goes to work on the "Morning Train," extending the train's traditional vocabulary as a bringer and taker of love. 2 Live Crew popularized the word "train" as a metaphor for group sex, possibly forced. Perhaps the most expertly crafted train song of the last three decades is Bruce Springsteen's "I'm on Fire," a steady growl of lust that consciously imitates the train as the singer pleads for orgasmic release: *At night I wake up with the sheets soaking wet / and a freight train running through the / middle of my head.*

The trope shows no signs of dying out. Soul Asylum expressed the angst of going the wrong way on a one-way track in "Runaway Train," while Beck invited listeners to ride a "Broken Train." Phish says, *See my face in the town that's flashing by / See me standing at the station in the rain* in "Get Back on the Train," and the Decemberists celebrate blue-collar love in "The Engine Driver."

And then, of course, there was "The City of New Orleans," which has never ceased its radio currency or its despairing message over an American railroad landscape that seems perpetually in eclipse.

> *The conductor sings his song again,*
> *The passengers will please refrain,*
> *This train's got the disappearing railroad blues.*

Not quite. The American passenger train has been supposedly disappearing for decades, and yet it still keeps running, quietly and stubbornly, even if the passengers aren't quite paying attention. A conductor on the *City of New Orleans*, Erin Higgerson, once told me that he'll sometimes sing a stanza of Goodman's famous song over the public-address system.

"This is the train that songs were made of," he told me. "But by far the biggest response I get is that people will just go, 'Huh?'"

The *Southwest Chief* was called for a 3:00 P.M. departure, and I went out onto the platform to board it. The carriages were two stories tall. They hummed with the potency of unseen ventilators. I stood waiting next to the tracks while the porter got into a loud argument with a squat man in a baseball cap who was insisting that his roomette number was different from the one she was pointing him to.

"Do you want to get on this train?" she barked at him. "Do you want to get on this train? Then you'll just step back and let me do my business!" I smiled at her blandly, and she pointed me toward a lower berth, which smelled of the usual blend of diesel and bleach.

The interior of this pricey roomette was pleasing in a tree-house sort of way. The design was 1970s glamour, though it was no bigger than an average clothes closet. Two foam-backed chairs sat facing each other. They were mounted on sliding rails and could be flattened out to make a bed. There was a second bed, a folding plastic crib that swung down from the ceiling and could be clicked back into place with a metal latch. There was a foldout writing table about the size of a paperback book, a coat hanger with gripper teeth, a speaker with a control knob bearing four audio channels that didn't work and probably had last played music when the Bee Gees were on *Soul Train*. A tiny closet had two hangers and a bath towel neatly folded at the bottom. Accordion curtains made of a kind of burlap covered the windows. There were two mini-bottles of water, a full box of Kleenex, two pillows with gauzy covers and a thin blanket the color of a Cub Scout uniform.

I sat in this padded cell and watched a strip of western Chicago pass by. And I thought that the little contraptions in this roomette were all derivative of what I had read of the innovations of a man named George Pullman, who at the age of twenty-two had been tossed around on a sleeping shelf during an overnight journey between Buffalo and West-field, New York. This was the usual way to sleep on a train: hope to remain unconscious through the jolts, which were, in the words of one traveler, "like riding a runaway horse." Ladies were generally shy about putting their feet on the benches, so they did the best they could in a sitting position, which made for awful nights.

Pullman wondered, *Did it have to be this bad?* He hired a wood-worker named Leonard Seibert from the Chicago & Alton to help him design a car with plush upholstery, upright sinks, box stoves for heat and riding on springs reinforced with rubber blocks for a smooth ride. But their great innovation was the padded upper bunk that swung on a hinge; it could be retracted to be a seat back during the day. The styling of Pullman cars—painted ceilings, varnished walnut, red-patterned carpets, little chandeliers—made a middle-class passenger feel enno-bled. Orders for Pullman's cars shot up after Mary Todd Lincoln used one to transport her husband's body back to Illinois after his assassina-tion, a sixteen-city funeral train that had become an orgy of grief. At the Pullman car's high point of popularity, nearly forty thousand people every night were going to sleep in one.

Pullman built his own "model city" he named Pullman next to his factory by the shores of Lake Calumet in Illinois, an army of captive workers matched in size only by the rolling brigades of African Ameri-can men he hired as porters. Unions complained that while the village green was indeed a little gem, the rest of the town was a Potemkin vil-lage: a pretty lie, hiding rotting slums that lacked running water and teeming with children who lacked proper food. One of the worst strikes in railroad history erupted over these conditions in 1894, when workers on twenty-nine railroads walked away from their posts, locomotives across the country ground to a dead stop, thirteen strikers were shot by the police and a national emergency was declared. Labor leader Eugene V. Debs served a prison term for inciting the violence, and George Pull-man died so hated that he had to be buried in a crypt covered with a thick layer of concrete to prevent his corpse from being burned.

He never got quite the adulation that he wanted, but few people in railroading ever do. Casey Jones—a man known for a single desperate act—has emerged as the only genuine hero in the industry's nearly two centuries of continuous operation. Other vehicles have no such shortage of illustrious figures. A list of famous ship captains, real and fictional, could go on for pages: Horatio Nelson, James Cook, Christopher Columbus, Vasco da Gama, Chester Nimitz, John Franklin, Captain Nemo. Automobiles have known Junior Johnson, Mario Andretti, Jeff Gordon, Danica Patrick. Airplanes, too, have a Valhalla of pilots, with Chuck Yeager, Baron von Richthofen, Eddie Rickenbacker, Antoine de

Saint-Exupéry and Amelia Earhart leading the ranks. Space capsules have their Neil Armstrongs, Yuri Gagarins, Alan Shepards, John Glenns, Richard Bransons and multiple others to claim as venerable personages.

Yet railroads are nearly bankrupt of heroes. George Stephenson, the chief engineer of the Stockton & Darlington, was once such a celebrity in Britain, but he remains obscure outside his home country except as a trivia question. In America there are some of the renowned nineteenth-century capitalists, such as Cornelius Vanderbilt or Jay Gould, but their financial cupidity obscures whatever accomplishments they may have contributed to the growth of the nation's rail network. A case might be made that the most public-spirited of the robber barons, James J. Hill, deserves a measure of respect, but his reputation for building the Great Northern from Minneapolis to Seattle is too often lumped in with the greed of the other plutocrats of his era. Jesse James and Cole Younger and other train robbers of their day are remembered as interesting rogues, but their real-life homicides make their claim to "heroism" a stretch. Their notoriety, in any event, had much less to do with trains than with the spoils within them.

The railroad is not friendly to the heroic personality. It is a pyramidal hierarchy controlled by either a government or a corporation and as such is inherently a collectivist enterprise and not individualist. The train runs according to a fixed schedule along a fixed line, and there is little room for deviation or creativity. Engineers are in effect imprisoned in a single dimension: they can just go back and forth. Even their speed is held in careful check. Only through originating actions—the invention of a new technology or the plotting of a new line—is there room for departure from accepted practice. And that almost never happens anymore on this country's railroads. Like correctional officers, railroaders are rarely acknowledged by the public when things go exactly right. Only in times of crisis or accident do they see any notice, and then it's mostly negative.

The capital irony of the railroad in America is that the machine that transformed the country is so free of the doctrine of the individual that lies at the heart of our national mythology. As it has ever been, the foremost superstar is the train itself. But the enterprise thrives on collectivism, its genetics are that of a timetable, its face is a corporate logo. It worships precision and is the obliterator of heroes.

I grew bored sitting alone in my Pullman-esque suite and wandered up to the observation car, whose lower story was a snack bar and whose upper story was a series of padded chairs underneath a canopy of shatterproof glass. A passenger could sit here and watch the landscape drift by in the company of others. These types of viewing cars used to be put last in the consist of old trains (a rear open platform was a favorite place for politicians to give whistle-stop speeches), but Amtrak has slotted theirs in the middle of the train and has done away with the platform.

I sat next to a pair of employees from the East Moline Correctional Center—known as "Sweet Moline" to the inmates for its light security—and they told me how they'd taken the train into Chicago the night before to watch a concert and get drunk. Out beyond the glass were tidy wood-shingled houses, a fire station, a pair of girls on the sidewalk wearing flip-flops and college hoodies, the old Santa Fe station at Naperville, a huge chestnut-colored tree that the assistant warden, in a flat-voweled accent, identified as a tree of heaven—a deciduous native of China, probably brought in as a street tree by some of the old village builders. We were at the outer edge of the sumptuary area called "Chicagoland," that loose collection of approximately thirty-five railroad suburbs that form the white Protestant backbone of the metro area today.

The hungover prison employees disembarked at Princeton to fetch their car, and I switched seats to face the northwest. The corn out here had been harvested early, the farmer writing it off to drought. At the horizon were restless clouds, and afternoon sun filtered through them in diagonal shafts that looked like an inspirational poster's rendering of the Almighty. Sunlight in the northern plains on a late-summer after-noon is marvelously serene, the light of meadowlarks and Canada geese and the unpainted sides of wooden barns. We arrowed through the countryside on course for the Mississippi River bridge at Fort Madison, the *Southwest Chief* running nicely on time.

For me, there is always a quality of homewardness about trains moving through the prairies, a Train Sublime that recalls all the hope-ful villages planted here by the Great Northern and the Illinois Central and the fresh caulking scent of a younger nation, when the locomotive was a vehicle for dreams. "That's my Middle West," wrote Minnesota native F. Scott Fitzgerald in *The Great Gatsby*, "not the wheat or the prairies or the lost Swede towns, but the thrilling returning trains of my youth, and the street lamps and sleigh bells in the frosty dark and the shadows of holly wreaths thrown by lighted windows on the snow." That ever-returning train is a part of the American collective uncon-scious, even if we never experienced it personally.

"Excuse me," said a voice to the right. I turned to see a powerfully built young man with a full black beard and the ropy vines of a tattoo creeping up his neck. "Can I trust you to watch my shit?" He gestured to his laptop and headphones on the seat next to me.

"Sure, no problem."

"I have to wash toothpaste out of my bag. The tube exploded all over it."

"That sucks."

"Yeah."

When he came back from the bathroom, his vinyl bag wiped out and wet, he started telling me about his life, which was currently a complete mess.

His name was Bryan, and he was twenty-five years old. He had been tiling bathrooms and making decent money, but there was a dispute with a business partner and he had vacated this afternoon, carrying with him everything he owned in two bags and leaving his furniture behind. His destination was Alamogordo, New Mexico, where his mother had beckoned him to live, though she hadn't seen him in more than a decade. "Yeah, it's a trailer park," he said. "Whatever, right?"

He composed dubstep music on his laptop and wanted me to listen to part of an album of his called *Remember Me*, and I obligingly put on the headphones prepared to be polite. But the music was surprisingly good—two electronic trills thumping and weaving in and out of each other in a pleasing contrast—and I kept listening longer than I expected, watching green rectangles of soybeans, a purple tractor-trailer rig parked in a field and a small-town Holiness church whiz past.

"Pretty good," I said, surrendering the headphones, and he nodded.

"Everything is rhythm, everything and everybody." He told me about Zoom R8, the program on which he composed his music, his struggles to get any recognition, his lack of patience for "other people's shit." On his forearm was a complicated tattoo in script that took me time to make out: THE ONLY PLACES WE CAN HIDE ARE IN OTHER PEO-PLE'S MINDS. He talked about getting a GED, but he had no idea about how to test for it. When I told him that applying was easy and searched for the number of the New Mexico test center for him on my phone, he told me I reminded him of the Andy Dufresne character from *The Shawshank Redemption*. Bryan looked and talked like a gangbanger, but there was a puppy-dog aspect to him.

He told me a story of working for $9.50 an hour in a slaughterhouse in New Rockford, North Dakota. The plant specialized in bison, which is lower in fat than ordinary beef; the animals had made a population comeback since the days when they were shot from the windows of moving trains. "I never saw one until I killed one," said Bryan. "They're kind of badass. I felt bad about it for a day. Then I didn't feel anything at all. There's blood and shit and legs everywhere, and you can't stop."

On his belt he had worn three knives and a hook. The knives were of surgical quality and would take a finger off if you weren't careful. The rules of the slaughterhouse were that if any of the meat was stained with urine or other bodily fluids, it had to be lopped off and left on the floor, but there were workers who were in the habit of taking some of these discarded steaks home and washing them off. Some of them were as big as encyclopedia volumes. Bryan began to do this, too, and he ate like a prince at nightly barbecues in his sister's backyard, pouring bison blood on the grilling steaks to keep them juicy. He quit the job only when a side of beef fell on top of him, cracking some of his own ribs. The slaughterhouse offered no health care.

We paused for ten minutes at Galesburg, and I longed to get out for a smell of the oncoming rain, but the porter who went by the name of Pinkie told me there was no time. This was the hometown of the journalist, poet and guitar strummer Carl Sandburg—an enthusiastic illegal rider of trains—who was born in a southside cottage near the Chicago, Burlington and Quincy tracks. I instead contented myself with a view of the Amtrak depot, which was a throwback built with public funds in the 1980s, a nostalgic echo of the peak-roofed stations that the CB&Q and the Great Northern had erected relentlessly along their string of prairie towns in the 1890s.

These rural stations were two-story Federalist blocks of brick, or perhaps a balloon-framed house with eaves and a long signboard proclaiming the town's name in large black caps: MARYSVILLE. TORRINGTON. HASTINGS. XENIA. Some western depots had been cabins built from logs cast aside by the track crews, or even converted boxcars dragged to the side of the tracks. They were the instant centers of activity in their hamlets. The parallel street outside was commonly named Railroad Avenue, and more often than not it would attract an eczema of new buildings around it: a hotel, a restaurant, a livestock pen, a grain elevator.

The station agent was kitted out in a paramilitary uniform, and he sold the tickets, worked the signals, handled baggage, cleaned the toilets, stamped the mail, helped load the freight, sold newspapers and sometimes cooked food. He was a wall soldier in a mechanical army, a man of consummate respect in a small town, as much as the local pastor or priest, and often more loose-tongued. He posted baseball scores received over the telegraph. Newspapers sent their reporters down to the depot every day to hunt for stories, in recognition that the tracks and telegraph were the only portals to a world beyond the dirt streets. The daily paper in Superior, Nebraska, emulated many small-town papers by publishing reports on who was coming through the station of the Chicago and North Western. The paper consciously evoked the railroad by calling itself the *Superior Express*.

These small-town depots became symbols of yearning, a place of waiting and action and possibilities. Sherwood Anderson, who knew the metaphysical longings of midwestern towns better than most, had his young protagonist reporter of *Winesburg, Ohio*, George Willard, go down to the depot at night to meet a man with a story to tell, who "danced with fury beside the groaning train in the darkness." And when it was time for George Willard himself to leave Winesburg for good, he did so from the same station, gazing out the window at the countryside which had "become but a background on which to paint the dreams of his manhood."

We approached the Mississippi River as the rain was beginning to fall, rounding a bend through cornfields that were as much a part of a vast industrial outpouring as were any of the coal mines in West Virginia. One last scruffy Illinois hardwood forest, a few breastworks of some flood-control levees, and then we were on the pivoting swing-span bridge that crossed the Father of Waters, which was looking about as tranquil and unmoving as a pond this evening. A few halfhearted raindrops hit the windows. Then we were past the square face of the Iowa State Penitentiary on the right, a denuded main street of the town of Fort Madison and, on the west end of the town, a depressing tin-sided depot.

Now, here was a real Amshack: the name that rail enthusiasts bestow on functional Amtrak stations that possess no grandeur or history. This one seemed like a wart on the dispatch center next door maintained by the BNSF, the Class I freight carrier that acquired the remnants of the Santa Fe, the CB&Q, the Great Northern and dozens of smaller regional lines that went bankrupt in the reorganizations of the late twentieth century.

I got out of the train and wandered amid the smokers for a few minutes, smelling the rain. Then we were rattling off again, cutting the corner of Iowa heading into Missouri and going at a forty-mile-an-hour clip in the near darkness when the train went into a rapid deceleration. I lurched forward a bit as we ground to a stop about twenty seconds later. For a train going our speed, it takes about a half mile of consistent brake application to cease all motion.

Suicide is not uncommon on American tracks, and Amtrak conductors are required by law to be the first responders to any injury caused by the train. "You have to get out and see what you killed," said one conductor to me.

I was once eating dinner on the *Sunset Limited* when there was a similar insistent stop outside the town of Lordsburg, New Mexico. We sat there for two hours before we moved again, and—though he was not supposed to talk about it—a conductor told me we had hit a young man. A passenger from the last car of the sleeping compartment told me the staff had tacked bedsheets up around all the windows, so nobody could see the gore outside. I later asked the state police for their report and learned it was Austin Tollens, age twenty, of El Paso, who had left a suicide note that also contained his Social Security number and phone numbers for his family. He had been walking across the track when, according to the engineer, he "stopped in the middle of the track, faced the train, crossed his arms and put his head down prior to impact." His father identified him by the tattoos on his arms. The report did not indicate what had driven him to the act.

Had the *Southwest Chief* just run over somebody? Two brothers from Massachusetts sitting near me had a Bearcat scanner tuned to the frequency of the conductor's walkie-talkies. "We didn't hit anything," one told me. "Apparently there was a pickup truck just sitting in the middle of an intersection. He squealed away when we got close." A high-school prank? I asked, and they shrugged. The train started its silent glide again, leaving behind mysteries.

I went to the snack-bar car for a scotch over ice and looked out at fences spooling by in the Iowa twilight, the loamy fiber that holds the continent together. For three seconds I saw a half basketball court next to a green-colored house, its concrete surface stacked with rusty farm implements, its hoop bare of a net. Had that court been built for some prodigal midwestern son who had cleaned out the bank account and gone to Las Vegas? Had he died and left a heartbroken father to fill the space? Had they just grown tired of basketball? The train is the bringer of ambiguous glimpses. It was like that old parable of time: A man lies on his back on a raft floating down a river, gazing up at the sky through a paper tube. A fragment of blue is all he can see. But he moves with the unchangeable flow of the river. That is our perception of the universe, so limited and slow and imprisoned.

It was near midnight when we got to Kansas City. The rain had stopped, and heavy pollen torpor was in the air. I got out onto the platform and looked at a giant Western Auto sign, its electric red arrow curved like a nautilus. "Homer sang of many sacred towns in Hellas that were no better than Kansas City, as hilly as Eteonus and as stony as Aulis," the critic Edward Dahlberg wrote of his childhood. "The city wore a coat of rocks and grass." Downtown was a small cluster of bank pinnacles on a bluff above the junction of the Kaw and Missouri rivers; long avenues with fountains in the medians were a matter of civic pride. This was the nearest NFL-level city to the geographic center of the lower states.

I walked past the coiled springs and huge wheels of the undercarriages toward the engines in the front: big P40DCs manufactured by General Electric. They were making a huge racket in the dark, expelling gray clouds of diesel exhaust. I was joined by a man in camouflage shorts who said he was from Milwaukee and who identified the locomotives for me. He spoke with a tone of authority. We both stared at a huge praying mantis crawling across the platform; it looked big enough to carry off a chicken. "Now, that's something different," said the man. Everything sang in its place; it all seemed lonely and perfect.

The westbound *Southwest Chief* passes through Kansas entirely at night, which is unfortunate, because the state has an exquisite feminine beauty of the kind best taken in the long draughts that a train can provide. I went to my compartment and slept through the gentle rise out of the green piedmont of the Kaw Valley and up into the plains, across the indistinct line that marks an annual rainfall of twenty-five inches a year and into the drier and higher spacious plains that marked the northern edge of the Dust Bowl, where fields had once turned to dirty powder and now-vanished railroads had encouraged farmers to plant more wheat than the nation could possibly consume.

There was no moon as we rolled past Dodge City, the old railhead founded by the Santa Fe Railroad in September 1872 to take on loads of live beef bound for the maws of the Chicago stockyards. The prior economy had been dominated by scavengers who picked up the white skeletons of buffalo* rotting on the prairie and sold them for fertilizer, but that quickly became small change in the flood of loose money brought by beef contracts. All history is publicity. And a blip of unruly behavior created by the railroads in this period became widely published and is now part of our national identity.

The cowpunchers who drove the longhorns up from Texas on the western branch of a dung-strewn road called the Chisholm Trail were hard-edged young men, typically orphans. They liked to wear kerchiefs tied around their necks to keep the dust off and Mexican-style sombreros to shield against the sun. After they arrived at the railroad feed yards at Dodge City or Caldwell or Ellsworth and collected their lump wage, they then went on binges of poker and rotgut and tramps,

---

* Many of them had been shot from railcars.

getting into petty disputes and shooting guns at one another and at any Pawnee Indian unfortunate enough to wander close. If this was happening in our own neighborhoods today, we'd call it a nightmare and a menace. Safely in the past, though, it's charming. And for all of the individualist myth that dime novelists would relish, the whole cattle-drive project had been a corporate enterprise from start to finish. Went the old song:

> *So we loaded them up on the Santa Fe cars*
> *And said Farewell to the old Two-Bars*
> *Come a-ty-yi-ippy ippi-ay-ippi-ay*
> *Come a ty-yi-ippi-ippi-ay*

Onward, then, past the beef-packing plants at Garden City and the town of Holcomb, where the writer Truman Capote had taken the Santa Fe Railroad out in 1954 to talk to the jailed killers of the Clutter family for his book *In Cold Blood*. Fruit trains from Colorado used to rocket through here on their way to Chicago, bearing jittering loads of apples and cherries. As dawn was breaking and the furrowed wheat fields became visible, we passed the invisible boundary west of the town of Lakin, where Central Time becomes Mountain Time. When I awoke with sun in my eyes and lurched to the dining car to get in line for breakfast, the conductor reminded me to set my watch back. This, too, was a legacy of the railroad.

Time had a loose and watery character in the days before the locomotive could travel long distances. Medieval popes had fixed the solar cycle at 365 days, and royal astronomers had established Greenwich Mean Time in 1648, but in an era without long-distance communication, the definition got hazier the farther one traveled from the King's observatory. In an era of ships and horse-drawn wagons, arrival times were measured in days, not hours—to say nothing of minutes, which nobody could agree on anyway.

The custom in most towns in nineteenth-century America was to guess the moment when the sun was at the midpoint in the sky and then set one's watch for noon. If the courthouse tower had a clock, it was much easier to find rough consensus. "Sun time" was always off by a few minutes, of course—sometimes as much as a half hour—which made early operations difficult for the railroads and added a considerable factor of danger. If one conductor understood the definition of 3:19 P.M. differently than a colleague on another line, it increased the chances that two trains would occupy the same block, and that was a potential killing zone. Precise measuring of seconds was vital to railroading as to no other business. Even when the timing was impeccable, global triangulation made matters difficult. The slight curvature of the earth meant that "noon" for the east and west borders of the city of Chicago were sixty-seven seconds apart.

Railroad companies clung tight to their own standards. The Pennsylvania Railroad used Philadelphia time for all its trains, which was five minutes behind New York and five minutes ahead of Baltimore. Union Station in Buffalo suffered the embarrassment of having to mount three clocks that told inconsistent times, one for each of the lines that called there. "The people of Kansas City," complained one local, "never did have accurate information on the arrival and departure of trains, except such as was gained by going to the edge of the hill and looking down on the railway station."

A professor named C. F. Dowd, who taught at the Temple Grove Seminary for Young Ladies, promoted the idea of "time belts"—giant longitudinal swatches that would rib the earth into twenty-four partitions, one for each hour of the day and all of it pegged to Greenwich Mean Time. But the idea didn't catch on until the railroads, who were now the acknowledged masters of time, could truly get behind it. That meant working with one another, which was always a difficult proposition for a business that considered competitors their mortal enemies. But the wrecks continued, and a consortium of railroad managers finally gathered in October 1883 for a General Time Convention.

There they agreed that 12:00 P.M. in Chicago on November 18, 1883, was to be tagged forever as the universally accepted "noon" and that the map of the United States would be chopped up into four time zones— Eastern, Central, Mountain and Pacific—roughly set along the 75th, 90th, 105th and 120th meridians. This arrangement was a long time coming, but people still groused. Much of the criticism came laced with the railroad hating common to the era. "The sun is no longer to boss the job," said the *Indianapolis Sentinel*, with heavy sarcasm. "The planets must, in the future, make their circuits by such timetables as railroad magnates arrange. People will have to marry by railroad time and die by railroad time."

November 18 became known as "the day of two noons." It was deliberately picked for a Sunday, when operations were at their quietest. Trains caught between stations were commanded to halt. Telegraphic instructions were wired to every station agent, and "their faces showed that something of an extraordinary nature was about to happen," reported the *Chicago Daily Tribune* from a westside depot. Churches in every city and town had been asked to ring their bells at the given minute. When a single electrical tap went out over the wires from the pendulum of an observatory clock in Allegheny, Pennsylvania, time zones were thereby pinned to the earth, giving recognition to the excruciating clock consciousness of the railroad.

The General Time Convention was, of course, a private association. The setting of clocks was not a binding act, and people were free to ignore it as they chose. But millions of clocks and watches all over the country were running on "railroad time" within the week. There were halfhearted measures to oppose it, including a mayor's declaration of local-time secession in Bangor, Maine, and a reverend in Tennessee who theatrically pounded his wristwatch into fragments on the pulpit during a sermon, but they were quickly forgotten.

When Congress created Standard Time and backed it with the force of law during World War I, it merely adopted the railroad time that everyone was using by then. Barely anybody noticed. The newspapers hardly bothered to report it. C. F. Dowd, the college professor with the "time belt" idea, was not around to witness it. He had been killed at a train crossing in his hometown of Saratoga Springs, New York, on November 12, 1904.

The best part of Amtrak is the dining car. And not because of the food, which is served on plastic dinnerware and is reliably mediocre. The wonderful part of the dining car is the enforced seating with strangers.

You make a reservation with the conductor and are given a little slip of paper. Then you show up at the appointed time and are walked over to a four-person banquette with a white tablecloth and a wicker basket full of salad-dressing packets. And if you're part of a couple, or alone, you'll invariably be seated with random other people you didn't choose, because seats here are scarce and the waiter doesn't like to visit multiple tables. The result is a near-mandatory conversation across the table from a fellow passenger, and it melts the layer of polite solitude that surrounds most people when they travel. Dining together is an ancient warming ritual—*Let's have lunch*—where amiability is the rule.

Amtrak scrambles the social order in this way three times every day, as did the dining stewards on nineteenth-century railroads. This custom of train travel seems to me an eminently civilized one: a reminder that all of us eat, that we're all going somewhere and that we can probably find a few life experiences or opinions in common with just about anybody if we can sit pleasantly together over eggs and coffee.

But whom you'll be eating with is out of your hands, and I never present myself at an Amtrak dining car without a little bit of anxiety about being bored silly, though the fear has never been proved out. Traveling through the Missouri evening the night before, I had been seated with Nicolas, a balding schoolteacher from France on his way to California. He had enthused in broken English about his love for the United States and how "it was zee cradle of world culture. . . . It is when you are out here that you can see how thoroughly American culture has penetrated the world." We talked of the upcoming election and the

French parliamentary system and the lasting impact of Napoleon's hubris on the European consciousness and drank to all of it, and both of us knew that we'd likely never see the other again but were spending a companionable hour together. The train is life.

And so at the far western edge of Kansas, I ate omelets with a middle-aged couple—Dave and his wife, D.A.—from Sioux City, Iowa. He wore a T-shirt with the legend WINGS OF EAGLES MINISTRIES, and they were going to see their son, who worked as a drug and alcohol counselor in Arizona. Dave was a high-school science teacher who was also a seven-day creationist, which meant that he did not personally believe in evolution and that the earth had been made by God in seven actual calendar days, no metaphor in service. I asked him if that put him at odds with the school board or if Iowa's official policy on the earth's age made him uncomfortable, and he said it wasn't a problem, because he had come to a peace with it. "I always make a disclaimer before that unit. I say, 'This is what the state says, and we're going to go by the textbook.' But I know who I am. And I know what I believe."

The talk turned to why we were all on the train, and Dave regarded D.A. with a smile. She looked at me and said, "I. Do. Not. Fly."*

Afraid of it? I asked, and she said no, that wasn't the problem. "I just don't have the patience for airports. You're in there for so long."

I gestured out the window. We were crossing a sorry patch of hardpan just west of the Kansas-Colorado border. A shallow pool of brown water lay at the center of a cracked field where the dirt was upturned in brownish shells. Our speed was about seven miles an hour—we wouldn't be in Flagstaff until long past dark. She nodded at the discrepancy and then gestured at the table with the coffee and the omelets, saying with a magnanimous hand, *Yes, but then we wouldn't have this conversation.*

---

* This put her in a rather large category of U.S. train riders. According to a 2010 ridership survey from Amtrak, about 11 percent of the passengers on any given long-distance train are there because they would rather not fly.

The imperceptible slope of the High Plains took us past sagebrush and cheatgrass on the dry ground and a farm with a stand of cottonwoods that looked battle-hardened from the wind. Past a line of low limestone bluffs looking like a row of library books or the ramparts of a house. Past a faded mural bearing cowboys and Indians in the town of Las Animas, whose name means "the ghosts." Past the turn of the Arkansas River where the brothers William and Charles Bent had set up a fort in 1833 to trade beaver pelts for cash with the Arapaho Indians, past the town of La Junta where a Santa Fe caboose was mounted up like a game trophy in the city park, and after that the prong of U.S. 50 lined up with the monoculture of the highway: McDonald's, Holiday Inn, Motel 6. The city fathers had zoned it all there many decades ago, creating a permanent quarter of easy commerce, what Bernard DeVoto called "motel town" that lights up the edge of every American town bigger than two thousand, and some smaller than that.

Then we veered southwest and into a long, lonesome spread of high grasslands. The Rockies were now a blue-green wall on the horizon, some seventy miles distant. Early travelers along this route described this first glimpse of the mountains with a mixture of poetry and fear. Some likened it to gathering thunderclouds such as they had experienced on the prairies now at their back. It was a view worthy of the Hudson River School artists like Alfred Bierstadt and Thomas Moran, who had been sent west by railroads to promote the glories of the landscape that had been recently opened up by the miracle of the train.

The Santa Fe Railroad had first pushed its crews through southern Colorado in 1874 on its quest to become one of the nation's "transcontinentals"—those megacorporations that linked the Pacific Ocean with the markets to the east. Like every other line of consequence, the Santa Fe had enthusiastically promoted the land alongside its line, setting up real-estate offices near the depots, running ads in overseas newspapers and essentially selling the southern plains to gullible newcomers. "Rain follows the plow," they promised. It wasn't true.

The droughts of the 1880s, in the words of Kansas senator John James Ingalls, left "empty trains running across deserted prairies to vacant towns." When wheat died too early in these places and busted settlers felt like quitting, the railroad that had brought them there was a common tool of suicide: it was simple enough to lay one's neck on the steel before the next train.

There have been few accomplishments in American history as celebrated as the connection of coast to coast with a continuous line of steel. Abraham Lincoln had signed the first Pacific Railroad Act in the midst of the Civil War, promising land grants to finance the construction, and within seven years, on May 10, 1869, the Central Pacific and the Union Pacific met at Promontory in Utah Territory. A single tap was sent out on a hastily erected telegraph wire to mark the photogenic moment when locomotives from the rival companies parked themselves nose to nose, the arriviste builders toasted with champagne in front of the Irish and Chinese work gangs and the dull-witted head of the Central Pacific, Leland Stanford, drove in a ceremonial golden spike that was quickly pried up and exhibited. The Liberty Bell rang at Independence Hall in Philadelphia, Wall Street trading closed for the afternoon, cannons fired in small towns and florid oratory spewed at rallies and parades. But did this accomplishment deliver all that it promised?

A history professor at Stanford's namesake university, Richard White, has argued that the transcontinental effort actually *harmed* America—it led to a speedy and reckless colonization of the West that in turn led to overgrazing, bubble economies, cattle die-offs and Indian slaughter instead of a more thoughtful and civilized process of westward movement. The railroad tycoons were building systems that made "no rational sense" but served as tools to raise vast amounts of money; the consequence of the tracks themselves was barely an afterthought, and the foolishly plotted towns and the killing of the buffalo and the ruination of the plains Indians could have been avoided. He writes in his book *Railroaded* that without the coast-to-coast frenzy of the last century, "there might very well have been less waste, less suffering, less environmental degradation, and less catastrophic economic busts in mining, agriculture and cattle raising. There would have been more time for Indians to adjust to a changing world."

For all the misery that these railroads brought to the West, they also brought the psychology of a united continent to a young nation and an unmatched thrill to the passengers of the day. They were making a remarkable crossing: coast to coast without touching earth, a journey that may be replicated today. These metal song lines engraved onto the American land may have come to us in shame and squalor and a pack of lies, but there is joy there, too. Joy in the feeling that track workers must have had on the clear, cold mornings holding a tin cup of coffee and seeing the blue Rockies, joy at the improbability of traveling across the prairies at top velocity, the buffalo grass blurring into dun indistinctness.

We came into the Picketwire Valley—a ranchers' corruption of the hard-to-pronounce and harder-to-fathom original name bestowed by the Dominguez-Escalante Expedition of 1776, the Río de las Ánimas Perdidas en Purgatorio, or River of the Souls Lost in Purgatory—and passed aqua-colored stands of Russian olive trees and farmers' ditches full of sluice water.

Trinidad was close by, a city at the base of a jagged peak and one that used to be the unlikely sex-change capital of the world, thanks to the rapid knife of one Dr. Stanley Biber, who died in 2006. Tidy homes with perfect chimneys signaled the approach into town. A stop of five minutes and then we were off again, the carriages rattling like an aircraft taking flight. We climbed past a football field with the painted legend TRINIDAD MINERS and a gold geodesic-dome gymnasium that was the pride of a sixties architect, and then we followed the route of Interstate 25 south out of town, ascending Raton Pass—its name means "mouse" in Spanish—a high notch in the Sangre de Cristo Mountains that had once been the gateway for migrating bands of Ute Indians.

The *Southwest Chief* trundled at a horse's pace up the piñon-covered notch that had once been fought over so angrily, and then it slipped through a tunnel* on the border between Colorado and New Mexico—right above an uncomfortable bald spot where I had once camped in a lightning storm seventeen years ago and over which used to pass the mule teams of the old Santa Fe Trail. A fire had been through here a few seasons earlier and turned the trees into charred sticks; I watched the damage roll by on the descent into a gigantic, airy valley.

I went into the dining car for lunch just before we got to Las Vegas, New Mexico, and a conductor directed our attention to an arcaded building with a big courtyard by the side of the tracks, boarded up and looking defeated. This was a "Harvey House," she said, shut down for years. The city of Las Vegas was still not sure what to do with it, and it remains most famous today for being the location of a climatic shootout in the movie *Red Dawn*. But it once represented something grand.

The railroad may have commanded time and space, but it could never completely master the rhythms of the human body. People still had to eat and sleep and use the toilet while they traveled, and American trains were forced to accommodate these biological realities, if reluctantly. Cargo was where the real money was made. "Freight doesn't complain" was a common saying among railroad men. James J. Hill, the builder of the Great Northern, had expressed his annoyance even more colorfully. "A passenger train is like a male teat—neither useful nor ornamental," he said.

The earliest passengers simply brought their food on board, pissed from the back of the carriage and didn't even think about sleep, because trips were too short to run at night. As routes got longer, railroad companies erected flimsy walls in the back of the carriage with a round hole

---

* More than a century of freight operations through here came to a stop in 2009 when the BNSF announced it would run its trains on a flatter route via Wichita, Kansas.

cut into the floorboards. If the passengers were lucky, there would be a wooden box on which to sit while doing necessary business.

Eating was an equally unpleasant act. There were no dining cars as such, so the custom was for passengers to be rushed out for ten-minute breaks whenever the locomotive was taking on more coal and water. In the stations were "buffets," greasy and expensive little stands, sometimes a tent, where passengers had to fight one another for attention at the counter and where the food was legendarily bad: stringy meat, stale bread, coffee so weak that the mint mark on a coin's face could be read from the bottom of a full cup. This had to be choked down in a matter of minutes or the passengers would be left there stranded with the sour waitresses and the flies until the next train came along, when half-eaten plates of food were topped off with fresh slop and served up to the new crowd of passengers, sometimes baked the following day into a disgusting mincemeat everyone called "railroad pie." The only alternative was to buy fruit or stale crackers on board from the prepubescent boys known as news butchers.* And in the carriages near the engine, the passenger had the choice of sweating in the stuffy air or opening the window and getting a faceful of smoke and burning motes. "You will turn blacker than the Ethiop with tan and cinders and be rasped like a nutmeg-grater with alkali dust," warned *Frank Leslie's Illustrated Newspaper.*

The hardships began to change only after the Civil War, when the Santa Fe hired a British-born former dishwasher and freight agent named Fred Harvey to clean up its second-floor lunchroom in Topeka in 1875. Harvey was tall, with a wispy beard and a nervous disposition, and he had certain ideas about how food should be served. Most radically, he insisted all ingredients should be shipped fresh from Chicago

---

* The most famous former news butcher was Thomas Edison, who said that his lifelong hearing problems had been caused by a blow to the head from an angry conductor.

and St. Louis and that the dishes be spotless. The arrival of each train was treated as a ceremony: a gong would sound, the wine would be poured into monogrammed stemware and the food would be brought out steaming and laid on sparkling china. Harvey was eventually given the contract to run the eating houses all along the line, in such places as Lakin, Dodge City, Winslow, Barstow, Albuquerque and in the magnificent La Fonda Hotel on the plaza in Santa Fe. Other railroads began to copy his style, but they could never match it. The Harvey Houses became America's first chain restaurant, though they bore almost no resemblance to the automobile-driven fast-food emporiums that would arrive after the decline of the railroad. Harvey's menu included both classic and regional cuisine with the best ingredients: chili enchiladas, filet mignon, chicken Vesuvio, albóndigas soup, foie gras, apple pies cut into quarters (*never* eighths) and the finest coffee around.

Harvey Houses ran late into the night, and the ease of round-the-clock railroading helped turn America into a twenty-four-hour nation. A substantial number of men on the graveyard shift began to live out a nocturnal existence, pulling the curtains of their homes against the sunlight when it was time to sleep.

Annoyed workers in the Union Pacific division point of Green River, Wyoming, demanded something be done about the salesmen who knocked on their doors throughout the day. City Attorney T. S. Taliaferro, who had previously worked as a Union Pacific stationmaster, drew up what became famous as the Green River Ordinance, which prohibits solicitors from knocking on a door unless invited. It survived a court challenge from the Fuller Brush Company and was copied by cities nationwide; Taliaferro wrote a colleague in Ohio that he had only been trying "to prevent contagious diseases being carried by promiscuous peddlers." But not all was pure in Green River. His son, Mayor E. L. Taliaferro, made a standing policy of collecting a monthly twenty-five-dollar "fine" from the prostitutes who welcomed callers into their houses alongside the tracks and then instructing the police not to bother them. "I made sure the money went to the town, not into somebody's pocket," he insisted later.*

The railroaders already knew something about that; they were legendarily reliable customers of brothels in stops along the way, and the story spread—probably apocryphal—that the term "red-light district" was named for the brakeman's habit of hanging his red lantern outside whichever cathouse he was enjoying that night so his colleagues could find him quickly in an emergency. The brothels ran all night, just as the trackside restaurants—the first prototypes for highway diners—started serving up eggs and hash browns around the clock, as well as whiskey for those who asked.

Along with its concern for fine cuisine, the Santa Fe had been an enthusiastic buyer of George Pullman's cars, especially for the California Limited, an "air line" inaugurated in 1892 to cement the railroad's status as the carrier of choice for Southern California. Promotional copy always emphasized the youth and pulchritude of the passengers, "a desirable class, persons you like to meet," said one ad, "successful men of affairs, authors, musicians, journalists, 'globetrotters,' pretty and witty women and happy children—these constitute the patrons of the *California Limited.*"

This was the Concorde or the Virgin Atlantic of its day, a western rival to the *20th Century Limited,*† which streaked overnight between New York and Chicago and welcomed its celebrity guests on board at Grand Central for a 6:00 P.M. departure with a carpet colored a deep Harvard red‡ on the platform of Track 23. Cocktails flowed freely in the card rooms of the *20th Century Limited,* whose black-painted cars traced

---

* The mayor was justifying the city's purchase of land south of the river, which he acknowledged was "paid for by community vice." The El Rancho neighborhood is now one of the more respectable neighborhoods in town.
† A fast train was typically called a "limited" because it made a minimal number of stops.
‡ Hence the phrase "rolling out the red carpet."

the edge of the Hudson River in the evening light "with the triumph of a proconsul," in the words of *New York Herald-Tribune* society columnist Lucius Beebe. On board were fresh flowers, a small library, a barber, a gleaming observation car, valets and china-plate dinners of chateaubriand, lobster and a specialty dish called "chicken à la century." But Fred Harvey and the Santa Fe were giving their customers a frontier experience the *20th Century Limited* never could, and no railroad could beat it for sheer artistry.

One of the youngest managers in the Harvey chain was a German émigré named Herman Schweizer, who had been hired at the age of seventeen to run the house in Coolidge, New Mexico, a day's horseback ride from the Navajo reservation. Schweizer had an eye for art, and he started buying up the blankets and pots that his Indian customers brought in, then resold them to customers passing through on the railroad. The sight always made a huge impression on California-bound travelers, who fell in love with this domestic exotica. Navajo "chiefs" in feathered headdress, chosen for their gregariousness, were eventually invited on board the trains to work a shift roaming the coaches and telling sanitized Indian legends to the passengers—a feature especially memorable to preteen boys, who got to meet a real Indian. For a poster mascot, the railroad created a cartoon Navajo boy they called "Chico." The backs of the checks in the dining car showed him writing "Thank You" on the ground with a handful of sand.

The "Santa Fe style" of the American Southwest—that distinctive mud-and-pole architecture, the chili peppers on the walls, the woven Indian baskets—was essentially spread through the country by the publicity department of the Atchison, Topeka and Santa Fe. Even as railroads compressed the countryside into mechanized funnels and tubes, they also remade and sugared its native culture for the popular tongue, making images of a way of Indian life they helped extinguish. The wistfulness of a conquering race was rarely expressed so colorfully—or profitably.

There was a drunk man in a porkpie hat in the observation car, and he stood in front of me with a challenging stance. "Excuse me," he said. "Are you going to get up out of that seat for me?"

I looked at him and then around at all the other empty seats surrounding me. We were winding through a shallow canyon in New Mexico, and the view was moderately interesting. But this was not worth fighting for, especially against a drunk, and so I moved out of his way. "Sure, pal," I said. "Plenty of room for everybody."

He sat in my seat, and I saw a bit of snot oozing out of his nose. Three of his friends, who had been rowdy for the last hundred miles, had brought their own beer on board and were deep into the case. At my side was Bryan, the slayer of bison and composer of dubstep music. He watched and shook his head. He'd made an earlier challenge to one of the drunks who had been spitting on the floor, and this situation had every potential for a fistfight.

But with a glance and a shrug, we decided to ignore them and watched the arroyo walls crawl by. Above them was a cobalt blue summer sky studded with cumulonimbus clouds; the pinkish walled earth and the occasional green juniper trees created a visual effect like Neapolitan ice cream. A few multiroom fantasy haciendas crawled past; the tidy adobe-painted exteriors and the Range Rovers and BMWs parked out front signaled the presence of big Santa Fe money approaching. There were doubtlessly a few Navajo pots and Kokopelli wall decorations in those living rooms. Inside the arroyo we passed a sign that puzzlingly advertised THE KILLING FIELD and then an older Anglo man who had taken off his T-shirt and was waving it over his head at the passing *Southwest Chief*, as if its coming were the greatest thing that had happened to him all day.

"This sucks," said Bryan. "I can't imagine living here. So boring and hot."

"But you're going to be living in this state."

"Yeah, dude, not excited about that. My mom called me last night.

She's getting really emotional about this, and I'm not sure how I'm going to react. I think she's going to want me to give her a big hug when I see her at the station, and that's just not who I am."

About five minutes later, his phone rang—his anxious mother, who had been out of his life for fifteen years and was suddenly omnipresent. He rolled his eyes and excused himself to take the call.

The drunk in the porkpie hat leaned over to me. "Excuse me," he said. "Come here, I want to tell you something."

Saliva pooled at his lips. He was wearing white socks and bedroom slippers, and there was a tattoo of a cross on his right hand.

"You can tell me from right there," I said.

"I want to say," he said, "that I'm sorry. It takes a lot for me to say that." He put a hand over his heart, then extended it. "I'm the lesser man here."

There was a drama playing in his mind that I did not want to interrupt. "It's cool," I said, shaking his plump hand. Then I turned back to the windows. Bryan reappeared, muttering about his rediscovered mother.

We watched as Santo Domingo pueblo clattered past. There were ceremonial earthen ovens in the backyards, looking like dromedary backs. Turquoise jewelry was a big part of the village economy. Southward was a hill scored with dozens of tracks made by ATVs and then, in the northern suburbs of Albuquerque, a man riding a motocross bike holding a twelve-pack of beer carefully balanced on the handlebars. "My kind of guy," said Bryan. He laughed. The Sandia Mountains were to the east, looking ragged and slightly hostile, as if they would draw blood from your knuckles if you brushed the back of your hand across them. And then Albuquerque and the combination Amtrak-Greyhound station with Moorish arches that had been put up to replace the old Alvarado Hotel and Harvey House, which had been bulldozed for a parking lot in 1970. I shook hands with Bryan and wished him well, silently hoping he would sign up for that GED test.

On the platform was some *Hecho en México* merchandise that some vendors had on display. A few painted turtles caught my eye, and the woman selling them told me they had been made by the Navajo. She shivered in her pullover. A monsoon was moving in—that strange kind of late-summer storm that gives the desert a violent dose of rain and kicks up enough dirt to make your teeth feel gritty. She covered up her goods with a clear plastic tarp.

I went back to the new Alvarado station and then, through the arches, saw Bryan in the company of a heavyset woman wearing big glasses. As he'd predicted, she looked teary and emotional. They both glanced over at me, perhaps a welcome pause in the awkward meeting, and I held up a hand to them. "Your son has a good heart," I called to her. "Oh, I know," she called back. Then they got into a Honda and were gone into a future that I would never know.

The *Southwest Chief*'s exit from Albuquerque took us past an industrial heath. At Isleta we turned to the west and climbed up the lip of the Rio Grande Valley and hurtled past red mesas that were lovely in the gray light. Rain arrived and then departed just as quickly. There were curtains of it hanging in the sky, drooping long legs. The Navajo called these summer squalls "the male rains" for their hammering effect. Everything in the universe has a hidden gender.

I sat in the observation car next to a fiftyish man with a long ponytail and a guitar at his feet, a teacher named Marcos who had been visiting his daughter and ex-wife. Outside the windows was the uranium town of Grants, its streets shiny with rain, the drilled-out mesas glowering down.

Marcos took up his guitar and began to brush his fingers across it. He played several indistinct chords and then found a melody that strengthened. It was a song that he'd written around the time of his divorce. His broken family was apparently on his mind, as the train pulled him farther from Albuquerque.

I've got this ring that's lost its meaning
And a knot I can't untie,
And I've got no more tears left to cry,
No more tears left to cry.

"That song is from life," he said when he was done, without further explanation. A few hundred feet away was a coal-fired power plant at St. Joseph, Arizona, shining yellow and hard. We were on the BNSF's double-tracked "Transcon" line that primarily ferried cargo from the port at Long Beach into the interior discount stores of America. It was about an hour to Flagstaff.

We would soon be passing through an enormous stand of ponderosa pine. There were dingy red, white and blue overhead lights in the observation car, looking like an aged set from *Space 1999*. Marcos leaned back in the bolted seat and began to play another song, singing softly as he felt his way through the notes. This one was from Woody Guthrie:

This train is bound for glory, this train.
This train is bound for glory, this train.
This train is bound for glory,
Don't carry nothing but the righteous and the holy.
This train is bound for glory, this train.

We rolled along like that, the words fusing with the motion of the rails, and I thought again what a miracle it was to have come all the way from New York on an unbroken runner of steel. The stories and the people are caroming around the nation on the rails every minute of every day, a miniature nation talking to itself.

When the conductor chased us out and Marcos reluctantly cased his guitar, I went back to my compartment near the front of the train, made up the bed and crawled under the sheets and the electric blue blanket. The elevation was more than a mile above sea level as we eased past Flagstaff and moody stands of ponderosa pines and down a long, dry slope toward the Colorado River, a metal caterpillar inching across the curved earth. If there is a more peaceful accompaniment to sleep than the tidal motion of the cars, the receding song of grade-crossing signals, the knowledge that you will wake up with a different country scrolling by outside your window, I do not know of it.

Crossing Arizona hadn't always been this pleasant. On another journey on these same tracks, I had been stranded on the *Southwest Chief* when the locomotive broke down in the darkness near Winslow.

I passed the time in the lounge car with a group of four people, one of whom was a short, graying man who had spent twenty years chasing storms across the Midwest with his son, packing chain saws in the truck and hiring out as freelance tree removers to slice up the windfall. His knee had been broken a few years back, and pain pills weren't helping. "I don't think I'd do it," he said, "but I now understand why people say they would want to hurt themselves." His eyes kept slipping shut, and he leaned in his seat so precariously that I had to get up to steady him. We had all been drinking lemon-lime soda, enlivened with belts of vodka with the brand name Dark Eyes, which someone had acquired from an Albuquerque liquor store and was sharing liberally.

The conductor told us the broken locomotive had to be replaced with one from BNSF, with a speed restriction of seventy miles per hour, and that we would be arriving in Los Angeles at least four hours late. Don't plug anything into the outlets—it'll drain the power. And by the way, the tables are for customers only. We ignored that last part, and he left. Then the lights blinked out and the reserve battery power came on. Purple emergency lights flickered on, and we sat together in the shadows, drinking more Dark Eyes.

"This thing is *archaic*," a man in a black cowboy hat complained. "This car came up from Cuba or somewhere. It's time to retire this. What the hell is *happening*?"

He raised a good question. Why is Amtrak limping along in a state of perpetual mediocrity, in a country that used to be so rich in railroads? The easy answer is that the spread of the automobile and Henry Ford's successful vow to bring one to every American garage made the train obsolete. But it does not tell the whole truth. America threw in its lot with the car only *after* a titanic program of government spending made it an inevitable outcome.

The key year was 1956, when oil and automobile lobbyists had urged Congress to pass the Federal-Aid Highway Act, an unprecedented twenty-year program to use gasoline tax money for expressways between and through cities. President Dwight Eisenhower eagerly promoted it, telling everyone how impressed he was by the German autobahns he had seen after the First World War. And in an era of the atomic bomb, he worried that cities might not be evacuated quickly enough in the event of a Soviet strike. But this policy choice was different from the course taken by the European nations that suffered the brunt of the war. Lower rates of car ownership—and the entrenched power of government railway ministries—meant that hard currency was devoted to fixing bombed-out tracks in Germany, Italy and France and upgrading those sections that had rotted during years of wartime austerity. The United States had not suffered such damage and was free to make investments that would most benefit Detroit and the powerful oil companies in Texas.

Herein lies a signal irony of American society. We think of the automobile and the peaceful suburban home as matters of individual choice—the way most families opted to live—and certainly the lifestyle they created has come to be regarded as synonymous with the ancient idea of liberty. But this was largely *not* a matter of individual choices or truly free markets. The automotive character of postwar America was actually decided by Congress. The psychological and economic guideposts were erected by federal fiat.

The long-range Boeing 707 debuted in 1958, making coast-to-coast air travel affordable to the middle class, and it caused even more trouble for the long-distance trains. The venerable Baltimore & Ohio, it of the lost cornerstone, announced that all passenger service north of its namesake city would end on October 4, 1957, which happened to be the same day Sputnik was launched. Six years later Pennsylvania Station was knocked down and turned to rubble. Conductors were actively rude to passengers, and speeds slowed to as poky as eight miles an hour. "The trains are absolutely disgusting," complained a British visitor. "They're filthy. They're invariably too warm or too late. The timekeeping is shocking." By the end of the sixties, only 450 daily intercity trains were in operation, and even the *20th Century Limited*, once the grandest ride of all, was carrying more porters than customers.

Freight rail, too, was going to the dogs. Trucking companies with new fleets and lots of WWII-veteran drivers were biting into the "less than carload" shipments in which small items, like a single barrel of chemicals or a few boxes of clothes, sat by themselves in a mostly empty boxcar. Shopping malls in the suburbs relied on quick turnover and tinier inventories—exactly the parameters that were most unfriendly to what railroads were good at doing.

There were also government troubles. The Interstate Commerce Commission, formed in another era to stop the abuses of Gould and Vanderbilt, forced railroads to give ponderous testimony on even slight price changes. But truckers could make deals quickly and without interference. Railroads had to maintain paperwork that was five times the volume as that for airlines, documenting in obsessive detail what they earned and spent. They made fruitless complaints about the government subsidies given to build roads and highways—$216 billion between 1921 and 1965—as well as city airports built with municipal bonds and run by federally funded air-traffic control, when they themselves weren't given a dime and had to maintain every inch of their own tracks.

And they had done a lousy job of this, too. Total mileage was barely a third of what it had been just four decades prior, and a lot of what remained was bending and cracking. A few trains suffered what was euphemistically called "a standing derailment," when sections of rotting track simply collapsed beneath them. Almost all the nation's commerce in wheat switched over to diesel trucks. The track sidings in front of midwestern grain elevators grew thick with grass.

The New York Central and the Pennsylvania Railroad, once archrivals, were forced to merge into a new company called the Penn Central in 1968, and the result was disaster. Executives got into petty disputes, tower signals were dangerously crossed, a fleet of Cadillacs on a flatbed was dumped down a culvert, an entire train was somehow lost for ten days on a siding and most of Maine's potato crop rotted in the Selkirk, New York, yards over the winter of 1969 when the car wheels froze to the rails. Locomotives were wheezy, unreliable, painted dull black and pitted with marks where people had thrown rocks at them. Meanwhile managers were borrowing heavily to provide the illusion of prosperity by paying dividends. On June 21, 1970, it became the largest bankruptcy in U.S. history.*

The crisis in passenger rail was "resolved" in 1970, when President Richard Nixon signed the Rail Passenger Service Act, which merged all the passenger assets under a government agency with the portmanteau name Amtrak,† with the expectation of profitability within three years. Transportation Secretary John A. Volpe predicted an "all-time comeback in the history of American transportation." Almost nobody believed him, and their skepticism was on target. After a ceremonial first run between Washington and New York in 1971, more than half of the 127 invited dignitaries chose to fly back to Washington rather than take the train. The array of worn-out carriages that the railroads had sold to the government—a ragtag lot nicknamed "the rainbow fleet"—

---

* Only Enron would top it in 2001.
† "American" and "track" pushed together and misspelled. The other contenders for a name were Span, Unitrak and Railpax. The last was a reference to the treatylike agreement that would create the agency, but federal officials worried it would be nicknamed "Railpox" by angry passengers.

had no standardized equipment. Hapless mechanics would show up to breakdowns or frozen pipes with no idea how to proceed. In 1975, *Elks* magazine felt compelled to remind its readers, "You may be surprised to learn that *any* rail passenger service still exists."

Amtrak invested in its own silver-sided cars designed to look like airplane fuselages and promptly racked up operating losses that exceeded $1 billion. A pattern was set. Amtrak would routinely come back to Congress like a drunk begging for more money and offering up promises to reform itself and in the meantime projecting volumes that even its own analysts conceded were fictional. Free plane tickets could have been given to each passenger for cheaper, it was said. At one point the agency secretly mortgaged the new Pennsylvania Station for $300 million in emergency operating cash—with no clear plan for paying it back. "I feel personally embarrassed at what I helped create," said Anthony Carswell, called the "Father of Amtrak" for his role in urging the passage of the 1970 bill.

President Ronald Reagan made great political theater of trying to kill Amtrak every year and sent his budget director, David Stockman, out to heap verbal abuse on the trains—"empty rattletraps," he said, which were nothing but "mobile money-burning machines." But this was to no effect. Too many powerful congressmen were there to protect their local routes (notably Senator Robert Byrd of West Virginia, who watched over the *Cardinal* as if it were his own private equipage). A 1997 reform bill did not stanch the bleeding. Amtrak president David Gunn went so far as to tell the *Toronto Globe and Mail* that Congress "doesn't have the intestinal fortitude to get rid of passenger rail service."

But for all its molded plastic mediocrity—and its status as a whipping boy for budget hawks—Amtrak had been a victim of false expectations from the start. No intercity passenger rail service in any country in the world actually makes a net profit. A somewhat defensive 2008 survey from the Amtrak inspector general found that European governments donate significantly more public money than the United States does for their own rail systems and that many of them falsely report "profits" by keeping things such as debt service, pensions and restructuring off their balance sheets. Germany's nationalized Deutsche Bahn ends up costing taxpayers ten times as much as Amtrak and France's rail system more than seven times, though cross-country and suburban trains are far more ubiquitous in those places.

I spoke about this with the president of Amtrak, a former city bus-system manager named Joseph Boardman, whose bearing was that of the classic high-level civil servant: smart, discreet and brisk. He had a tidy gray mustache, and his office in a third-floor corner of Washington's Union Station had a lot of old-time train bric-a-brac and a prize view across the lawn to the U.S. Capitol—where, he acknowledged, there were "five hundred thirty-five members of my board of directors," meaning every voting member of Congress, which sets the budget for him.

These were days of clover (relatively speaking) for America's perpetually bankrupt passenger rail company. The system was $1.2 billion in the red, but passenger growth between New York and Washington had been steadily growing in the decade since the September 11 attacks, as air travel had become more cumbersome and expensive. Even in the Northeast Corridor, Amtrak still operated at a net loss, but it was able to make $200 million in profit in this sector on the higher-speed Acela train once the above-the-track costs were deducted—that is, labor and maintenance of the locomotives and coaches.

Boardman summed up his agency's task thusly: "mobility and continuity for our citizens across the nation," before going on to tell a folksy parable. "When I was a kid, I remember coming out of the barn after milking cows and saw a Greyhound bus going past our house. And I thought, 'What a waste.' And my dad said, 'Son, you're wrong. There are a lot of people in this country who don't have cars, and they need to get somewhere.' That's true today. Those trains are the lifeline for the communities they operate within. We have to connect them for the common good."

That may be true in the heavily urbanized ribbon from Boston to

Washington—"BosWash" to futurist thinkers—the home of a densely packed 50 million people and a regional culture that still thinks of commuter trains as a possible way to get to work. Eighty percent of Amtrak's revenue comes from here. But for coast-to-coast passengers, Amtrak still functions more like a "a rolling national park," a way of keeping a certain national heritage on a breathing machine, in the same way that price supports and crop subsidies prevent thousands of midwestern family farms from going bankrupt every year.

The most reliable constituency is made up of the hard-core train fanatics—middle-aged or elderly men mostly—who call themselves "railfans" but whom Amtrak conductors call "foamers," as in one whose mouth starts to foam at the sight of a locomotive. The term is not charitable, and most Amtrak employees regard them as nuisances. Railroad crossing signs and engineer caps decorate countless workshops across America. I once visited a friend who owned a home in Protection, Kansas, that had been made from a restored depot; the doorbell was rigged to sound like one of the lonely horns in the night that had first enchanted me as a child.

There are about a quarter of a million owners of model railroads in the United States and many more sets than that sold every year to amateurs—not just the trains but miniature depots, storefronts, pine trees and dioramic filigree of all descriptions. "This gives people the opportunity to be the engineer, to be part of something larger than life," said Neil Besougloff, the editor of the well-read enthusiast magazine *Model Railroading*. There are corporate histories written for railfan readers, featuring loving technical accounts of locomotives and carriages and scores of homemade videos showing trains barreling across the countryside and, especially, passing each other on opposite tracks, which is a kind of money shot.

One of the nation's biggest marketers of train films is Dick Eisfeller of Greenland, New Hampshire, who has endured snow, rain, sleepless nights and harassment by cops to produce an impressive library of 239 videos documenting everyday operations everywhere from the Bailey

Yards in North Platte to the Moffat line in the Rockies. The labels on his videos make a pornographer's promise: "No more mindless runbys. Our tapes & DVD's show the whole train."

I asked Eisfeller why watching a video of a train lumbering past a grade crossing would appeal to his many viewers. He shrugged and chuckled at the obviousness of my question. "Heavy equipment moving fast," he said.

In the café car of the Vermonter a month later, I put the same question to a confirmed foamer, an earnest man in a commemorative railroad hat and T-shirt, whom the conductors were treating badly. Why do trains have such aesthetic appeal? He hesitated before he answered. "I guess some people say it's the way the train moves," he told me. "It's like the canter of a horse or the walk of a woman. . . ." He trailed off, unable to complete the thought.

Other passengers find the appeal equally hard to explain, and yet their addiction is lifelong and it is shared by many. According to a 2010 ridership survey from Amtrak, 16 percent of passengers cited "the uniqueness of the train" as the primary reason they were on board. Amtrak tried to cash in on this nonspecific yearning in the 1980s with a television campaign that used a jingle telling viewers, "There's something about a train that's magic. All aboard, America!"

Heavy equipment moving fast: this is still the sine qua non of the passenger train, which today, in America, is fueled primarily by sentiment. Long-distance Amtrak routes don't have much relationship to supply-and-demand thinking, but then again neither do public schools or homeless shelters or famine relief—or any other endeavor where cold, close-by realities take a backseat to a distant romance.

Our trains will keep running in America, even if in a terrarium.

The Mojave Desert is a fittingly apocalyptic place to conclude an overland journey, a savage expanse of aridity at the hind end of the continent dotted with Joshua trees and creosote, and I awoke to it somewhere west of Needles with a gradual awareness that there was a faint smell of rain. This was unusual on any Amtrak Superliner, where any trace of the outside air is usually smothered in a vague chemical scent. I glanced at my cell phone: 4:00 A.M.

I lay there in a restless haze until the lights of the station at San Bernardino invaded the curtains, and I knew I ought to give up. I spread the curtains and looked at the giant sharp-edged Spanish Mission station and the chemical tank cars and the boxcars filled with God-knows-what in the BNSF yard, and it hurt my eyes.

I took coffee in the compartment and watched the far margins of the urbanized territory of greater Los Angeles emerge. "This baby Italy, more straw than stone," as the poet Karl Shapiro once put it, and the city and its civic satellites have since grown to contain a population exceeding that of Italy. The *Chief* went through corridors of shabby houses outside Victorville colored so dull that they appeared to have sprung like plants from the desert caliche. We passed tire emporiums, a Hostess bread outlet, an estate liquidator with boarded-up windows, broken telephone poles with their wires drooping, men stabbing at Russian thistles with long pikes, a cinder-block building with graffiti that said ONCE I WAS IN LOVE / THEN I DECIDED TO LIVE IN MY OWN PRIVATE HELL, and then the early light on the young slopes of the San Gabriels.

I walked with squinted eyes and bed-tousled hair to the dining car and waited to be seated for breakfast, annoyed at the jolts beneath my feet. Though I loved trains, I wanted to be home, and knowing that Los Angeles was so close made it seem that much farther away.

"Good morning," I muttered to my table companion, an elegant-looking woman in her fifties. "Where ya coming from?"

"I'm coming back from the Santa Fe Opera. We saw Verdi." She spoke carefully, though with a trace of an incipient joke behind her eyes.

"Taking the train to the opera. Very 1890s of you."

Her name was equally of a different era: Florence Horton. She worked for Sacramento County in an agency that dispensed emergency aid to the homeless and sought to find them transitional housing. Other social workers I've known have told me that repeated contact with the down-and-out—especially the accomplished liars—had turned them cynical over time, and I asked if that had happened to her.

"Oh, no," she said. "Some were very beautiful and kind. Do you know what I saw one day? It was raining, and this older man came in, not doing very well. He was staggering, but there was a blond woman with him. She was very tall and elegant, very Italian-looking. They were leaning on each other's shoulder as they walked. His prescription had run out, and he was badly in need of his medication. They had to wait there for a few hours while we took care of it, and they just leaned on each other the whole time. That was humanity right there."

She told me this story as we wound through Cajon Pass, one of the best keyholes to the Los Angeles Basin in existence. Lieutenant A. W. Whipple, posted out from Fort Smith, Arkansas, had surveyed this narrow earth gate for a transcontinental railroad in 1853, and he wrote in his journal, "Proceeding through groves of yuccas beautiful as coconut and palms of southern climates, and dense thickets of cedars, by a gradual ascent, averaging probably sixty feet to the mile, we reached the summit of Cajon Pass." It would probably not be as expensive to build tracks through here as he feared, though he noted that he wished it led to a more attractive place than the village of Los Angeles, which was then a fly-specked ranchero prone to seasonal flooding.

I was fully awake now and attuned to the kimono glimpses of greater Los Angeles, which is far more of a blue-collar town than its coruscating image suggests—the "Know-How City," as Jan Morris puts it. The basic pathways of the fabled L.A. freeway system, as a matter of fact, follow the tracks of the old Pacific Electric railway, which had been the most extensive trolley system in the world. It became a sacrifice** to

---

* The 1988 animated movie *Who Framed Roger Rabbit?* was a comic retelling of this real-life incident.

progress in 1953, when, after a period of financial struggle, it was sold to a shell corporation for General Motors. The tracks were ripped out and replaced by gasoline-burning buses.

The *Chief* wound through the trellis that made it all work: fabrication plants, poured-concrete slopes for trucks leading into numbered bays, the hidden assemblies. Beside one dusty shed, a few Jet Skis poked their rumps out, a taste of the nearby ocean. Sun winked off new pickups in a lot with colored pennants that looked like Tibetan prayer flags. A business advertising "BBQ Islands and Hot Tubs." A Del Taco advertising crispy shrimp tacos. Behind a wall of condominiums, in a place invisible to the occupants (but visible to us), a few homeless people had arranged a hospitable square of couches. The horn sounded more frequently after we passed the earthen dam that stopped up the Santa Ana River, and then we were into a carpet of Orange County affluence: hillside homes with blooms of bougainvillea, swimming pools, the lovely diffuse light prized so much by filmmakers. The *Chief*, late of Chicago, moved through it all like a disinterested party guest shouldering through a crowd.

We called at Fullerton for ten minutes, our next-to-last stop, which had a café with the Santa Fe's old cross logo in front and some outdoor tables shaded by umbrellas. I stood on the upper level of the observation car with my hands in my pockets, looking out the window through a few date palms and over the walls of a condominium, but in the flat L.A. Basin there was no view of the fake alpine peak I knew was just five miles to the south: a marker of the stupendous monument—and secret tombstone—to the American passenger train.

Walter Elias Disney was born in 1901 in Chicago, but when Walter was four, his father moved the family to a wheat and apple farm near Marceline, Missouri.

These four childhood years in Marceline made a deep impression on Disney: he remembered the Main Street branching from the depot, the park with a Civil War cannon and a gazebo, and he especially remembered the Santa Fe tracks that led out of town in both directions, to which he would press his ear, listening for the hum and rattle that signaled an incoming train.

But these were also not years of unbridled happiness. His father, a tough and flinty man, was prone to beating young Walt, who found escape through sketching horses. He left Missouri on the Santa Fe Railroad in 1923, heading to Hollywood in hopes of founding a studio. A bit of company legend has it that the first sketches of Mickey Mouse were made in a Pullman car after Disney learned that a rival studio was stealing one of his first characters, Oswald the Lucky Rabbit.

Though blessed with wild commercial success and a genuine love for other people, Disney suffered from hyperactivity and depression, and his doctors recommended he take time away from the office. That usually meant tinkering with an elaborate miniature railroad he had built in the backyard of his house at 355 North Carolwood Drive in the Holmby Hills section of Los Angeles. After the art film *Fantasia* had bombed with critics and at the box office, Disney lost interest in making animated movies and became "almost weirdly concerned with the building of a miniature railroad engine and a string of cars in the workshops of the studio," observed Bosley Crowther, a visitor from the *New York Times*. "All of his zest for invention, for creating fantasies, seemed to be going into this plaything." He would pilot it in a pair of bib overalls and an engineer's cap, sometimes after eating a doughnut dipped in scotch, his favorite snack.

Disney called it the "Carolwood-Pacific," and it ran over trestles and through a winding tunnel under his wife's flower garden, for which he made a show of securing a legal "easement." Walt loved hosting backyard parties for children, and the highest honor in his small circle of friends, it was said, was to be made an "honorary vice president" of the Carolwood-Pacific, which came with a printed certificate. It occurred to Disney that his backyard was a more welcoming place for children than the local amusement lots with cheap midway games and staffed by sleazy-looking characters. He made some preliminary sketches for "Mickey Mouse Park," to be built behind his studio in Burbank, which would be designed around a railroad depot and a village green: a clean and nice place, like the Marceline of his invented memories.

But his strongest inspiration was the Chicago Railroad Fair of 1948, in which thirty-eight of the nation's railroads sought to make a show of their contributions, even as their share of passenger traffic was hemorrhaging. Disney took the *California Limited* across the country with his friend and fellow railhound Ward Kimball to the city where he was born. Somewhere in the middle of Arizona, Disney was invited to come to the locomotive and blow the whistle, and, reported Kimball, "I had never, ever seen him so happy."

The railroad fair was located at the shore of Lake Michigan near the site of the 1893 World Columbian Exposition, and some of its "villages" took their cues from previous world's fairs, but its basic layout would now be familiar to any visitor to one of Disney's theme parks. There was a re-creation of a sandy Florida beach, with palm trees, an orange-juice bar and a diorama celebrating Stephen Foster's "Way Down Upon the Swanee River," constructed by the Chicago and Eastern Illinois Railroad; a fake dude ranch with a steam-pipe version of Old Faithful sponsored by the Northern Pacific; an aromatic French Quarter of New Orleans from the Illinois Central; a display of locomotives by Union Pacific; and what may have been the pièce de résistance for Disney: a giant mud-and-pole pueblo village staffed with Navajo medicine men and ceremonial dancers from five other Indian tribes, sponsored by the Atchison, Topeka and Santa Fe, an act ripped straight from Fred Harvey. The connecting thread between all these villages was, of course, an old-timey railroad: the Deadwood Central, a tribute to the western mining roads of the 1870s, which ran on a narrow gauge and cost a dime to ride.

Disney began to have second thoughts about "Mickey Mouse Park." He had already seen children's parks that he liked, but his recent experience seemed to have brought it to a full-scale vision: a snow-globe version of America, divided into different lands and all of it linked by a friendly train. On the ride back to California, he was talking of little else. "Disneyland was already forming in his mind," said Kimball. "Of course, he thought it should have a full-sized steam train . . . that he could have fun operating himself on days when the park was closed." Lillian Disney always told friends she was convinced Disneyland came into being because of her husband's childhood obsession with the Santa Fe Railroad.

After seven years, $17 million and many experiments with tamed-down carnival rides, Disneyland opened in a former citrus grove in Anaheim,* looking eerily similar to the Chicago Railroad Fair. There were four original "lands"—Fantasyland, Frontierland, Adventureland and Tomorrowland—and the centerpiece of Main Street USA, which was based directly on Walt's gaslight memories of Marceline, Missouri. Encircling the whole park, at a length of one and a half miles, was the "Santa Fe & Disneyland Railroad," a steam train with tall stacks and cowcatchers that provided the quickest route between the lands.

Tracks were embedded in the very gears of the park. The core of a Disney ride—from It's a Small World to Mr. Toad's Wild Ride to Pirates of the Caribbean—was a rail system that conveyed the visitors at walking speed through a series of wildly decorated rooms animated by singing mechanical puppets in a seven- to ten-minute fantasy. With no apparent irony, Tomorrowland contained the most rail-oriented rides, including a People Mover, sponsored by Goodyear Tire and Rubber Company, and a Mark II monorail connected by "beamway" to a nearby hotel.

---

* The original location choice had been the land near Union Station in downtown Los Angeles.

Rail transportation remains the invisible skeleton of Disneyland, which celebrated an America whose substance was already fading away.* The park was on a vanished orange farm astride a major California freeway and could be reached only by car. The parking lot charged high fees with the goal of discouraging the "loafers and other undesirable characters" whose presence was a feature of most actual railroad stations and who were presumably too poor to afford cars.

The nation's dying passenger railroads were in effect cryogenically frozen at Disneyland: a perfect specimen of the past captured in a time capsule for the amusement of the public. In this way the Magic Kingdom has a lot in common with Amtrak. They are charming and expensive, and they both require a certain dose of good humor.

The *Southwest Chief* stole into downtown Los Angeles on its final bended joint, paralleling the northwesterly route of Interstate 5 along a corridor of steel-pipe yards and pizza-dough factories at a rate of seventy-nine miles per hour. We slowed at the west bank of the slimy old Los Angeles River, a trickle in its cement cradle, and then curved around an abandoned Mission-style tower on one side and the gray walls of the Men's Central Jail on the other. Though we finished at a crawl, the journey in from Fullerton had been one of the speediest daylight trips into downtown I had ever experienced.

I tipped and thanked Pinkie, shook hands with the French schoolteacher, shouldered my pack and walked through the tunnel into Union Station, a soaring hall of terra-cotta and travertine marble in a Mission Revival style, finished in 1939 and called "the last of the great railroad stations." For years, Jack Benny had a gag of broadcasting a radio show from Union Station and being interrupted by the voice of Mel Blanc announcing, "Train leaving from Track 5 for Anaheim, Azusa and

---

* The Atchison, Topeka and Santa Fe had to withdraw its sponsorship in 1974 amid declining revenues, and the train became known simply as the Disneyland Railroad.

Cuuuucamonga." But the walls in the waiting hall are lined with cork, which creates a strange hush, and sunlight streams through the front doors in the afternoon for a reddish-golden effect. Local folklore has it that this was the point of disembarkation for herds of would-be starlets, soon to be corrupted and discarded by the Hollywood beast.

"Certainly I know of no other city in which arriving passengers leave the station through an open patio, filled with bright flowers, shady pepper trees, and flanked with tall palms," wrote a visiting architect named Paul Hunter who arrived shortly after its completion. "This scheme undoubtedly originated with publicity men, but they have certainly hit upon the ideal introduction to Southern California."

The city of Los Angeles has done an exceptional job of repurposing it as a hub for buses and the Metrolink commuter trains, though the north ticket hall is roped off. A Harvey House restaurant remains shuttered, except when crews rent it out for location shooting. The movies *Star Trek: First Contact*, *Blade Runner* and *Pearl Harbor* all have scenes that were filmed here.

In fact, Union Station makes such an appealing background for movies that it has its own portfolio agent. On approximately one hundred days out of every calendar year, various films are being shot here. Historical dramas and science fiction are by far the most popular genres for this place, the last of the great stations.

BLOOD ON
THE TRACKS

Moscow to Vladivostok

Almost everyone in Russia who heard me say I was going to ride all the way to the Pacific Ocean looked on me with pity. You don't understand, they said. So *boring*. Nothing to do for seven whole days. Bad people on the train. Crowded. Smelly. Why don't you fly? It'll be easier.

I didn't listen. This was a train journey nonpareil, nothing else like it anywhere. Nearly six thousand miles of unbroken iron across the Eurasian landmass. Russia would never have become Russia without the easy access it provided to mineral and agricultural wealth. It is the longest unbroken railroad in the world and spans sixteen time zones. As the sun sets on one end, it is not far from rising on the other. Even the name has panache. *Trans-Siberian*. It sounds like a teleportation across the steppes, an easy glide past the snow and birches.

But this railroad is not beloved in its home country. For one thing, the term "Trans-Siberian" is not even used here; it is the foreigners who call it that. For those who live in Siberia, it is the only real choice for traveling long distances, as the roads are shabby. They tend to associate it with going to a relative's funeral or getting to a hospital for surgery. Older Russians recall it mainly as a link to Stalin's gulags, a belt of misery. A traveler generally boarded only when under compulsion, and not as an experience to be enjoyed. Few but eccentric tourists or true aviophobes ride the whole way.

But how bad could it be, really? Though it was November and snow was everywhere, the train would be warm and the scenery would be unique, if monotonous. I was certain to meet some Russians with interesting stories. If nothing else, it would be a good chance to sit and read for a few days and make some notes. My destination was the Pacific port of Vladivostok, Russia's easternmost city of consequence.

Practically every rail journey from Moscow through Siberia starts from Yaroslavl station, a handsome hulk built in 1904 and designed to look like a Russian Orthodox convent. Peddlers sell food and radios from the stalls outside. I took a train down from St. Petersburg, ate a final restaurant meal of Stroganoff and thin beer and walked to the platforms at Yaroslavl to find my train. The ticket I held was for *platskartny*, otherwise known as "hard class," the cheapest type of Russian train ticket, purchased the previous day after a round of pantomime with a sour woman behind smeared glass.

Once I'd shown a guard my passport, I was pointed to the wrong seat in a carriage jammed with Russians stowing away their plastic luggage and getting ready for the slog. Young women peeled off their high-heeled leather boots and changed into rubber slippers; unshaven men in zippered tracksuits dealt cards to each other, the first rounds of many. The car itself was basically a long hallway divided into eight sections of benches and bunks. The bunks were coated in vinyl and padded with approximately two micrometers of stuffing. They appeared long enough to comfortably accommodate a horse jockey. Small squares of lacquered wood were wedged between the benches, meant to be used as tables. Though the train was not yet moving, a strong odor of coal smoke and human body pervaded the carriage.

I smiled at the heavy grandmotherly type sitting across from me and introduced myself in English. She said something back in Russian, and I nodded and said *zdravstvuite* ("hello," which is about the pathetic extent of the Russian I speak) and then added "Vladivostok" to explain where I was going. She looked at me like I was crazy.

One of the car attendants—a *provodnik*—came by and informed me I was in the wrong seat, and I was reseated in the next car beside two young men, one of them dark and squash-shaped and the other who looked like a blond Iowa farmer with broken teeth. Tolia, the farmer look-alike, wore a floppy red soccer jersey displaying the letters of the old Soviet Union (CCCP) and spoke a tiny bit of English. He introduced me to his friend, Roma. They were chatting away like old pals, and it wasn't until we were clear of the outermost ring of Moscow suburbs that they grew bored with each other and I learned they had just met.

Tolia broke the ice by cracking a half-liter tallboy aluminum can and setting it in front of me. The can bore pictures of violet berries popping open like airborne bubbles. The contents smelled like room freshener. I guessed it was a concoction of vodka and sugary fruit juice. On the side was a brand name that a Russian-speaking friend in the United States would later tell me meant that the drink was essentially a form of local moonshine, made of flowers and stale bread.

"Cocktail," said Tolia, smiling. I sipped it, and it tasted as if enough of them would fry the liver into oblivion. I raised the heavy can to him, and he nodded. "Very good," he said with the gravity of a sommelier. He opened a package of dried fish and his own oil-can-size cocktail. The customary Russian chilliness, which wraps the public persona like a layer of tree bark, gave way to warmth and solicitude—as it generally does when enough face time and alcohol are in play. They taught me the Russian word for "beautiful," which I applied, to their amusement, to the birch forests drooping with fresh snow beyond the passing factories.

It went on like that for about three hundred miles. The sun sank, and harsh overhead lights shone down on the silver fish of the train as we passed through the cities of Petushki, Vladimir and Kourov. We raised more cans of floor cleaner to each other. Tolia's supply of it seemed inexhaustible. But we couldn't communicate much beyond gestures and toasts and simple harmless words. He would ask me a question in Russian, and I would answer him in English and vice versa, and we both nodded and laughed as if we understood. We toasted Putin and then Obama and LeBron James and anybody else we could think of that we had in common.

Out the windows, icy to the touch, were scenes of men burning branches. The flames were little orange pyramids in the snow. There were brown cabins through the trees, and in places old men and women struggled along paths with canes. These Russian freeholds rolled along like a filmstrip behind the slab of cold glass, and it occurred to me, even in my growing drunken stupor, that I was passing by quite arrogantly. I saw for a few seconds the land these half-seen people had known intimately for decades.

I would later come by an observation from Victor Hugo about his first train journey in 1837 that reminded me of this helpless feeling: "The flowers by the side of the road are no longer flowers but flecks, or rather streaks, of red or white; there are no longer any points, everything becomes a streak; the grainfields are great shocks of yellow hair; fields of alfalfa, long green tresses; the towns, the steeples and the trees perform a crazy mingling dance on the horizon; from time to time a shadow, a shape, a specter appears and disappears with lightning speed behind the window: it's a railway guard."

We clicked past a line of petroleum tanks and through the station at Nizhny Novgorod, the nation's fourth-largest city, and then across a wide sheet of dark water smeared with bridge lights. This was the Volga River, the bloodstream and the major watershed for most of western Russia. Tolia and Roma fell silent. I wanted the train to stop so I could walk to its edge, dip a hand into its freezing and oily water, breathe harsh November air into my lungs and try to get sober. But in three minutes we were over it and gone back into another enveloping of drab suburbs and birches. In another day we would be crossing a much more arbitrary line over into Asia and thence into Siberia.

In the medieval Russian imagination, Siberia was a sheet of howling emptiness, the vanishing point of the horizon out of which had ridden the apparition of the Mongol murderers of the thirteenth century. They had sacked Riazen and Moscow and Kiev, beheading the princes, slaughtering the male inhabitants and turning the women into sexual slaves. The Mongols ruled here as khans, exacting tributes of gold and sheep, for a hundred fifty years until they were refused their tributes and beaten back eastward by a coalition of petty Russian-speaking nobles, allied in 1480 under the rule of Ivan the Great.

His grandson, the illiterate Ivan the Terrible, then started the conquest in reverse, marching eastward against an offshoot band of Mongols, known as Tatars, with a gruesome battle at the fortified city of Kazan in 1556. Fur traders were given permits to settle and build log forts on the broad and barely moving rivers of what was already being called "Siberia," after the Sibir khanate that lay on the other side of the Ural Mountains. This first attempt to annex the east marked the beginnings of monarchical Russia.

Peter the Great decided as early as 1722 that Siberia would be an excellent place to warehouse thieves and political opponents, and he forced them to work in the silver mines around Daurya. This was the beginning of the infamous gulag system, later used by czars and Communist Party bosses alike to condemn people to squalid eastern jails for crimes as vague as "being incompatible with public tranquillity." The trip out to Siberia with a cart and team could take up to a year and left the passengers open to exposure, disease and bandits. When they arrived, they were housed in grimy and freezing cabins amid roaming bands of native huntsmen.

Such was the state of Siberia—a loose constellation of mines and prison forts amid a blanket of grass and snow—when the growing influence of China convinced Czar Alexander III to toughen his hold on it in the 1890s. The idea for building the Trans-Siberian—the railroad equivalent of a mission to Mars—belonged to Count Sergei Witte, who bullied and bluffed his way through chancery politics up to the position of finance minister and persuaded Alexander that Russia's only cure for backwardness was to borrow heavily, tax heavily, adopt the gold standard and build massive public works.

The cornerstone plan was to be a six-thousand-mile railroad from St. Petersburg to the Pacific, which would stitch together the vast territory into one nation, much as the Union Pacific and Central Pacific had done for the United States in the 1860s. Such a project, while opulent, would eventually pay for itself in the new farms and mines that would be opened near its tracks. Because all that wheat and iron ore certainly couldn't be hauled in an oxcart. "Money can only be found by spending it lavishly," Witte was fond of saying.

This was a proto-version of Keynesian economics in flower, four decades before John Maynard Keynes found fame by advocating state spending as a vital function of national health. Witte was in an excellent position to experiment, because he enjoyed access not only to the czar but also to the royal treasury and the mint. To build the Trans-Siberian, he adopted the suicide regimen of simply printing more rubles to pay his contractors.

On Sunday, May 19, 1891, the son of Alexander, the future czar Nicholas II turned a ceremonial shovel of dirt at the Pacific port of Vladivostok, marking the official beginning of construction. A proclamation written by his father said the project would "connect the natural abundance of the Siberian lands" with Russia's European side. Which meant the train was basically a straw through which to suck money into St. Petersburg. While other European nations were quarreling with one another for African spoils, Russia would colonize its own backyard. The locomotive, not the gunboat, was the chosen vessel of imperialism.

When a statue of Alexander III was later cast and erected in St. Petersburg, he was shown wearing a railway conductor's uniform.

About a third of the nation's production of pig iron was diverted for the project, either hauled on wagons or railcars to the end of the line or shipped by steamer to Vladivostok. Wells had to be drilled through the permafrost to find water for the engines. Even a basic natural element, mature hardwood for the ties, was nowhere to be found in large stretches. Count Witte wanted this line built fast and cheap, so young green wood was laid down on the rail bed, which sagged over the many brooks it had to cross. When the track gangs of ill-paid Russians, Koreans and Chinese had to be beefed up, the czar ordered forced prison labor. More than fourteen thousand prisoners would eventually serve at least part of their sentences in filthy railroad camps where the food doubled as live-stock feed and where they were forced to trundle iron and haul stones in the freezing cold that could dip below minus fifty Fahrenheit.

The earth was tough as granite until the middle of July, when the ditches carved next to the tracks ran high with meltwater and became breeding pools for the mosquitoes and gnats that made an average work-day intolerable. Cholera, anthrax and even bubonic plague broke out, and hundreds deserted into the wilderness to join the roving bands that locals called "General Cuckoo's Army," the vagrants and thieves who made their living from robbery in the late-spring thaws when the first cuckoos began to sing. Count Witte's aggressive schedule ensured that the railroad would be finished by 1901, but the green-wood ties warped and the cheap iron bent upward, causing wrecks at a rate of three a week. Engineers felt safe running their trains only at thirteen miles an hour.

But Siberia did begin to grow. Land near the tracks was sold for a pittance when it wasn't simply given away. A ticket for a trip across three thousand miles was offered for twenty rubles, only about a month's savings for a farmer. The fifth-class cars became "stables on wheels," as up to 5 million settlers flooded into the territories and became New Siberians.

Some of those who rushed to take jobs at the rail stations soon became disillusioned with their life in the midst of nowhere, and many turned to embezzlement, theft of cargo and heavy vodka drinking to take the edge off their poverty and boredom. Others simply walked away from their jobs to join General Cuckoo's Army or to hitch their way back to Moscow. In a short story entitled "Champagne," Anton Chekhov wrote of the misery of a station agent whose only relief was the occasional passing of a train when he might catch a glimpse of a beautiful woman behind the frosted glass. "In summer the solemn peace, the monotonous, strident chirping of the grasshoppers, the clear moonlight nights from which there was no concealment wrought in me a mournful sadness; in winter the immaculate whiteness of the plains, their cold remoteness, the long nights, and the howling of the wolves oppressed me like a painful nightmare."

Even more isolated were the flagmen, who had one of the most boring jobs imaginable. The rule book said that engineers must be waved ahead by a spotter with a green flag, and so an army of flagmen were hired to live in little cabins beside the tracks—one every thirty-five hundred feet so as to be within sight of each other on a clear day. Most often it was the flagman's wife or daughter, clothed in a shift dress and barefoot, who would rush out in all kinds of weather with a worn green flag wrapped around a stick. There were approximately nine thousand of these flag holders, a chain of human beings that stretched along the tracks from Moscow all the way to the Pacific Ocean, a distance of 5,776 miles.

The debut party was held not in Russia but in Paris. Czar Nicholas wanted the rest of the aristocratic classes to see his new creation, and so he spent lavishly for a display at the Universal Exposition of 1900. Replicas of the sleeping cars—complete with velvet sofas, lamps and blazing gold curtains—were displayed amid papier-mâché mock-ups of snow-capped mountains.

Romance and orientalism beckoned. The carriages were decked out with Louis XVI furniture and frescoed ceilings, the library stocked books in four languages and the gym car featured dumbbells and a rowing machine. But the unstated psychological appeal was the hint of danger in the Wild East in Russia. On day trips away from the railroad, cautioned the Baedecker guide, "It is desirable to carry a revolver."

The Russian promoters had an enviable publicity model to imitate— the *Orient Express*. This splashy train across Europe had been the brainchild of a Belgian travel agent named George Nagelmackers, who realized that the decline of the Ottoman Empire made it possible to start exploiting the fez-and-sword images of the Islamic world to paying customers. In 1884 his Compagnie Internationale des Wagons-Lits* ordered a fleet of Pullman sleeping cars and fitted them out in high bordello style: mahogany moldings, handblown glasses, champagne in ice buckets, heavy red carpets, obsequious waiters wearing buckle shoes, breeches and monkey jackets. Departing from Paris's Gare de l'Est, the train crossed Europe and the Balkans and in eighty-two hours arrived at Istanbul, where steamer tickets to any Asian port could be purchased.

One regular passenger was King Boris of Bulgaria, a serious foamer who had his own pair of canvas work overalls custom-tailored in Paris. Fascinated with the steam engine, he loved nothing more than to ride in the locomotive and ask all kinds of questions of the driver and the fireman. The directive eventually came down: anyone who let King Boris talk his way into the cab would be fired on the spot. The king retaliated by ordering the train stopped by the military once it had crossed into Bulgaria. Then he would seize the controls and "defy anyone to stop him from driving a train across his own kingdom," reported journalist Martin Page. The sneaky child-king was part of the lore† that

---

* French for "International Sleeping-Car Company."

† No homicide on the *Orient Express* was ever recorded, though an attaché for the U.S. Navy named Eugene Karpe disappeared from a successor service to Bucharest in 1948; his body was found trackside in a tunnel in the Alps. Whether he fell or was pushed was never determined.

grew up around the *Orient Express* and made a ride on it a guaranteed story at a dinner party.

But the Trans-Siberian was no *Orient Express*. The first travelers complained about the mediocre quality of the coaches and the food and, more impressive to the senses, a feeling of awe bordering on outright despair at the ceaseless plains out the window, scenery that barely seemed to move.

A bon vivant travel writer named Harry De Windt passed the time in the company of Russian cavalry officers, whom he considered "capital fellows," as well as the women of the petite noblesse who sang in the dining car. "Nearly every one spoke French, and the time passed pleasantly enough, for although the days were terribly monotonous, evenings enlivened by music and cards, followed by cheery little suppers toward the small hours, almost atoned for their hours of boredom," he wrote. "This train has one advantage, there is no rattle or roar about it, as it steals like a silent ghost across the desolate steppes."

The journalists of that period, especially the British, competed with one another to describe the boredom of Siberia in new and creative ways. Images of desolation flew thick: endless plains of grass, sad crowds of dark-coated peasants clustered at the stations, the monotonous views of the continent-long boreal forest called the taiga. Villages were like "hems of rubbish," the train was a "fly trailing across a hemisphere," which traveled at a speed "which an able-bodied cowboy on his bronco would outstrip."

Some preferred to sink into their own imaginations and allow the train and its symbolism to transport them elsewhere. John Foster Fraser stood in a freezing vestibule in 1901 and let himself daydream. "I confess the railway, a twin thread of steel spreading over the continent, began to fascinate me as nothing had done for a long time. Here is a land one and a half times as large as Europe—forty times indeed as big as the United Kingdom—that has lain dormant through the ages but is at last being tickled into life, as it were, by the railway, as a giant might be aroused from slumber by a wisp."

Few, however, wrote more eloquently about the passage of time on the Trans-Siberian than Peter Fleming (Ian Fleming's brother and a much better writer), who in a trip to Manchuria in 1933 made several allusions to his velvet coupe as a kind of coffin and himself as a ticket-holding dead man.

"This small, timeless moving cell I recognized as my home and my doom. I felt as if I had always been on the Trans-Siberian Express," he wrote. "There is no need to get up and no incentive either. You have nothing to look forward to, nothing to avoid. No assets, no liabilities. . . . You lie in your berth, justifiably inert. Past the window plains crawl and forests flicker. The sun shines weakly on an empty land."

Laziness and dissipation are inevitable on the Trans-Siberian; what matters is how well you can pass the time. I found very few people in hard class who spoke more than a few functional phrases of English, and I had nothing more than a few phrases of restaurant Russian to repeat endlessly. When I grew tired of reading and unable to focus, I looked out the window at the moving scroll and thought about the intense physical labor that had gone into building it and felt guilt at how little of that energy I was personally exemplifying by sitting still and staring out the window.

I had grown used to the smell of sour feet and onions and had done as almost everyone else was doing by the way of meals—that is to say, avoiding the dining car. Instead I bought cartons of sodium-soaked ramen noodles from the babushkas who gathered by the tracks. We made them with hot water from the samovar, the giant pot of boiling water at the end of every carriage, at the opposite end from the generally disgusting stainless-steel toilets that dumped straight onto the tracks and were ritually locked when we were stopped in the stations.

It was just as well that overwatered ramen became my staple. Peter Fleming had written about the gastronomic cycle on this train in 1933, and not much had changed for those making long journeys. "We sat and ate, with dull, heavy eyes," he wrote. "If you had been told to name the outstanding characteristic of this cross-section of the New Russia, you would have put it down as constipation. You would not have been far wrong."

After Tolia had staggered off the train, giving me the peace sign as farewell, Roma fell silent and put his head down on the small table in between the benches. He offered up a deep, bored sigh every ten minutes or so, an exhalation that became as anemic as the regular *tap-a-de-tap* of the rails underneath. After a time I couldn't listen to him any longer, and so I got up to pace the length of the train. We were beginning to ascend into the Ural Mountains, and the floors were at a slight slope.

The dining car was dim and purplish; the only people within were a dark-haired female bartender and a hard, square man with a leather jacket and one metal tooth. Both were watching a Russian soap opera on a television mounted above the bar. As I wove through, a lurch made me stumble against the man wearing the leather jacket. I smiled, uttered a *whoa* and gave him a pat on the arm. That was a mistake. He took the touch as a challenge and gave me back an angry, ironic pound on the shoulder that sent me reeling. Then he uttered a Russian phrase I didn't understand. His eyes were inebriated, and his mouth twitched. Repair seemed impossible; I kept walking, hoping he wouldn't follow.

In the next car, I met a wispy-mustached English speaker named Arsin who told me that he had worked for Russian Railways for several years before quitting.

"They are okay to their passengers," he said. "But they are awful to their employees."

What did he mean? I asked, and he thrust his hips forward once while whistling like a cuckoo: a gesture of forced sodomy. Arsin had worked as a *provodnik*, the attendant who rides along in every carriage, responsible for cleaning the toilets, sweeping the floor, selling candy bars and beer and generally keeping order. Russian *provodniki* of both sexes are notoriously rude and prickly—though, to be fair, it is a grind-ingly hard job. They typically get only two to three hours' worth of sleep a night. Not to mention that holding this job is basically a life sentence to the excruciating boredom of the Trans-Siberian.

There were a bewildering number of regulations to follow, said Arsin, as well as the need to deal with the rowdy drunks. When thirty-two ex-soldiers, recently discharged from the front at Chechnya, came across the platform like a tank in a storm, he thought, "Please, God, not me." But they were indeed assigned to his carriage, and they piled in. The vodka came out. And in the night, as he was drooping in his chair into his cherished hour of unconsciousness, he heard the sounds of a fight beginning.

"They would have killed me," he said, "so I went up to them with a big smile." The lead troublemaker started throwing punches at him, wild haymakers that were easy to duck. Arsin then used a move he had learned from his own time in the military: He grabbed the drunk by the lapels and rammed him into the bulkhead, knocking the wind out of him. Then he gave him a rap against the nose for maximum pain value.

This ended the fight, but Arsin went back to his chair with a deep sense of dread. Even though he had been right, there would be a prob-able reprimand or firing. But a few hours later, the same drunk came back around, with a cold bottle of beer pressed against his wounded nose. He introduced himself as Leonid and spoke the closest thing to an apology he was capable of. "Thank you," he said. "I was drinking." A letter on military stationery was indeed forthcoming, but instead of complaining, it praised Arsin's performance, calling him "a good peace-maker."

Soldiers on the Trans-Siberian are to be avoided, he told me. "They do nothing for a year, and then they have a party. This is the first place they come."

He told me he wanted to show me something, and so I followed him back through the dining car, where the drunk man in the leather jacket was again contemplating the fuzzy soap opera, a cigarette smoldering in front of him. He paid us no attention. I told Arsin about the hard slap he'd given me, and Arsin told me that the man was an undercover security guard who worked for the railroad.

"I know him," said Arsin. "He is angry at the world."

We were by this point in a freezing vestibule, and our breath was cloudy. Arsin withdrew a flat key from his pocket and opened several of the compartments to show me what was inside: supplies, toilet paper, coal chunks for the samovar, a few wires. He had stolen the skeleton key from his days working for Russian Railways. He then used it to open the thick door that opened to the outside, where a dark blur of birches was whipping fast. A frigid wind filled the vestibule, and I stepped back a bit. Arsin grabbed hold of a bar and leaned out of the train, hanging himself out to the wind for a moment.

Then he thought better of it. "I guess that's dangerous, isn't it?" he said sheepishly, pulling himself back inside.

Arsin got off a few stops away from Yekaterinburg, at one of the closed towns where Russia stores old uranium and plutonium left over from the Cold War. But I remembered his warning about soldiers when a group of them came and sat next to me on my bench, laughing and singing.

They, too, had been stationed in Chechnya. One of them showed me a video on his digital camera that had been taken from a moving vehicle cruising through the blasted remnants of a village; he had added a hard-driving rock-music sound track. The soldiers were all in their late teens and were passing around a 2.5-liter bottle of beer with a picture of a white bear on the label. When it came to me, I smiled no and passed it along.

One of them, a young Asian man in camouflage sitting next to me, spoke a little English and asked where I was from.

"Do you like black rap?" he asked. I nodded. He started to recite, word-perfect, a song from Jam Master Jay.

Then he asked, "Are you carrying any money?"

"Sorry?"

"Money? Are you carrying any money or jewelry?"

"No," I said.

A soldier on the bench across from me scowled as I refused another pass of the warm beer. Suddenly it felt like time to go back to the dining car. And if there was no reason, I would have to invent one. The soldiers let me get up, accepted my nod and didn't follow.

I stared at the wall in another carriage until close to midnight, when we reached the mining city of Yekaterinburg, which had grown into one of eastern Russia's wealthiest places because of the ore hauling made possible by the railway. In the dark, somewhere that I did not see, we had passed the small, towerlike monument that marks the hydrological division line between Europe and Asia.

This pillar was emotionally significant to travelers on the Trans-Siberian in its earlier days, enormously so for those on their way to prison. There used to be a custom for convict trains to stop for a rest at the little stone marker, which turned out to be an object of intellectual torture to those who feared they would never know the warmth of their homes or families ever again, and that all that lay ahead was the chartless misery and loneliness and ne plus ultra of Siberia.

"No other boundary post in the world has witnessed so much human suffering, or been passed by such a multitude of heart-broken people," wrote the American gulag investigator George Kennan in 1891. Many, he said, would place their lips on the European side of it, as they would kiss the portrait of a saint or scratch the names of their wives or children onto the white plaster before being ordered back into line.

I got off in the spotlight cones of Yekaterinburg and made my way over the ice to a Communist-era travelers' hotel across the street from the station. But before going to bed, I wanted to make a pilgrimage. The spot was about a mile south of the tracks and not terribly difficult to find.

Czar Nicholas II, who had turned the first spadeful of dirt for the

Trans-Siberian, was forced to give up the monarchy in the revolution of 1917. He and the rest of the Romanov family were arrested and taken quietly on the Trans-Siberian Railway to Yekaterinburg, where they were received, warily, at a freight depot by members of the Ural Regional Soviet, who had arranged for them to be held in the house of an engineer named Nikolai Nikolayevich Ipatiev, who had helped build the local section of the railway.

The Bolsheviks kept them hostage in this house for seventy-eight days, debating what to do, until the approach of a legion of the Czech army along the railway tracks convinced them to take an irrevocable step. On the night of July 16, 1918, a squad of revolutionaries, after a night of drinking, led the Romanovs to the basement, blindfolded them, read an execution order and then opened fire. The bodies of the czar and his family were dumped down a mine shaft in the forest.

Nicholas had been a tone-deaf king at a time of sweeping change, and he had approved the exile and execution of thousands. But his Christian faith in an era of atheism, plus the naked pathos of an entire family's slaughter, including the four daughters and a hemophilic son, made this house of regicide a place of curiosity until a local party boss (Boris Yeltsin, of all people) ordered it razed for a road-widening project in 1977 because it was "of insufficient historical value."

The Orthodox Church has since canonized the Romanovs as saints, despite their many unsavory aspects, and a mammoth new house of worship with golden domes and high windows—"Church on Blood in Honor of All Saints Resplendent in the Russian Land"—now sits atop the basement where they were gunned down. The cavity has long been filled in with dirt. As far as sacred places go, this one was eerie.

I wandered around outside the gaudy church for a while, my boots crunching in the snow. No cars passed on the road. Everything was utterly quiet. Nicholas had spurred the railway to life; it would be complicit in his end.

But even more than Czar Nicholas II, the Russian who had the most ironic and even fatal relationship with this new method of travel was Count Leo Tolstoy.

He distrusted the way they turned the view of the countryside into a long tube, disliked the speed and hustle they brought to the old way of peasant life in its horse-path niches and hollows, and the leveling force of modern values, which he considered a toxin in the blood of the Russian people. He saw the train as a colorless and alien intrusion, a "nasty" conveyance that cheapened the leisurely perambulations that previously characterized getting from one place to another. "The railroad is to travel as the whore is to love," he complained in a letter to his friend Ivan Turgenev in 1857. "It's just as comfortable, but just as horribly mechanical and fatally monotonous."

This was an appropriate comparison for Tolstoy, a sexual buccaneer in his youth, who later became a prominent—though not always consistent—advocate for celibacy. His true attitudes toward the convenience of the railroad were just as changing and complicated, as a matter of fact, as his lifelong struggle with the material pleasures of the flesh.

At the age of forty-four, Tolstoy was settled into married life with Sophia Behrs at his estate Yasnaya Polyana. Their relationship had been madly passionate from the start and fraught with some guilt; he was sixteen years older than she, and on their wedding night he famously made her read his diary of past conquests to understand what a rake he had been. With that, and the word galaxy of *War and Peace* behind him, he was happy in his newfound domesticity but still restless to write "a first novel" (he did not consider *War and Peace* to be of this category) that aimed to capture the panorama of the individual human experience.

His inspiration came in 1872, in the form of grotesque news from a neighboring estate: a nanny named Anna Stepanova Pirogova, who was said to have been left by her boyfriend for another woman, threw herself under the wheels of a passing locomotive. Tolstoy saw her body laid out in a railroad station, and while he didn't record his feelings about it in his diary, he soon after began writing the opening chapters of his greatest achievement, *Anna Karenina*, in which the title character first meets her eventual lover, Vronsky, in a train station on the same day that a guard is crushed between the cars of a train. "An evil omen," thinks Anna, who is eventually proved right.

The train, in fact, becomes a powerful symbol throughout the book for a multitude of things, mainly negative, that Tolstoy hoped to convey through both mood and action. The primal forces of sex and death are packaged in the steaming black locomotive, but they trail a cloud of other urgent references. The literary critic Sydney Schultze has pointed out that scenes involving the train in *Anna Karenina* contain signposts of crippling modernity: heat, excitement, the color red, the French language, telegrams, disorientation, emotional instability. The train is eerily unseen for most of the book, "something heavy in the distance." After all the tumult and unhappiness caused by Anna's infidelity, she takes herself to the depot. "A freight train was approaching," wrote Tolstoy. "The platform began to shake and it seemed to her she was riding again. And suddenly, remembering about the crushed man on the day of her first meeting with Vronsky, she understood what she must do." In one of the most famous acts in Russian literature, she throws herself under the wheels of the engine, as she had plunged into the irresistible force of the love affair.

Tolstoy was only channeling an idea that had lurked in the subconscious of nineteenth-century writers almost since the birth of the train: the sense that it housed death—metaphorical and actual—in its bellows and cranks.

Part of this surely had to do with the physical novelty of the thing. Man had never traveled so fast before, and at such risk of a sudden and devastating stop. There was the routine nature of everyday accidents reported in the newspapers—brakemen and engineers who saw their own legs sheared off by the blades of the wheels, tramps crushed by the force of carriages slamming together, passengers hurled across rows of seats when two trains collided at a diamond. A journey by train was an existential distillation of life itself, a thoughtless glide through time and space over which always hung the possibility that everything could be cut short by a force the rider was utterly helpless to affect, all the while tugged along by a dynamo that could not be seen except for trails of smoke and cinders. To a passenger in his berth, the engine was as invisible as God.

A French scientific encyclopedia, although generally enthusiastic about railroads, made the following observation in 1845: "Steam power, while opening up new and hitherto unknown roads to man, also seems to continually put him in a position best compared to that of a man who is walking along the edge of a precipice and cannot afford a single false step."

Yet even as the first generation of rail passengers saw death in the wheels, they also could not help but find sexual energy in the hum and rumble and rush of the coaches sliding upon the rails and in and out of tunnels and the brute force of the engine barreling forward. It surely contained Thanatos, the death force, but with a healthy dose of Eros, and writers found that dynamic irresistible.

"I like to see it lap the miles," wrote Emily Dickinson. "And lick the valleys up." This poem, one of her more playful creations, was called "The Railway Train," and it imagined the train as amorous companion, crawling up slopes and fitting itself into crevices, at once "docile and omnipotent," both submissive to control and yet uncontrollable.

Sigmund Freud, of course, saw sexual ghosts in every direction, and his career as a psychiatrist paralleled the railroad's golden age in Austria and in England. He had already observed that many of his patients were seeing train journeys in their dreams as a symbol for dying, and now he pointed out an enduring feature of childhood playtime. "It is a puzzling fact," he wrote, "that boys take such an extraordinarily intense interest in things connected with railways, and, at the age at which the production of phantasies is most active (shortly before puberty) use those things as a nucleus of a symbolism that is particularly sexual. A compulsive link of this kind between railway-travel and sexuality is clearly derived from the pleasurable character of the sensations of movement."

For a few travelers, the rails were an experience of controlled stimulation without climax. The Freudian analyst Karl Abraham recorded the case of one of his patients who took long train journeys and always stayed awake "in order not to lose his pleasure." The following night would bring on what Abraham called, in the medical jargon of the day, "a pollution"—a nocturnal emission.

This anonymous patient was far from the only one who traveled on trains for a sexual thrill. The cheapening cost of travel, the involuntary touch of crowds in the stations, the introduction to attractive companions in the same carriage, the escape from the stern watch of friends and family—all of these brought thoughts of assignation to the Victorian mind. A popular cartoon trope of the era involved a stolen kiss in the darkness of a compartment when the train passed through a tunnel. One pulp story classic of the 1890s, "Raped in a Railway Carriage," received wide underground circulation, as did the even more explosive *My Secret Life*, the purported "sex diary" of a respectable gentleman named Walter, who claimed to have slept with twelve hundred women, some of whom he wooed in the intimate public space of the railway carriage. In one scene he wordlessly communicates his intentions to seduce a twenty-three-year-old fellow passenger. "I kept my eyes on her for she was coarsely handsome, was opposite to me, and our knees nearly met. Soon I put foot and knee against hers, and a thrill of desire shot through me directly they touched. . . . A soft uneasy look came then into her eyes, and she looked round anxiously at the other travelers, twiddling at the same time her third class railway ticket nervously."

The trysts were not only between strangers. Couples both married and unmarried booked sleepers to themselves for the express purpose of making love during the journey; a tip to the porter was enough to ensure privacy. Such was the popular understanding of the dynamic between eroticism and the iron horse that readers of E. M. Forster's *Howards End* needed no elaboration when his female protagonist yearned for the "low rich purr of a Great Western Express . . . that moved so easily and felt so comfortable." The sensual atmosphere of the railroad, concluded the writer Peter Gay, "became, for the nineteenth-century bourgeois imagination, a favorite actor in the theater of libido."

Tolstoy's renunciation of his own sexuality in later years found stern expression in *Anna Karenina* and in its famous climax, when the heroine surrenders herself to the train as she had earlier given herself over to adulterous coupling. At the moment of her impulsive decision, while the locomotive noses closer to her, "the platform started shaking; it seemed to her that she was *in* the train again." And then with a light step, she descends to the rail bed, crosses herself and sticks her head underneath the rolling wheels.

Tolstoy's own marriage to Sophia was a tumultuous one, particularly in its last days. They quarreled constantly after he broke with the Orthodox Church and proclaimed a new utopian version of Christian socialism, which included a life of vegetarianism, sensual abstinence and the general rejection of personal property: an even stronger response to the same corruptions of modernity that he had railed against in *Anna Karenina*. Sophia tolerated most of it, even his wearing of peasant clothes and boots, but she protested vehemently against his plans to let the copyrights on his works lapse into the public domain so they could be available as an inheritance to the Russian people over his family. She felt he was failing to provide for her and their children. When the clamor grew too loud for him, he decided to leave on the morning train with only his doctor as a companion. While Sophia slept on the night of October 10, 1910, he packed a few articles, put the equivalent of seventeen dollars into his pocket and left her a note:

> My departure will distress you. I regret it; but please understand
> and believe that I cannot act differently. My position in the house

has become unbearable. Apart from everything else, I can no longer live in these conditions of luxury in which I have been living, and I am doing what old men of my age commonly do: leaving the worldly life to spend the last days of my life in peace and solitude.

After spending a day with his sister at a convent, he traveled southward in third class with the peasants, planning to go to the shores of the Black Sea to spend those last days in a commune that some of his followers had established. But while he scribbled in his diary, he was recognized by those who shared the carriage—Tolstoy was one of Russia's most visible celebrities—and the chill wind that blew through the windows made him feel sick. Before long he had fever and shakes, and his doctor advised him that to continue on the journey was to risk death. They got off in the small rail village of Astapova, where the stationmaster said it would be his "duty and honor" to let Tolstoy sleep in the bedroom hung with pine branches that he kept at the station.

Tolstoy lingered there with pneumonia for nine days. The news of his whereabouts leaked almost instantly, and correspondents from the world press dashed to the obscure rail siding, where they set up camp and filed regular updates on the great man's health. "Please delete that Tolstoy ate two eggs, incorrect: drank only milk tea," one correspondent wired his editor. After an unsuccessful attempt to drown herself in a pond, Sophia made a dramatic arrival in a private railcar but was not permitted to enter her husband's bedchamber. She slept instead in her railcar, which was ringed with the tents of the reporters and a crowd of mourners next to the tracks. "There huddled together were relatives of the dying man, Tolstoy disciples, villagers and many churchmen, among them Abbot Varsofonius, who did not lose hope until the end of extending to him the olive branch on behalf of the Church," wrote the man from the *New York Times*.

Tolstoy had always said he believed that the telescoping last minutes of a person's life were highly significant—the haunting banality of *The Death of Ivan Illyich* must certainly have been on his mind—and he seemed to be aware the end was coming for him, though he could not recognize the doctors. He tried to cough some final words through his illness. "Truth . . . I have much love . . ." he said, before falling into a coma. Sophia was allowed to come see him, and he died shortly before dawn.

The doctors told the crowd of journalists that his face was clear of pain. Telegrams of sympathy poured in. Even the czar, a frequent target of Tolstoy's invective, sent a sympathetic note. Sophia tried to have a requiem said in the chapel of a nearby school and fainted when she was told it would not be permitted. Instead, wrote the man from the *Boston Daily Globe*, "The platform of the railway station was covered with fir boughs, spread by the peasants of the neighborhood."

A Tolstoyan mist of sex lingered around the train in Russia, but it also sported a halo of blood. The czar's execution was only one of millions of killings that had been enabled by this iron contrivance. The railroad's use as a tool in warfare had been seen shortly after its invention, and among its first victims were the Russians, in a conflict where Leo Tolstoy had been an early witness.

During the Crimean War in 1854, several hundred Russian troops took refuge in the city of Sevastopol while British and French troops pounded away at the lines until supplies ran low. Horses died three a night, after having chewed their tails down to stumps from hunger. The ground "was everywhere covered in twisted gun carriages with the corpses of Russian and enemy soldiers crushed beneath them," wrote a young Tolstoy, and cannons were "half-buried under mounds of earth, shells, cannonballs, more corpses, craters, split beams, casements and yet more silent corpses in grey and blue greatcoats." A railway contractor named Samuel Peto read about the disaster in the London papers and had a flash of insight. Why not build a quickie railway? And within seven months, the British had pounded thirty-nine miles of track up to the plateau. Locomotives hauled in fresh food and guns, and the Russians were forced to surrender. The minor war that would become most famous for producing Florence Nightingale's medical reforms and the suicidal romanticism of "The Charge of the Light Brigade" left another lasting impression on Russia: the supreme usefulness of the railroad as a logistical weapon.

The czar's strategists noted that many of the battles in the American Civil War had been fought for control of railway junctions. And so he built his tracks with a gauge of five feet—pointedly refusing the standard gauge of four feet, eight inches common in Europe—so as to frustrate invading armies who might otherwise have run their troop trains on captured Russian lines. But this was of no help during the revolution of 1917. Immediately after Nicholas II was forced to abdicate, the German government approached Vladimir Lenin, then living in exile in Zurich, and allowed him to ride in a "diplomatically sealed train" through Germany, feeding him extravagant meals to impress him, and then to the Finland station in St. Petersburg, where he gave a rousing speech in the czar's own extravagant waiting room. "We must fight for the social revolution, fight to the end, till the complete victory of the proletariat. Long live the worldwide social revolution!" He succeeded far beyond the Germans' expectations.

Those same interlocking railways that brought Lenin to his destiny might also have made the carnage of World War I inevitable. Germany's famous Schlieffen Plan, a blueprint for a two-front war that had taken years to coordinate, called for a speedy defeat of France in the west and then a redeployment of divisions in the east before Russia could fully respond. "The railways have become an instrument of war," General Alfred von Schlieffen proclaimed. But the "war by timetable," in historian A. J. P. Taylor's memorable phrase, left Germany's leadership paralyzed because it allowed for almost no flexibility once the first shot had been fired. Any halt to the deployment would have created a break in the lines that an enemy could exploit, making a diplomatic resolution extremely difficult. Once in motion the trains could not be stopped. And neither could the war.

The Schlieffen Plan bogged down into a ghastly trench-fighting stalemate in France, where fresh troops were brought in by rail. The soldier-poet Wilfred Owen wrote of the despairing rail journey to probable death: "Down the close, darkening lanes they sang their way / To the siding-shed, / And lined the train with faces grimly gay." The continuing significance of the railroads in WWI was such that Marshal Ferdinand Foch had a special train poached from the *Orient Express* that he used for his field office.

As the war dragged to its end in November 1918, that same train was rolled to the forest outside Compiègne, France, and the Armistice was signed at 5:00 A.M. on the eleventh day of that month, inside Railway Carriage 2419. Foch refused to shake the hands of the German delegation and told them, "Well, gentlemen. It is finished. Go."

On their march into France twenty-two years later, in the opening days of World War II, the invading German army was instructed to find Railway Carriage 2419 and roll it to the exact same spot on the tracks at Compiègne so that the humiliated French government could sign their own surrender papers inside it, which they indeed did on June 22, 1940, to Adolf Hitler's great satisfaction. He stood in the car and listened to the ceremony but left the actual document signing to his underlings and went off to pose for photographs in front of the carriage, which was later taken into Berlin for public exhibition.

In Eastern Europe, meanwhile, the railroad would soon see its darkest use.

Long before the Final Solution was put into action in January 1942, Nazi planners realized that railroads were the essential appliance for transporting Europe's Jewish population to special processing centers, or concentration camps, located, as SS general Reinhard Heydrich put it in a memo, "in cities which are rail junctions, or at least are located along railroad lines." The assistance of the national rail network, the

Reichsbahn, would therefore be important, as its formidable system had to be linked to the systems of conquered territory in France, Poland and Russia and its rolling stock used to transport human cargo en masse. On January 20, 1943, head of the SS Heinrich Himmler wrote a pointed letter to a state secretary in the transportation ministry discussing plans to evacuate Jews from occupied areas of Russia. "Help me and *get me more trains!*" was the last line.

The Germans forced their prisoners to pay third-class fare to the Reichsbahn, meaning that people bought tickets to their own exile and probable execution. The classing and sorting in this giant people-moving operation was made easier by punch-card machines supplied by IBM's German subsidiary, Dehomag, which tabulated freight-car capacity, schedules and the location of virtually every train in Europe. IBM had already helped the Reich identify the Jews within their society in a 1933 census; it now made the trains run efficiently.

The knock at the door of a Jewish home was typically followed by a quick escort to the train platform, where refurbished boxcars were waiting. Soldiers and rail officials learned to quickly recognize which of these cars were to be loaded with humans; the narrow ventilation windows were fringed with barbed wire.

Conditions in the boxcars ranged from the barely tolerable to the horrific. Up to sixty people might be packed into a single car, where it was standing room only and the stench of waste filled the air. "In the semi-darkness, we were terrified by our own numbers," wrote Sala Pawlowicz. "Some people went berserk and bit each other in a rage." The lines leading to the larger camps were bottlenecked, packed with human freight, and cars were often shunted to a siding for days waiting for the lines to clear. German soldiers sometimes fired their machine guns into the cars for amusement. Thirst and starvation also claimed many before they even arrived at the camps, and the survivors finished the ride with corpses lying among them. The Treblinka camp was located strategically near a major rail junction at Malkinia, and when one well-informed fourteen-year-old rail buff on Saul Kuperhand's train realized they were turning there, "many of us broke down and lamented the certain death we now knew awaited us."

Approximately half of all the Jews killed during the genocide were taken to their doom by the railroad, and with a daily efficiency that came to seem routine. "With great joy I learned from your announcement that, for the past fourteen days, a train has gone daily to Treblinka with 5,000 members of the chosen people," wrote SS-Obergruppenführer Karl Wolff to a colleague. Informed of the atrocities by the intelligence work of Polish resistance officer Witold Pilecki,* Allied war planners debated whether to bomb the tracks leading into Auschwitz, but such a measure was rejected, partly on the reasoning that Nazi combat engineers would repair the damaged tracks within hours.

There is a reason that signature photos of the gate at Auschwitz always show it with the tracks in the extreme foreground, the iron rails pointing toward the death camp like an arrow. A full-bore genocide would have been impossible without the train. The efficient people-moving skills it had demonstrated throughout the century turned it into a conveyor belt to the gas chambers. No other kind of transportation would have been feasible: forced marches would have faltered; truck caravans would have been too disorganized and prone to rebellion; village-by-village massacres—such as those committed by the SS before 1942—would have been widely noticed, and the news would have spread. Only the brisk efficiency of the train could have been responsible for the industrialized deaths of 6 million Jews and 5 million gays, Gypsies, Communists, Jehovah's Witnesses, the disabled and others whom the Nazis wanted to disappear, and this in the midst of a

---

* An underappreciated spy hero of World War II. He was the only known person to have *volunteered* to be a prisoner at Auschwitz. As he would write in his smuggled report, the horrifying moment the boxcar door slid open at the camp to reveal bright lights and barking dogs was "the moment in which I had done with what had existed on Earth so far, and I began something which was probably somewhere outside me."

shuffle of cars so routine that the high officials of the Reichsbahn found it possible to claim they had no idea that a death machine was humming within their timetables.

The head of the Reich Transportation Ministry, Julius Dorpmüller, was captured by the Allies after the war and spent time in a prison near Paris. One day as the inmates talked about the scale of the concentration camps, Dorpmüller turned to his former head of purchasing and said, conversationally, "Tell me, Pless, did you know about that? I didn't."

Other rail officials were not so willfully blind. Walter Stier was a member of the Ostbahn, the rail division that served a network of camps, where the trains were known euphemistically as "soap delivery." Stier privately concluded from the statistics that something bad was happening, because the boxcars were going to the camps fully loaded and often coming back empty. Sometimes the returning boxcars contained clothes, or women's hair. But he said nothing. Also silent was the man responsible for the station at Auschwitz—and the spur of tracks that led to the gate—who was fearful of jeopardizing his career or being perceived as a traitor. He remarked, "I want to emphasize that it was my job to ensure that the wheels rolled and not to concern myself with what was being transported." The "banality of evil" documented by philosopher Hannah Arendt was rarely expressed so cogently.

The railroad car in which the hated armistice had been signed had been exhibited at Berlin's Lustgarten, a spacious public square where Nazi rallies were held. As Allied bombs began raining down on the capital, this trophy of the previous war was spirited away to the small town of Ohrdruf and jealously guarded. When Germany's defeat became inevitable in the spring of 1945, a retreating column of SS troops doused Railway Carriage 2419 with gasoline and set it on fire, burning it down to the chassis.

The ceiling was about a foot away from my nose in the top bunk, and I watched a small seam of rivets sway during the times the Trans-Siberian was moving in the middle of the night. Sleep was elusive. A drunk had stumbled against the side of the bunk at around 3:00 A.M., awakening me from a vodka doze, and I couldn't find a comfortable position on the hard open rack. The car was an old East German survivor from the 1970s and not built for comfort. Our progress across the midsection of Siberia had been steady but almost invisible, like a man growing older but not understanding when, exactly, the aging had taken place.

Novosibirsk was approaching. This was the third-largest city in the nation, one of those places "tickled to life" by the Trans-Siberian in 1893 as a shantytown for workers building the mammoth bridge over the Ob River. The usual motley crew of trappers, bankers, prostitutes and priests came in and started a boomtown named for the czar which lasted even after the four years it took to finish the bridge. After the revolution, Stalin turned it into a major mineral and manufacturing center and gave it the name that translates as "New Siberia."

Lenin had once said, "Railways are one of the manifestations of the most striking tie between the city and the country, between industry and agriculture." This was certainly the case in Novosibirsk, whose stature was like that of Chicago. Without the railroad it would have been a bush-league town. Triumphantly wide avenues leading from the station converged on a drafty opera house in the center. On the outskirts a hydroelectric dam stood in front of a giant artificial lake, on the shores of which was built an academic research facility to turn out innovations in space technology, wheat seeds and diamonds grown inside high-pressure machines.

We crossed the new steel-framed bridge over the Ob, which seemed to go on for nearly a kilometer, and downtown loomed on the banks. I was aching to get off, so I disembarked into the station, with its sleek orb-shaped lamps and polished floors, and took a commuter train out to the western suburbs to visit the West Siberian Railway Rolling Stock Museum, a collection of old steam engines lined up in a row. I wanted to talk to the director, maybe find an engineer who spoke English and could tell some old war stories.

The guard smoking at the gate was dressed in camouflage, with two scruffy dogs milling about his legs. I approached and through a combination of gestures and a few English words managed to get across that I wanted him to show me the office. He nodded and bade me to follow between a set of decommissioned locomotives. I walked with him about five paces before I felt an excruciating pain in my right calf, which radiated up my entire leg.

"*OWWW!*" I yelled, and looked down to see one of the stray dogs attached to my pant leg, chewing away at my flesh. The guard made a disgusted sound and clapped his hands together. The angry dog bolted away, underneath one of the railcars. That revolver mentioned by the Baedecker guide might have come in handy here.

I let a stream of curse words fly, for I knew exactly what this meant, even before I rolled up my jeans and saw the ugly red wound. Rabies is not uncommon in Russia, and it is a wretched way to die.* Once the first symptoms appear, there is nothing that doctors can do for a victim except sedate him and make coffin measurements. There is only one certain way to stop it, and that is a series of vaccinations, which must be taken at precise intervals over the course of two weeks, to prevent the infection from taking hold.

I limped into the director's office, which was located within one of the railcars, and let her know in colorful terms how displeased I was that a dog had bitten me inside her museum. She spoke no English but caught the gist of what I was saying (it would have been hard not to). She then demanded to see my ticket. I hadn't thought to purchase one, as I hadn't been coming to look at locomotives but to speak to the director. The guard tried to explain this, but she was iron-eyed. My lack of ticket exempted the museum from any responsibility. End of story. I left then in the back of an ambulance van they had called for me, too exhausted to holler any further.

---

* A brain encephalitis brings seizures and insanity before death. Victims also suffer a strange terror of water before they perish.

A doctor in town told me what I already knew. A vaccine course was necessary, and I would be far better served to return immediately to the United States, rather than face dying in Russia. Rabies was known to be in the area. He wrote me out an indecipherable prescription with these instructions, along with the type of serum ("anti-dog") that I was supposed to have. Part of me wanted to ignore this mandate and hope for the best down the Trans-Siberian, but I knew I should succumb to better judgment. At an Internet café next door, I checked the schedules for Aeroflot and calculated the times. There was one that would have me back in the States safely inside the infection window.

My trip on the Trans-Siberian ended thusly—roughly half the way through—with my leg bandaged and my forehead pressed against the window of a painfully exorbitant coach seat looking down at the vast expanse of land that a railroad had dragged into the modern age. This violent railroad had taken a jab at me, too, though in absurd fashion. And somewhere down there, too, was a stray dog I did not wish well.

The week after I returned for two weeks of shots, somebody bombed the *Nevsky Express* in the same corridor where I had ridden from St. Petersburg to Moscow.

As the train passed a remote part of countryside at 10:32 P.M., a bomb equivalent to fifteen pounds of dynamite exploded underneath the first carriage, which trembled and then fell off the rails, pulling the rest of the train with it, fourteen cars in all. Twenty-seven people were killed, including elected government officials and businessmen.

Though this rail passage has been used continuously for more than a century and a half, and between the two most prominent cities in the nation, there were no roads leading into the accident site. Help was slow to arrive; some passengers lay four hours in the wreckage. Emergency crews in Jeeps had to navigate muddy tracks spotted with huge puddles full of snowmelt. The high-speed *Sapsan* took most of the wounded to a hospital in St. Petersburg. Relatives who called for news were given the brush-off. "When we asked for some contact phone numbers, the lady told us that it didn't fall within her job description," one told a reporter.

Federal police later said the bomb had been set off by a device triggered by a cellular phone, leaving a small trackside crater that journalists were not allowed to inspect. Six months later the police announced that they had shot or arrested most of those responsible, who had apparently been linked to the Chechnyan separatist figure Said Buryatsky.

Train bombings were a long-acknowledged act of war in Russia. The *Nevsky Express* had been hit with a bomb hidden in a toilet two years prior, and few thought then that it would be the last time.

THE ROOF OF THE WORLD

Beijing to Lhasa

The minister produced a piece of vinyl from his pocket and spread it on the table.

"This new plan we are trying to accomplish is rather large in scale," he said dryly, and lit a cigarette from a red velvet case. "As you know, we have a very big population in China. We need railways to match it."

The vinyl cloth was the Ministry of Railways' master plan for rail development through the next decade, and it told a story of near-imperial expansion. Three major links from Beijing spread out like vertical girders—to Shanghai, Shenzhen and Harbin—and a fourth went out from Shanghai to Shenzhen. Four more belted the country horizontally. And between them were slashed hundreds of secondary routes, a total of 120,000 kilometers, about double the current capacity. And for this the Chinese were borrowing heavily, ready to spend up to $292 billion before it was all over.

China is preparing, in short, for a possible oil shock in the medium-term future, and it wants to have a system already in place in which goods and people can be moved by very little fuel while the rest of the world remains locked to the private car. And even if an energy apocalypse does not happen, the rails will still be useful for tamping down highway congestion and keeping the skies from being jammed with flights. The Chinese Communist Party sees this as a crucial strategy for maintaining prosperity—and internal control—well into the next century.

The minister's name was Dai Xinliu, and he was a midlevel official with the Economic and Planning Research Institute of China Railways, the state-run monopoly in charge of the expansion. He had tousled hair and wore a houndstooth jacket. He puffed on his cigarette while I studied the map.

"Only a small percentage of our people are ever going to take airplanes," he said. "Railroads are still a first choice for us. I feel confident to say that even our old people have the belief that the railroad system of China can help this nation grow. We should be the most hardworking department on this question. Everyone here is working harder."

The magnitude of this project was already putting strains on the treasury. The amount of money invested in railroads here has grown faster than any segment of the economy and has helped fuel China's relentlessly marching growth, rising a reliable 7 to 8 percent each year. A major part of this $292 billion investment is being spent on Japanese-style "bullet trains" capable of speeds of 220 miles per hour and above. These trains are aimed primarily at business travelers and come equipped with Wi-Fi and smartly dressed service hostesses. Their lead cars are needle-nosed, their trailing bodies majestic and sleek as swans. They eat up the distance from Beijing to Shanghai—a longer journey than between New York and Chicago—in slightly less than five hours.

There is no nation on earth that has more firmly tied its destiny in the new century to a device whose basic features debuted in an English coal town in 1825.

"We are putting energy and passion into this because of the practical situation of China," said Dai. "We have a lot of land and a big population, and we are still short of resources."

One line on the map stood out among all the others, if only for its isolation. It dangled like a fishhook on a thread from the town of Golmud, in the far western province of Qinghai. I did not need to ask Dai about it, because I already knew what it was—the $4.3 billion connection built across seven hundred miles of high plateau, much of it covered in permafrost.

This was the highest-elevation railroad in the world. It also made no economic sense whatsoever and played no role in a larger transportation or energy strategy. But since it opened in 2006, it was now China's strongest link to the disputed province of Tibet, whose hopes of independence China had been trying to smother for sixty years. Not only that, a funnel for troops and tanks would make the foothills of the Himalayas an excellent base for maneuvers against nearby India or Pakistan in the next century, should geopolitics take a turn in that direction.

Sensing the spot on the map I was looking at, Dai said, "This is a top priority for us, to connect these areas with the better-developed eastern part of China."

Tibet is a vast snowcapped plateau at the southwestern edge of China, once governed by a feudal theocracy but today as a ward of the Chinese Communist Party, which has struggled to quash any remaining sentiments that the region ought to be independent.

The rugged topography made the place inaccessible and near mystical for most of its history. Living at an average elevation of thirteen thousand feet above sea level, where few cash crops could grow, Tibetans survived the centuries by raising yaks for their hides, fillets and milk. The Mongol and Chinese empires were kept largely at bay, and the Buddhist faith that had been brought up from India in the south had crystallized into an elaborate hierarchy of monks, led by a figure called the Dalai Lama ("Ocean Priest"), who was said to be the reincarnated presence of his predecessor.

Tibet's spectacular isolation crumbled in 1903, when Britain sent a colonial captain named Francis Younghusband to secretly occupy the plateau for the king. He did so only after murdering* several hundred monks, reasoning that "all this trouble had arisen through the Tibetans being so inaccessible and keeping them so much apart; and now I meant to close in with them, to break through their seclusion." Tibet meanwhile became the world's most famously isolated penthouse, its reputation cemented by the 1933 novel *Lost Horizon* by James Hilton, which described a serene cluster of happy monks occupying a lamasery called Shangri-La.

The plateau remained independent, at least in name, until 1950, when the Chinese Communist Party moved in troops and proclaimed a "liberation of the serfs" from the forced-labor polices and high taxes levied by the lamas. They denounced the "yellow robbers and red thieves," a reference to the saffron- and mustard-colored robes worn by the monks, who ruled as feudal overlords. The 14th Dalai Lama, then a teenager, was turned into a semi-puppet ruler until 1959, when he received an invitation from the Chinese army to "see a play," which he interpreted as a pretense for his kidnapping. With the quiet help of the CIA, he fled to the town of Dharamsala in India, where he and his associates set up an exile government and continue to press for a relaxation of the Chinese fist.†

In Tibet the Chinese were left with a rump hierarchy of monks and a mountain shelf they could never really master. What was really needed was a mechanized funnel to draw out the minerals and bring in the soldiers, and Mao Zedong once confessed to the king of Nepal that he wouldn't be able to sleep soundly until he had built a railway to the edge of the Himalayas. But the project suffered from false starts and a lack of money, as well as the permafrost that lay on top of the plateau like a hard candy shell. Earthmoving would warm the soil and turn it to

---

* Younghusband later regretted his violent past and turned to a religion of free love and "cosmic rays," proclaiming all men to be divine.

† In recent years he has called for a "middle way" of limited autonomy while recognizing Chinese authority; Beijing refuses to meet with him and calls him "a splittist" intent on stirring up unrest.

muck. How could you put down tracks when the ground was barely a degree away from thawing in most places?

The ministry did finish a hard-won railway to the base of the Kunlun, but the project was defunded in 1979 as Deng Xiaoping decided that a better way to keep Tibet hugged tight to China was the constant upkeep of the potholed two-lane highway first built by the People's Liberation Army shortly after liberation. But when Jiang Zemin became president, he instituted a policy called "Go West," which sought to modernize the poorer western provinces and exploit them for minerals. This also involved a fresh attack on the lingering Tibet problem. Engineers were summoned to the Ministry of Railways in October of 2000 for a planning conference.

There a fifty-four-year-old junior engineer named Zhang Luxin stole the show. His colleagues had been agitating for a southerly route through Yunnan, but Zhang had been studying Tibetan permafrost for nearly three decades on a mission that had come to seem hopeless. Once, he and a colleague were out in the trackless nowhere surveying a grade when they got lost in an ice storm and nearly died. Zhang now faced the possibility that a lifetime of research might become futile. He stood up to speak, breaking protocol and acting imprudently.

"The route from Yunnan, many parts of it, no one has ever been there," he said. "We don't know anything about it. But the Qinghai-Tibet Plateau, we've been traveling it for forty years, we know every inch of it." An ordinary rail bed might indeed heave upward on the permafrost, he conceded, but science had advanced to the point where the soil could be kept hard by constantly chilling it with chemical ventilation pipes. The bed could also be made of loosely packed granite, through which air could flow and keep it from getting soft.

Zhang's speech was rude but convincing. From that afternoon, wrote the journalist Abrahm Lustgarten, "there was an almost irrational sense of urgency." The central government dumped more than $4 billion into a chain of contractors, work agencies, suppliers and twenty-two separate bureaus. Overseeing the project was Liu Zhijun, a former track worker from the countryside who also happened to be a good calligrapher. He wrote beautifully rendered letters for his less educated bosses, who rewarded him with promotions. With round-the-clock work habits and a gift for flattery, Liu ascended to the top by 2003 and was running China's rail expansion with a blowout budget and bidding protocols that were impossible to understand by all but the best-connected. He insisted on speed and delivery and tolerated no dissent. "To achieve a great leap, a generation must be sacrificed," he said, earning him the nickname "Great Leap Liu" and inspiring flattering portrayals in the state media.

By April 2003 the rails from Qinghai advanced past the jagged peaks of the Kunlun range and the train itself carried steel and workers to the farthest point of advance, much as the Union Pacific Railroad had been its own supply line in the race to build the U.S. transcontinental in the 1860s. No fewer than 681 bridges had to be built, and their pillars had to be wrapped in wool blankets to get them to set properly in the cold. The cement had to be mixed with boiling water, which made clouds of steam under the glare of the lamps that allowed crews to work all night long.

At least a hundred thousand migrant workers were given railway jobs, which required only muscles and an even temperament. "They had no time to enjoy the beautiful scenery around them," said an official history. "To them the beautiful natural sights were hardships and dangers. . . . News of one victory after another could not catch up with time." Still, there were casualties. Men often became sick from the altitude, the "mountain sickness" that first manifested as a headache above eight thousand feet and, thanks to a lack of oxygen in the blood, could progress to stroke, heart attack or swelling of the brain. Tibetans have been shown to have a genetic capacity to move more oxygen in their bloodstreams and are thus largely immune, but the Chinese enjoyed no such disposition. The government said there were no fatalities from altitude sickness, but rumors persisted of trackside graveyards.

The first detailed geological surveys of the plateau had shown reserves of up to 40 million tons of copper, another 40 million tons of lead and zinc, a field of oil shale of undisclosed size, some natural gas and billions of tons of iron. "These deposits will fundamentally ease China's shortages of mineral resources," Zhang Hongtao, vice director of the China Geological Survey Bureau, told the *People's Daily*. The same tracks that would ease human migration to Tibet could also soon create their own method of payback. Official propaganda called the train "a line to wealth" and a "golden path to prosperity." Native Tibetans were given pamphlets warning them not to trespass on construction sites or tamper with the tracks, and meetings were held to foster an atmosphere of "praising the railroad, protecting the railroad, loving the railroad."

On July 1, 2006, almost a year ahead of schedule, the line was formally opened for business, and General Secretary Hu Jintao cut the ceremonial ribbon at Golmud. In the orotund style of party speeches, he called it "an important expression of the constant increase in the comprehensive national strength of our country" and "enhancing ethnic solidarity and consolidating the motherland's frontier defense." The Chinese perspective on Tibet has always been one that emphasizes the benevolence of the Han people shouldering difficulties to help lift one of the poorer portions of their sovereign country into prosperity while still preserving the unthreatening parts of its culture. Their claim is like that of the American government's protectorate over the Sioux in South Dakota, who were allowed to have a few defanged tribal councils but were forced to surrender most of their grasslands and the minerals in the Black Hills.

The Dalai Lama had a different view when he was asked about the Qinghai-Tibet Railway the year before. "Some kind of cultural genocide is taking place," he said.

The train was going to bring in waves of ethnic Han Chinese, there to work the mines and build the cheap new high-rises and mediocre urban sprawl characteristic of the rest of the nation, diluting and eventually obliterating everything that was unique about Tibet. For those who held out lingering hope of independence, this train was the coffin lid slamming down.

The Chinese Lunar New Year, whose festivities typically are held in late winter, has been described as the largest annual movement of human beings in history, and most of it takes place on the rails. This is the only time of year when the factory toilers are free to go back to their villages for reunion dinners. Almost all of them do. The number of personal rail journeys in this forty-day period—an estimated 1.4 billion—exceeds the entire population of China.

My train to Tibet was scheduled to leave near the start of the holiday, and the tourist company through which I had to book my ticket picked me up at my hotel in a black livery car with leather seats. This was a make called Red Flag, the favored car of Communist Party officials. We passed Tiananmen Square in the dark and waited in clogged traffic for more than a half hour before creeping close to the eleven-story monolith of Beijing West Railway Station, which was overflowing with young couples in puffy coats, old men with canes, grannies in shawls, frightened children, tough teenage boys lugging bags the size of love seats and a few beleaguered soldiers in green caps trying to shout orders over the din.

Ticket lines can last for three days in the New Year, and sellouts are common. Family members have been known to lose sight of one another in the immense station crowds, and these are usually the people laboring in the gargantuan factories that most upper-class Chinese shun. In one of the occasional exposures tolerated by the Communist Party, the *Guangzhou Daily* newspaper was allowed to run a photograph of railway officers struggling to lift and cram extra passengers through the open windows of a train to Xinyang. Two directors were fired over the incident, but an online poll of readers revealed that 84 percent had approved of the rule bending. Most viewed it as a compassionate act.

The escort handed me a visa to get into Tibet—it had been stamped four times—told me the number of the gate and bade me good luck. I waded through an immense sea of homebound pilgrims toward the platform where the T27 was ready to depart. Though its mission was extraordinary—a train about to make the highest tracked climb on the planet—it looked entirely normal, with its string of carriages headed up by two diesel locomotives.

I found my place in a soft sleeper, where there was a pitcher of water, a mounted television with ten channels, a dainty coat hanger with silk padding and a pink ribbon and, tucked into the wall, a flexible plastic oxygen tube to fit into the nostrils in case I should become weak from the altitude in a day and a half. A magazine on the table carried a glowing piece about tourism in Tibet. "The cleanliness and beauty of the train matches the best in the nation," said the article, "and it is well worth the money to sit in such a comfortable compartment to enjoy this unique view of the Qinghai-Tibet Plateau." We pulled away from the platform, and I fell into a trance watching the lights of Beijing recede. Eventually the trance became a muddled half sleep.

The next morning I went into the dining car for tea and started talking with Li Jijian, going home to Longzhou for the holiday. He wore a blue-striped shirt with orange fuzz sewn into the insides of his sleeves. Li showed me a cell-phone picture of his parents' house, a rectangle of white stucco backed up against a ridge. Within a day, he told me, they would probably have him plowing soybean fields behind a mule team.

Li slowly and almost painfully gnawed an apple down to the seeds while I ate an oversalted plate of beef. We watched the country scroll by: yellow prayer towers, grape stumps, a river with a scum of dry ice on the top, bags of coal stacked by the right-of-way, a few houses with hip roofs that were hardy old survivors of the Qing dynasty. A few of the hills had strange-looking terraces; entire sections of turf had been cut away in geometric order, and the slopes looked like accordion folds. The clay in the soil was used to bake bricks for houses. In one of the larger towns, I saw buildings spray-painted with a single character 拆, pronounced *chai*, which means "to demolish." Construction officials use this simple marker to indicate where the next high-rise is going to be next year.

Li started to grow pale, quickly excused himself from the table and came back apologetically in a few minutes. He insisted on giving me one of his apples, a package of instant noodles and a few orange plastic tubes of sausagelike meat that he'd bought for the trip. Trains made his stomach nervous, he explained, and he sometimes had to vomit. "I try not to waste food," he said. "I know the farmers have a hard life."

Feeling guilty for eating in front of him, I asked what he did for a living and could not have been more surprised to hear him tell me he was an engineer for China Railways. His pass allowed him to board for free, and the conductors were pretending not to see that he was sleeping in the dining car. How could he deal with the train sickness at his job? I wanted to know, and he said it was a matter of ignoring it as best he could during his twelve-hour shifts. Dimenhydrinate tablets were also of some help, though not now.

Before going back to my berth, I talked in the corridor with a salesman named Zou Wei, who told me that the route of this train through Shaanxi province was following the Silk Road, which had connected the Far East with Persian marketplaces in the first century B.C. This part of China has a reputation for producing tough country people—if China had cowboys, this would be its Texas. We passed a line of adobe greenhouses where bamboo mats had been rolled out over the roofs at sunset. Wei talked about the strength of China, which he felt was tipping out of balance toward too much materialism. "We have hard power, but we need to develop our soft power. We need what comes from inside." He patted his chest and smiled.

After the city of Xining, a conductor knocked on the compartment window and asked me to sign a statement certifying that "my health condition can adapt 3000 meter above high elevation area travel." The light had faded, and the fields were turning to indigo; chlorine-colored street lamps bathed the hillsides, and the train slipped underneath them, wheels slapping against the welds, making a continuous chant: *dear boy, dear boy, dear boy.* I wanted to stay awake to look at Golmud, the famously squalid town in a high salt desert that had served as the bus terminal for the teeth-jarring overland journey to Lhasa. Never attractive, it was said to be even deader now that this train had rendered it obsolete. But the bed was soft, and the soporific effect of the train's rocking soon put me under again.

Light through the window woke me, and I pulled the curtains back to see the Tibetan plateau, called the Chang Tang. We were now at an elevation of somewhere above fourteen thousand feet. Stretching away was a tabletop of bright nothingness, terminating on the far horizon in a snowcapped ridge so far off that it might as well have been a mirage. The oxygen port built into the bulkhead was emitting a steady hiss, and I could feel a slight headache, though this might also have been the power of suggestion. Aspirin took care of it in a hurry. A loudspeaker announcement in both Chinese and English told us that we were passing near the glaciers that were the source of the Yangtze River. Then it described a nearby, and unseen, monument to Jiang Zemin, the originator of the "Go West" policy.

"You must have a strong impression of the spirit of the Chinese people, which is to withstand anything and march straight ahead," said the voice.

China was trying to subdue Tibet with a railroad, the same device that had once been the cause of significant internal misery.

British traders pried their way into China during the Opium Wars of 1840–42 and 1857–60, when the East India Company struggled to find something to trade for all the tea and silk they were buying. A ring of local aristocrats who called themselves the *cohong* agreed to accept chests of Indian opium, which could be smoked with tobacco for an impressive high. This vice, once an indulgence of the lazy rich, soon became a fad among all Chinese classes. The drug reached into even the most remote villages, tucked into merchants' wagons along with sacks of rice. The consequent addictions made the opium trade a reliable profit stream, which the British refused to give up. When the imperial government tried to seize the opium chests, the British sent in the Royal Navy and opened fire. China was forced to legalize opium, pay restitution and hand over the island of Hong Kong.

Then came another humiliation: China's first railroad, which began with a lie and ended with a near riot.

The British firm of Jardine and Matheson and Co. had bought up a strip of land leading from the port of Shanghai to the nearby town of Woosung, telling everyone they were building a "carriage road." On February 14, 1876, they made a surprise run of a locomotive they called Pioneer, and a few days later a soldier either threw himself or was pushed under the locomotive. Government officials promptly bought up the tracks and ordered them ripped out of the ground while they watched from their hand-carried sedan chairs to show their contempt for any form of machine transportation. A temple to the Queen of Heaven was built on the site of the station, and the tracks were dumped to rot on the island of Formosa.

The Chinese were suspicious of this "fire cart" that threatened to flood the interior with British goods, disrupt the spirits with dynamite and upend the peasant way of life that had existed for three thousand years and whose harmony depended on an interlaced series of covenants among families, aristocrats, the ancestors and heaven. Confucius had said that these relationships were the glue of the universe.

An intellectual named Yen Mao looked at the Westerners and their locomotives and was not hopeful. "They rise at the crow of the rooster to seek profits wherever profits are to be found, but where there are profits, the relationship of prince and minister and father and son cease to exist," he wrote. "This is the reason why Europe has twice the profits of China and why Europe has more disturbances than China. Thus China should not build railways."

This fear of the railroads touched one of the deepest fears in the collective unconsciousness of the Chinese ruling class. This was *jao min*, which is roughly translated as "disturbing the people." Mass gatherings, rural uprisings, food riots, a rejection of the "mandate of heaven" that sustained the government—all of these were anathema to those who occupied the throne and, truly, one of the only historical forces that was ever able to achieve a change in regime. Wrote Chang Tzu-mu, "The peasants in the fields of the south, the miners in the mountains of the north, and those who haul the carts and man the boats—these number millions of people. They bear the calluses of their struggle to survive. If machines are suddenly introduced, they will lose their livelihood. Won't they join together to cause disturbances?"

Other Chinese thinkers were more worried about the naked greed that would come from railways. Ching Len argued that the iron bands would be like needles to foreigners eager to suck out Chinese natural resources. Boatmen and carters would also lose all their freight business and become angry. On a diplomatic mission to London in 1877, Liu His Hung offered a list of reasons that railways would never work in China: the peasants were too poor to buy tickets, the volume of freight was too small, people would steal from the boxcars and the necessary construction loans would be too much of a burden. None of these proved correct except the last one, which was all too prophetic.

A capable diplomat named Li Hung-Chang emerged as a powerful critic of the British, though not necessarily of railways. He had already told the grandees he thought their railroad agenda had far more to do with politics than commerce and complained about the foreign "clocks and toys" being sold to poor people. But he thought the Chinese needed to command the new technology for themselves instead of rejecting it outright. He got permission to build a standard-gauge coal line from the mines at Kaiping, far away from the treaty ports and their corrupt atmosphere. Military tacticians also argued that "one soldier can have the impact of a dozen" with the help of a railroad, which could be used to fight Westerners and put down countryside insurrections.

The royal court ultimately surrendered to the inevitability of railways and the modernization they promised. But the resulting debt to foreign contractors was a major contributor to the collapse of the monarchy. Surveyors were sent out to map long-distance lines from Peking to Shangahi, Ningbo, Wuhan and Canton. But hardly a line could be built in China that didn't cross an ancestor's grave, which was a form of blasphemy to rural families. Eager to be done with these nuisances, the railroad paid damages. One British manager complained, "It is found that if the natives learn in advance of the location of a new line, that the more enterprising among them, if so unfortunate as not to have a family burying-ground in the way, will borrow from their neighbors the temporary loan of a few grandfathers whom they will quietly rebury in advance of the work."

The network they built was impressive, but it turned out to be a spectacularly bad deal. In 1894 the national debt to railways was the equivalent of $325,000; within seventeen years it had metastasized to $71 million. On the Shanghai-Nanking line, the interest payments alone were gobbling three times its revenue. Foreign banks were only too glad to repossess the foreclosed property, and especially all the land near the stations. In a crowning humiliation, the entire system was under foreign control by the turn of the century. A radical group called the Society of Right and Harmonious Fists rose up against foreign influences, particularly the railways that had been stealing public money and disturbing ancestors' graves, and the instability led to the fall of the Qing dynasty in 1911.

The revolutionary leader Dr. Sun Yat-sen tried to find a road out of the wilderness. He proposed a nationalized system and confidently proclaimed he had "found a new law in railway economics" in which the profits from new lines would pay for themselves with revenues—the same flawed reasoning that had gotten China into trouble. The Ministry of Railways was given enormous powers to refurbish the system and to encourage domestic industries by paying off Chinese suppliers with bonds. And hence the growth of one of the tallest silos of power within the Chinese state apparatus, an agency nicknamed *tie laoda*, or "Boss Rail." Mao Zedong's policy of the "iron rice bowl"—lifetime guarantees of food, education and health care—was best exemplified by the railway ministry, where the jobs were passed down from fathers to sons and where even the incompetent were never fired.

Boss Rail had access to enormous cash reserves, as well as the ability to favor one region or another and condemn whatever land it pleased. It had a private police force and its own court system. It learned to be secretive and conservative and to accept cash bribes with impunity from middlemen, who took their own cuts. The ministry had an internal saying: *Feishui bu wang wai liu,* which translates as "Don't let your fertilizer run off into the neighbor's fields." In other words, don't share power, money or information.

"The Ministry of Railways was conservative and closed-minded," said Rong Chaohe, a professor of transportation economics. "Whoever has to deal with them is never very happy with it. They are like a semi-army. They had a built-in profit center. They could depend on people's willingness to take trains."

Any outsider who wanted to do business with Boss Rail had to rely on the ancient principle of *guanxi*, which means, roughly, "connections" or "juice." A person's *guanxi* could be measured by the number of friends he had in the right places who could find him a job, a business partnership, the ear of the government. Personal acquaintance and favor trading is the same loose currency of any civilized society, but it is especially important in hierarchy-minded China and absolutely crucial in a walled kingdom like the Ministry of Railways. Even in an era of promiscuous contracting, not knowing the right people means not getting the deal.

Five years after China made an all-in bet on the future of railways, a bolt of lightning from a summer storm hit a signal box. That tiny event revealed the fatal limitations of the *guanxi* principle.

The bolt had struck at 7:30 P.M. of July 23, 2011, on the *Harmony Express* tracks that led to the city of Wenzhou, and it damaged a signal box. Fuses blew inside, one of which was keyed to the lights that informed passing drivers of any hazards on the tracks ahead. One light froze on the color green, for "go."

That section of the track also lost its ability to send train-detecting signals back to the dispatch center at Shanghai. In itself this is not a remarkable occurrence: it only created a temporary patch of what is called "dark territory," meaning that drivers must navigate by sight without guidance from the dispatcher.

When a high-speed train with the code number D3115 approached this section of the track, its safety systems shut it down automatically. The driver had been warned about this over the radio and had been instructed to restart the train and proceed at slow speeds. But he had trouble firing his engines and could not alert Shanghai, where a dispatcher named Zhang Hua assumed the train would soon be emerging from the dark territory.

Zhang then cleared another train, D301, to proceed. The driver of that train also saw the green signal, which ordinarily would have been red. When the first train emerged from the dark territory at a crawling speed and reappeared on the monitors in Shanghai, there was a moment of intense panic. A fundamental rule of railroading as old as the Liverpool & Manchester had just been violated: two trains should never occupy the same section.

"D301, be careful!" yelled a dispatcher. "D3115 is ahead of you. Be careful!"

At that moment D301 plowed into the back of the first train, knocking three carriages off the viaduct, killing forty people, including the driver of D301, who was impaled on his own emergency brake. There was an immediate blackout of information—the state media version of dark territory—and the line was running again within a day as if nothing of interest had happened. Newspapers across China were directed to run only brief stories on the crash. "Do not question, do not elaborate," warned the Department of Propaganda in a memo. One of the mangled carriages was immediately buried on the scene, and when accused of trying to whitewash the catastrophe, authorities explained unconvincingly that they had needed the extra ground for rescue staging.

Prime Minister Wen Jiabao promised to get to the heart of what had happened, and in December 2012 the government released an uncommonly blunt report that concluded, "The disastrous crash was caused by serious design flaws in the train control system, inadequate safety procedures implemented by the authorities and poor emergency response to system failure." The government fired fifty-four employees of Boss Rail, but the top management was already gone. "Great Leap" Liu Zhijun, the architect of the Tibet line and the massive railway expansion, had been arrested on corruption charges five months before the crash, accused of pocketing at least $155 million. The practice of illegal subcontracting—taking bribes to hire "construction firms" that were poorly trained and supervised—was rampant throughout the ministry. Liu had also arranged for his brother, Liu Zhixiang, to receive protection, even though he was a suspect in the stabbing death of a contractor who had threatened to expose corrupt bidding practices. The party also accused Liu of "degenerate morals," which was widely understood to refer to his multiple mistresses. In a separate case, one of his aides who officially earned less than $15,000 a year was able to buy a luxury house in Walnut, California.

The flamboyant corruption inside Boss Rail raised questions about how fast the system had been constructed and what other deadly flaws might be hiding inside the biggest public-works project in the world since Dwight Eisenhower's buildup of the U.S. interstate highways. The high-speed trains had been reverse engineered from Japanese designs and were being pushed to speeds they were never meant to achieve. Officials announced that trains on the Beijing-Shanghai route would be slowed down to a top speed of 186 miles per hour, significantly below the 236 miles per hour that had been previously announced. Cheaper tickets were also offered. Railway Vice Minister Hu Yadong said that "the satisfaction of the people" would now be "the basic requirement for evaluating railway work."

China—unique among today's major world powers—has the advantage of being able to take a pen and draw train lines at its pleasure, with the ability to ignore free-market forces or local political trouble. The authority of the Chinese Communist Party has shown it will go even into the Himalayan permafrost to extend the reach of its sphere of influence. Not since the days of Czar Alexander III has a central authority been so ambitious with long-distance railway diplomacy.

But this railway-by-fiat is exactly what makes the short-term prospects so uncertain and what had also permitted the bloated budgets and the spread of corrupt bidding. A line that serves a national interest may not be the best idea for the factory owner or the rice farmer, and the oceans of leveraged government cash have none of the natural competitive checks upon them that a free bidding process would ensure. "Socialism with Chinese characteristics" was the vague formulation that Deng Xiaoping's intellectuals used in the 1980s to explain how Marxist ideology could be harmonized with the kind of free-trade reforms that have enabled today's consistent growth numbers.

This has made for some awkward compromises: politically guided railroads with no clear business plan. The World Bank flagged this as a potential problem in a confidential report. "The availability and sources of railway finance are major challenges," it said, "particularly since many of those proposed railway projects that are driven by regional and economic development aims are likely to be not commercially viable, irrespective of their wider economic and social benefits."

One example is that as much money was being spent on debt service for the Qinghai-Tibet Railway as was on construction. Yet the Chinese see future benefits in speedier internal travel that cannot be expressed in a straight balance sheet. The Chinese rail strategy is actually a national-development strategy in disguise, said Keith Dierkx, director of the IBM Global Rail Innovation Center in Beijing, whom I met for coffee at a Starbucks near the Pacific Century Center. "This is going to become a center of production for them," he told me.

Faster access to the archipelago of factories around Guangzhou, for example, means that containers full of goods can be shipped more quickly to the ports. In manufacturing, a day's advantage can translate to hundreds of millions of dollars. Mineral traffic has already doubled since 1990, thanks to better rail service, which means that more coal seams in the Datong Basin can be opened. Taking people to work faster in the mornings expands the horizons of where they might conceivably live and—as railroads always do—boosts the value of the land near the stations.

One of the nation's railroad lenders, the Asian Development Bank, has language inserted in one of its loan documents describing a new railway in the Guangxi Autonomous Region that could have been lifted from the mouth of a silver-tongued nineteenth-century promoter of the Chicago and North Western: "The project will improve local people's standard of living and influence all aspects of their daily life, directly or indirectly, in a positive manner."

But the exuberance had left some fearing a replay of the disaster of 1912, when China found itself with an opulent network, an empty treasury and a government reeling before a mass of angry citizens. These worries were only exacerbated by the Wenzhou crash and the acknowledgment that the lines had been built with poor oversight. A few academics are willing to openly criticize the bonanza, especially in high-speed spending, and I found one of them at Beijing Jiaotong University. Zhao Jian is a professor of transportation economics, who wears thick glasses and speaks in a booming voice. His office on an upper floor of a Maoist-era tower is bare of any decoration. An older computer is covered with a shroud.

"We can't afford this in China. How can America?" he said in a near shout. "You should wait and see how this turns out in China—you could learn some lessons from us!"

Zhao said he didn't believe the government's line that getting people to their destinations faster would create benefits. Long-distance travel was better done in the existing sleeper cars, tickets for which were cheaper than high-speed tickets, which cost about three-quarters of a peasant's daily salary. And if the bulk of China's population rejected the new trains, the debt would become runaway.

"This is a toy," he scoffed. "It's like a three-hundred-million-dollar Hollywood movie that nobody sees. If this has such an economy of scale, why are only thirty thousand people taking it each day? That's ten-percent capacity. That's a railway heading for bankruptcy, and we will have a real debt crisis."

Zhao's outspokenness has gotten him into trouble. None other than Great Leap Liu has warned him to tone down his criticism, and the university's president has also chided him for his imprudence. "He told me not to continue to voice my opinions," Zhao said to Evan Osnos of the *New Yorker*.

One of the main complaints among Chinese is that the high-speed trains were built not for the working people but for the burgeoning middle classes and for the rich. A new piece of slang is starting to be used in Beijing: "You have been compelled to take high-speed rail." This is roughly equivalent to "You're screwed!"

"If it can't make money, it will be a waste," conceded Rong Chaohe of the College of Economics and Management at Beijing Jiaotong University. "In China decisions aren't always about economics. Things are built based on an order from the government. And they believe this is durable technology. Real-estate prices are going crazy, and so they figured they better do it now, before land acquisition becomes unrealistic. Settlements must still be paid."

Still another matter is the geologic delicacy of the hard-won line to Tibet. Seven hundred miles of permafrost may have temporarily held firm, but could it last for years, particularly in light of global warming? The average temperatures were only one degree below the freezing point in many places; even a slight uptick could destabilize the tracks.

Wu Ziwang of the Chinese Academy of Sciences told a state news agency, "Due to the melting permafrost, I am worried that after ten years the railroad will be unsafe. Fast thawing of frozen soil in the plateau might greatly increase the instability of the ground, causing more grave geological problems in the frozen-soil areas where major projects such as highways or railways run through." The best comparison may be the Alaska Railroad Corporation, which operates a line from Seward to Fairbanks built in the 1910s and now must spend more of its budget on track rehabilitation than almost any other railroad, because of the bulging soil and bent rails. Tibetan activists have speculated that China may just have paid for a useless railroad and taken on an astonishing level of debt for it.

The closest official breakdown of the financing I could find came from Dai Xinliu at the ministry, who showed me a policy document in English but would not let me photocopy it. It said the following, which says nothing: "Besides the investment from central government, state and railway companies and local governments, railway construction is financed by stocks, bonds, insurance, trust, capital from enterprises, private sector and foreign entities."

A top official at the ministry agreed to meet with me for tea, but only in an unfashionable restaurant away from his office at 3:00 P.M., when the place would be deserted. He also asked that I keep him anonymous, because he was talking about the sensitive matter of financial risk, though he gave me what was, more or less, the approved party line.

"There are a lot of expenses, and we're taking a lot of loans," he acknowledged. "There are going to be operational costs. We're aware of this. But from a psychological point of view, it can improve the economy and economic development. We have to make a fundamental investment. When you consider the benefits to the entire society, it will pay itself off."

The loans have been easy to obtain because banks have been successfully convinced that railways are ingrained into the Chinese mentality, and that 1.3 billion people won't all become rich enough to afford plane tickets. Manufactured goods and the people who assemble them will be able to zip around quickly and boost China's income, in the classic way of all industrial revolutions. Those parastatal supercompanies like China Railway Engineering Corporation and China Railway Construction Corporation,* having grown fat on government contracts, will be well positioned to build systems all over the globe—in Latin America, Africa and eventually even in the United States.

The runaway expansion has also created a freakish efficiency, this official told me in our meeting the year before the Wenzhou crash.

"We're getting good at this," he said. "The biggest thing the world can learn from us is efficiency. What takes five years in Europe takes four years here. We do it straight through. We work twenty-four hours a day. We are industrious. You are lazy." Then he laughed.

Riding through the Tibetan plateau inside a train compartment feels like cheating. The hard physical trials of Tibet that used to function as a test of character have been neatly erased. All a traveler needs to do these days is gaze out the window at the unfolding subarctic plain where he never belonged but nevertheless has a kind of unlikely intercourse.

I was the only non-Asian on the train, and since few people I could

---

* This company won a contract in 2009 from the Saudi Arabian government to build a high-speed line between Mecca and Medina, which will cut the travel time between Islam's two holiest cities from five hours down to thirty minutes.

find spoke English, I spent long hours in the dining car watching the bare and blank hills go by. My government permit to stay in Tibet would last for only three days, and I had been warned not to bring up any topics that might be seen as controversial. It was best not to mention the Dalai Lama, for example, or ask too many questions about Tibetan autonomy. Spies and informants were everywhere, I was told. Even ethnic Tibetans had been paid to point out suspicious activities by their neighbors, or foreign tourists whose movements might be questionable.

This section of the line was double-tracked, and I saw a field of rocks arranged in little squares: this was part of the aeration system that kept cool air flowing through the rail bed and stopped the permafrost from melting. A scattering of concrete tubes lay discarded to one side, and farther away were the mud-walled pens for yaks and a few ponds with ice floes jutting upward like rock candy. A woman in a hooded garment was bending over to pick up a disk of yak dung which is used as everyday household fuel. I smelled some in a fireplace later, and it burns as clean and odorless as balsa wood. Muddy tire tracks scissored across the plains.

I ordered a dish off the menu called "braises in soy sauce the chicken" and watched in solitude until a youngish Chinese man sat down across from me and introduced himself as "Phoenix."

He said he was a financial analyst from one of the big eastern cities and that this was his vacation. He wore a black turtleneck sweater and there was a small blossom of blood on his lower lip, which he licked away a few times. Around his neck was a camera with the brand name Sigma.

We talked about the train for a while, and I wondered out loud about the subject that most puzzled me with regard to modern Chinese rail policy: whether the fares or the freight would ever help pay for the $292 billion the government was investing.

"Are you implying that the central government had a strategy?" he asked abruptly, leaning forward.

"Hey, I'm only asking."

He seemed to relax a bit. "This is a symbol of China's reign over Tibet," he said. "The supply chain this train will establish is the most important thing. It will never make money on fares. The government doesn't need a reason. They expect the people to follow. Where they want a line to be, there will be a line."

He then inquired about where I had stayed in Beijing and if I had liked it. We retreated into less exciting topics for a bit.

I asked him about the schedule on this line, and he named the villages along the way where we would be stopping before we got to Lhasa. It seemed to me he had either memorized a map or knew this train well. I also wanted to know what he was doing here by himself in the midst of the New Year celebrations, when people everywhere in the nation typically go home to be with their families. He told me he had developed a fascination with Tibetan Buddhism and wanted to study it up close but offered no further details. We then both awkwardly looked out the window.

At a station called An Duo a few minutes later, I remarked that there wasn't much of anything surrounding the platform.

"Oh, there will be," said Phoenix.

Then he raised his Sigma camera, and before I could protest, he took my photograph.

A consultant who had helped build the train from Wuhan to Guangzhou summed up for me what was distinctive about the Chinese method of railroad construction.

"There is absolutely no change in the completion deadline," he said. "The project is always delivered on time. Period. The management is totally autocratic. I remember we were three weeks behind on a tunnel. This tunnel was six miles long. I went to the boss and told him that if the delay continued, I would have to go to the Ministry of Railways and make an explanation. Well, I think this guy would rather have hanged himself than lose face. He made phone calls all night long, and by the next morning there were five hundred extra people at the job site. Within a week the project was back on schedule."

The cost overruns that are a feature of Western civil engineering—and where the real profits in contracting are made—are practically unknown in China. The price bid is the price paid. And no contractor would ever think to go to Boss Rail to ask for more time or cash. He would simply have to finish the project at his own loss. The alternative would be never to work on a government project again.

The Wuguang Passenger Railway, as it was known, is part of a longer line that will reduce the travel time from Beijing to Hong Kong from its present twenty-four hours down to about eleven. It was built religiously level and almost entirely on elevated pillars and prefabricated girders, which keeps the tracks lofted above the innumerable roads and dirt paths that stripe across eastern China. This elimination of "grade crossings" means that the train does not have to slow its pace, except for at the fourteen stations along the way, and the chances that a train might plow into a wayward automobile or farm wagon have been reduced to zero. There are an estimated two hundred thousand pillars like this all over the nation, each separated from the next by a uniform 248 feet.

The manager on the Wuguang project told me he was surprised and fascinated to see the number of people carting no more than shovels and wheelbarrows hired to build the most advanced railroad technology in the world. "There's not much mechanical equipment on those job sites," he said. "You won't see it because there are certainly enough people in China to do the job. About forty percent of them are women, too. It's the mentality of the people that they will use only mechanical equipment as a last resort. They have people, and people are cheaper."

He showed me photos of workers hauling flagstones and pouring wet concrete out of handcarts, even as the slab on which the tracks were to run would cost up to $30 million per mile. It was the strangest melding of the super-fast and the primitive.

The railway gold rush has created a huge demand for muscle across China, and I later talked to one of these modern-day rock breakers standing outside a building in the city of Xi'an, looking for day work. His name was Xiao Qin Zhou, and he was just over forty. We shared an early lunch of noodles and beer.

"I use a wheelbarrow to haul stones, probably two or three tons every day," he told me. "I think I am strong enough, and I can handle it very easily. I suffer a lot for my family so I can have a better life. No matter what the work, I can do it. And if you don't think I'm strong enough, then I will fight you and prove it to you."

I told him I didn't want to fight him.

There were three teeth in the front part of his gums. He wore a black jacket zipped to the neck, and there were sores on his hands. An ugly bruise purpled under a fingernail. He had most recently labored on the new line from Tongchuan to Yao Xian, and was paid about ten dollars a day.

"Very horrible things have happened to me," he said. "My wife died from cancer, and I have two daughters. Now that I'm old, I have to do any kind of job to support them."

He was born in 1969 in a small farming village in Shaanxi province. His childhood nickname was "Puppy." From an early age, he loved trains and cars—"anything that moved"—and an early ambition was to be a driver. But the family suffered at the hands of the Red Guards set loose in the countryside during Mao Zedong's Cultural Revolution. They had been discovered trying to farm a small piece of land all by themselves instead of sharing it, so the guards drew a line in chalk around their house and forbade them to leave—a virtual prison. They survived on smuggled food and rations for months, while being beaten periodically.

Xiao passed his exams in school, but his parents couldn't afford to educate him past the age of fifteen, so he went to work on the various construction jobs blossoming in the big cities. What he had to offer was his muscles. His marriage was arranged to a neighbor girl back home, but they never quite got along. For starters, she was sexually disinterested most of the time. And he never seemed to make enough money. The best parts came when she would accompany him to a new city; it felt like an adventure.

An opportunity came along when Xiao was offered the chance to operate a small store down the street from a middle school, where children could buy notebooks, pencils and candy. But the principal of the school decided he wanted a piece of this trade and opened his own store. Furthermore, he threatened the students with academic punishment if he saw them going to Xiao's store.

"This was a small thing," Xiao told me. "The bigger thing in this society is that if there's a conflict between me and the boss on any job, I'll be instantly fired, even if I am right. I am just a common person. If you don't have any money or connection, you can't go to court." The pervasive *guanxi* principle at work yet again.

His wife died in 2004, the victim of breast cancer discovered too late. It was only when she was gone that he realized how much he missed her. "I wasn't there to help her," he said.

Railroad work pays relatively well, and the routine takes his mind off his problems. There is a trick from ancient laborers that he has mastered, a way of breathing in short and rhythmic strokes, that keeps him going for twelve-hour shifts. Other men on his gang—they call themselves "the geniuses" as a joke—tend to be afraid of the explosives, a fear Xiao does not share. In fact, he makes the charges himself and enjoys the nitrate blasts. He sleeps out in a tent near the railhead for weeks at a time and is paid in cash by the boss of the work gang; the arrangement is only semilegal. Nobody ever bothered to teach him how to drive the heavy equipment the bosses occasionally bring in.

Boring nights are enlivened by bottles of beer and rice wine, and

playful tussles turn into punishing brawls when the drinking gets serious. Xiao himself can drink a dozen beers without getting blurry. When
the job is done and the rails have been fastened to the sleepers, he looks
at it with no pride, as anybody could have done it. What he now wants
most is a wife who can understand what he has been through. "She
ought to be divorced, or a widow, someone who has had a hard life.
I want her to understand my situation. Someone who knows what life
is really like." He is a Christian—a rarity in China—because a missionary once came to his village and preached convincingly; Xiao's own
approach to the world seems an especially glum version of Calvinism.
His theology is unceasing work.

Nobody sings on the railroad crew, but a song sometimes plays in
Xiao's mind as he hauls rocks in his wheelbarrow, a melancholy theme
song that played over the opening credits of a television drama called
Thirsty Hope that was popular in the 1980s. Chinese of a middle-aged
generation tend to know the words:

> *Long, long years,*
> *It seems the years are so confused.*
> *Some is true, some is false,*
> *And it's hard to make a decision.*
> *Happy or sad, together or apart,*
> *It happened, but we keep going.*
> *Tell me why*
> *The roads of life are long.*
> *You are always asking for something,*
> *Hoping in your heart and leaving real life,*
> *And who can tell me, right or wrong?*

After talking with Xiao, I went out to look at the farthest extension of
the line from Xi'an to Langzhou, which knifed across the wetlands of
the Wei River and came to a dead halt above a series of shacks. The

concrete rail bed, vaguely triangular and looking a bit like the platform for the Disneyland Monorail, stuck out from the last piling like an outstretched tongue. The landscape to the west, in the fading sun, was an Asian urban mélange: oil-storage tanks, a field of rapeseed, tall apartments, dirty-paned greenhouses, some gravel quarries, the tower for the airport.

A few of the people who lived in the shacks beneath the half-finished bridge came up to talk to me. Work had halted for several days because of the Lunar New Year but would resume with its usual intensity next week. They told me they had been paid a few yuan to watch the site during the holiday. "This will be done next year," said one man. "We're not sure what it's going to be, but we know it's going to be good."

Tibetans are perhaps the most constitutionally friendly people on the planet. I experienced this for the first time after wandering back toward the end of the train, into a car that the train stewards were reluctant to clean. Spit-out sunflower shells littered the floor, as did wrappers from processed-food packages and empty aluminum cans. I was only trying to get away from my photo-happy dining companion but was quickly boxed in by at least a dozen teenagers who seemed mesmerized with every banality that came out of my mouth. They wore jerseys that zipped up to the neck.

The boys told me they were coming home from playing in a basketball tournament—their team was called the Lhasa Yaks—and they were in a high mood, despite being knocked out early. They gleefully recited the names of at least a dozen American hip-hop singers. I was asked if I knew Lady Gaga and then President Obama, and I had to say no, not personally.

"He is a Nobel winner," one boy said upon mention of Obama. "We have one of those, too." Then he folded his hands and mimicked prayer. He meant the 14th Dalai Lama, who is usually invoked here through euphemism and nonverbal gestures. Photos of him are strictly forbidden, though many Tibetans keep them in secret places in their homes, as contraband.

They asked me to sing a traditional song from America and sat ringed around me expectantly, arms draped over one another. I ended up giving them a few creaky stanzas of George Strait's "Amarillo by Morning," and they drank it in as reverently as though it were a lost canto of the *Iliad*. A smiling monk, clutching beads, came by to listen. Then they sang me one of their own songs, which was significantly more up-tempo than mine. Only once in this whole exchange did their faces grow stony, and that was when a uniformed Chinese military officer shouldered his way through the car and glared at them.

"Attitude," one of the basketball players whispered to me.

We were getting close to the valley of the Himalayan foothills that weaves toward Lhasa, and the Chinese presence was becoming more intense, even overwhelming. The tabletop of the plateau opened to a high, Colorado-like valley of brownish peaks looking like pyramids of sugar molasses. Along the river were hideous institutional superblocks such as the Russians had pegged on the Mongolian steppes, alienated from any purpose in the landscape other than exterior control. Cinder-block houses decorated with prayer flags appeared in clusters. Some of the rainbow pennants had torn loose in the wind and floated in the river like leaves.

On the far bank of the Kyichu River was a slab highway of new Chinese construction, with advertisements in Mandarin characters painted in red and gold on the sloped flagstones. And on our side of the river, quintupled tracks and a cavernous freight depot at West Lhasa where packages and containers were stacked high: manufactured toys and clocks from China flooding into this kingdom as surely as into any midwestern Walmart.

Within minutes we could see the thronelike Potala Palace, the old seat of the Tibetan theocracy and the boyhood home of the 14th Dalai Lama, who has not seen it since he slipped across the border more than forty years ago. Shaped like a thirteen-story trapezoid, painted maroon and white and strangely reminiscent of a human head swaddled in cloth, it drapes across a hill called Marpori and has been built in stages since the seventeenth century. Most of the artifacts were stripped away during the Cultural Revolution,* and then a 2002 "restoration" made it even more sterile—a husk of a monastery more noteworthy as a post-card icon than a living seat of spirituality.

The T27, its incredible journey now finished, then eased into a slot next to one of the most remarkable stations I have ever seen. The Chinese architects had taken a lesson from the nineteenth-century railroad executives in America and Britain who sought to make their depots like cathedrals, the embodiment of their worldly ambitions to conquer time and space.

As a theater of power, it is hard to beat. The station is a quotation—even a parody—of the Potala Palace: a backward-reclining trapezoid, though with clean lines and floors polished to a high sheen. The Ministry of Railways had spent $35 million on this showcase for arriving passengers, a reminder of who was really in charge. The grand waiting hall was bare of anyone actually waiting for anything, and the presence of blank-faced soldiers watching the passengers detrain did not seem to welcome loitering or even eye contact. Like the gutted palace that it imitated, it felt more like a museum than a human place. I hustled out into the crisp sunlight, across a wide, empty plaza and found my assigned tour guide, who showed me into a taxi van.

The Chinese influence, both military and commercial, seemed to be everywhere. Our ride into town was interrupted by a convoy of army trucks, their emergency lights turning, on their way out of the South-west Command headquarters, which is a close neighbor to the railroad station. A squadron of soldiers in black uniforms stood at attention in

---

* The exterior was left relatively undamaged, reputedly on the orders of Foreign Minister Zhou Enlai, who feared international condemnation.

the beds of the trucks, their riot shields held at eye level. They looked like robot troopers.

Men and ammunition are shipped much more easily here on the train, as are all the steel girders and gypsum and caulking that have boosted the population of Lhasa, once a medieval backwater, today embracing the generic alabaster nothingness of a Shanghai suburb. The city is now said to be nearly three-quarters Han Chinese, many of them young people lured by new jobs. Chinese economists have called it "state-sponsored urbanism." Tibetan activists liken it to "the second invasion of Tibet."

One thing that both sides have agreed upon, however, is that the railroad has worn down the physical barriers that preserved a residue of Tibetan specialness that had lasted through the worst periods of Chinese political oppression. The commercial assault, however, is a much harder force to fight.

The van took us down Shangbala Street, paved as wide as the Champs-Élysées, lined with hotels and noodle shops and mall-like shops blaring Mandarin characters, with elevators behind towering plate glass, and selling video games, gummy candies and brand-name shoes. Umbrella banners advertised Pabst Blue Ribbon and Coca-Cola.

In the middle of the 1980s, Paul Theroux could write that the "main reason Tibet is so undeveloped and un-Chinese—and so thoroughly old-fangled and pleasant—is that it is the one great place in China that the railway has not reached. The Kunlun Range is a guarantee that the railway will never get to Lhasa. That is probably a good thing. I thought I liked railways until I saw Tibet, and then I realized I liked wilderness much more." Those words now seem quaint.

My tour guide—required under government rules—watched me check into my hotel, draped a fringed white prayer scarf around my neck and then left me for the afternoon. I wandered over alone and, I believed, unwatched to the Barkhor, the public square at the epicenter of the old Lhasa. Dozens of Tibetans were making repeated ritualistic prostrations on their stomachs in front of the Jokhang Monastery. The flagstones had been prayed down into little troughs over the decades.

At the edge of the square near the monastery is a pillar protected by a low fence. It was erected to commemorate a treaty signed in 815 and its legend is now pathetic. ALL TO THE EAST IS THE COUNTRY OF GREAT CHINA; AND ALL TO THE WEST IS, WITHOUT QUESTION, THE COUNTRY OF GREAT TIBET, it says. HENCEFORTH ON NEITHER SIDE SHALL THERE BE WAGING OF WAR NOR SEIZING OF TERRITORY.

The Barkhor had been the scene of a rally for independence by monks in March of 2008 that turned into a minor uprising across the plateau and brought embarrassment to the Chinese as they were preparing to host the Summer Olympics. Now the buildings surrounding the square are mounted with security cameras, and every now and then the helmeted head of a Chinese army sniper can be seen peering over the edge at the happenings below. That ancient fear of uprising, the *jao min*, is an ever-present loathing here at the end point of the Qinghai-Tibet Railway.

OVER THE
MOUNTAIN

Lima to Cerro de Pasco

Alberto Benavides de la Quintana has a bad back and can no longer roam the cordillera like he used to, when he would set off for days with just a pack and a donkey studying the hills for minerals, but at ninety years old he is still the president of Compañía de Minas Buenaventura, and he remains unapologetic about his decision a decade ago to terminate all the contracts with the freelance truckers who used to haul the company's loads of silver, zinc and bismuth concentrates down the western slope of the Andes.

"Our mentality, as Peruvians, is one of independence," he told me in a voice that was a low rumble. "Everyone wants to own their own business. And the truckers were no different. I had also been convinced the railroad was no good for Peru. It was too small and too slow. Inimical for mining interests."

The only railroad up the central Andes at that time was a bad joke. The Ferrocarril Central was a state-run entity with hopper cars so worn and decrepit that approximately 3 percent of every shipment of concentrate was falling out of the floors, where the sheet metal had rotted into a latticed state like Swiss cheese. "All the yards looked like the surface of the moon," recalled one visitor. Powdered ore glinted in the sunshine, and employees shoveled it away as waste.

The route itself was a ludicrous piece of work. From the Pacific port at Callao, it rose to a height of 15,804 feet at the summit of the Andes before dropping into the valley smelter town of La Oroya. Locomotives derailed frequently on the "zigzags"—a series of switchbacks blasted into the slopes at the steepest points, which the trains used like stepladders. They could not use them in the rain because the wheels spun on the wet tracks.

Then Benavides, known in mining circles as "Don Alberto," got a phone call from an associate that changed his mind. Peru was looking to sell off its corroded mountain railroad; one official compared it to an "old lady" that should be euthanized out of mercy. But if it could be repaired and its books brought to order, Don Alberto thought, it might be a reliable method of transportation the truckers could not match.

Eleven years later the privatized Ferrocarril Central Andino was taking zinc and lead down to Lima and ferrying coal back up to the Andes. All the truckers got fired.

The story highlights a central truth about the railroad: there remains no better mechanism for hauling heavy commodities.

The basic physical economics remain much the same as they were in the coalfields of northern Britain in the 1820s. And as long as the world continues to consume raw materials like iron and copper and to produce manufactured goods for export, a system to move them overland will be necessary. No truck has yet been invented that can outperform the railroad in terms of energy efficiency and cost per ton. And nations around the world are increasingly looking to their old rail legacies as a means of restarting their economies.

Don Alberto was wearing a brown sweater and black gloves the day I was taken to see him in his mansion behind high walls in the Miraflores neighborhood of Lima. A blanket was on his knees. He had been rolled out in a wheelchair next to a table laden with family photographs arranged around a lamp with a pattern of musical notes on its shade. I could hear the sound of city traffic over the walls, as well as the high heels of a woman walking somewhere overhead on a wooden floor.

He had a reputation for being sentimental about some of the copper mines that he found during his days wandering the cordillera, refusing to shut them down even after they had clearly reached the end of their economic life, finding excuses to keep them open. But he was not soft-hearted with the trucking companies who had taken the zinc down to Lima. "The truckers were a nightmare," he said. "They gave us a Porsche when we needed a truck. With the railroad, per ton of ore, it is not expensive. It is very competitive."

He grew even more animated talking about a proposal to build one of Peru's first new freight lines in years: a link to a gold deposit at Chupaca. Bridges and tunnels would be necessary, and a consultant's report had put the price tag at $5 billion, but Don Alberto was confident it could and should be done in the next decade, even if he might not be around to see it.

"I have become quite fond of the railroad," he told me.

Taking ore by railroad is one of transportation's crudest acts—moving rocks by force—and a freight train has no frivolous touches. Nothing is without a function. The chassis on which a car rides is a steel frame called a "bogie," which is a rectangle of beams and axles, with flanged wheels and huge coiled suspension springs growing like tumors from the sides. The couplers on both ends look like dead fish with gaping mouths. Locomotives are nothing but platforms for big diesel engines; even the cabs look like they could be washed out with a high-pressure hose and suffer no damage, except for the clipboards hanging from hooks.

Yet freight trains are still awesomely beautiful—in the same way that the deadly contours of a shark are beautiful—and their efficiency has been the subject of considerable poetry through the years. One of the world's serious train aficionados became an investor in the reconstituted Ferrocarril Central, and he invited me and a few other visitors to ride with him on a run of six cars of coal up the face of the Andes.

Henry Posner III is the president of the Railroad Development Corporation, based in Pittsburgh, which has made a specialty of buying and revitalizing legacy cargo railroads. Along with Juan de Dios Olaechea, a well-connected friend of Don Alberto, he owns 35 percent of this former Peruvian state asset. Posner already has a sizable inheritance from his family, who made their money putting up billboards around Pittsburgh and bottling Pepsi in Wisconsin, but his job in the late 1970s was as a train master for Conrail in the South Bronx, and he decided to make a career of it. He has since bought up shares in clunky state-owned railroads in Mozambique, Estonia, Guatemala and Argentina.

"I *love* the smell of diesel in the morning," he told me, relishing the phrase as we got on board the coal train called "1010" on a foggy morning in the junction town of Chosica. The locomotive was a General Electric model with a cracked windshield, purchased at a deep discount from a line in Venezuela. Posner had ordered a refurbished office car called "the Paquita" set in the tail position, and it had all the genteel fittings that a nineteenth-century rail tycoon might enjoy: a dining room, brass chandeliers, polished wooden finishing, buzzers to summon the help and a smiling llama painted on the side.

We sat on wicker chairs on the back platform, rocking slowly, watching lower Peru slip away along the tracks, the whistle far ahead, old men hacking at potatoes in the gardens and little kids running behind the train before growing bored. Dogs paused, stared at us and moved on. Below, in the nadir of the valley, was the thin blue trickle of the Rímac River, whose course the tracks paralleled for most of the way up to the summit. We passed a sign at a road that said OJO PARE CRUCE ("Look, stop, cross"). There were no electric signals on this route and no crossbars; the budget did not allow it.

"The compromise," said Posner, "is to just go slow and blow the horn."

This railroad now hauls about 80 percent of Peru's zinc, a mineral used in appliances, vitamins and for putting a coating on steel so it won't rust. An average car contains twenty-six pounds of it. Peru is the second-largest producer in the world, and zinc makes up more than half of the total export economy.

"We provide a low-cost, safe, environmentally friendly way of building up Peru's exports in the world market," said Posner, going into corporate mode. "And we also help reduce transportation costs for domestic producers like cement. Unlike trucks, we don't congest the highways." He was wearing glasses with plastic shields on the side, a baseball cap with a railroad logo, a blue button-down shirt and a suit jacket that he'd bought in a thrift store for five dollars.

The crops gave way to fields of prickly pear, and the valley walls soared to a V-shaped precipice as we slipped into the Andes. We crossed a bridge named after Dr. Daniel Carrión, a medical student who had been trying to find a cure for a mysterious disease affecting railroad workers now known as verruga peruana. In 1885 he injected himself with the disease and died a month later. The creek shimmered below, about the drop of a twenty-story building. Once we crossed it, we were into a curving tunnel braced with steel beams. Flocks of bats fluttered in the trail of the diesel smoke.

Out in the sharp open air, and at the first of the zigzags, a brakeman named Aldo Matins jumped down, ran forward and cranked a switch on the rails so the locomotive could ease up the incline before starting to reverse itself at the second level—a maneuver not unlike a car making a three-point turn. There are no centralized controls here; every switch must be turned by hand. "We have to do this ourselves," said Posner. "Twelve times a day."

We soon came to the town of La Oroya, which is one of the filthiest places I have ever seen. The cliffs surrounding the town have been wiped clean of all vegetation and sport a bizarre white coating that looks as if ten billion tons of bird guano or cake frosting had been dropped on them and slowly oozed downward. This is the remnant of the sulfuric-acid clouds from a nearby smelter.

The children of La Oroya suffer a high rate of mental retardation because of it. Lead levels in the water are 50 percent higher than what is considered safe, and studies of the air have revealed eighty-five times more arsenic than in healthy air. The Doe Run smelter, built in 1922, is owned by American billionaire Ira Rennert, who is perhaps best known for also owning the largest single residence in the United States, a sixty-six-thousand-square-foot mansion in Sagaponack, New York. To be fair to him, the ninety-year-old smelter had been belching out toxic fumes long before he bought it. The Ferrocarril Central has a side business taking captured sulfuric acid from the now-idled stacks down to Lima in tanker cars. About nine hundred tons go down every day.

We paused for an hour and then kept climbing, upward and upward in the Andes, at grades as high as 4.2 percent, among the steepest in the world, past terraced villages that clung to the rocky hillsides: Tamboraque, Cacray, Río Blanco, Chicla, Saltucana. Barracks painted with pastel colors anchored some of these villages, but others had a shantytown look, with mud paths winding through mazelike barrios. The tracks here, as well as some of the villages, were vulnerable to mud slides in the rain. When boulders fall onto the line, especially on a curve, it creates a nasty surprise for the locomotive driver. If the train derails in one of the many narrow spots between a cliff and a drop-off, the emergency crews have a difficult time setting the pulleys that can inch a locomotive back on the tracks. In these cases, one official told me, half wistfully, it would be cheaper just to push the locomotive down into the ravine. A few years back, a giant mud slide—in local parlance a *huayco* as opposed to a smaller mud slide, a *derrumbe*—came barreling down the mountain and tore a bridge in two. Repairing this mess halted traffic for four days.

At Ticilio we passed a lake full of heavy-metal contamination. Talus from the highest peaks lay draped in fringes of maroon, chocolate and coral on the slopes. The oxygen was growing weak, and I could feel my head start to pound. The temperature had also dropped to just above freezing. A waiter came out to the back porch to serve cups of tea brewed from coca leaves, and it numbed the inside of my mouth.

The air smelled of wet grass and fresh metal, and as we climbed, the sky became a weird pastiche of angled sun and clouds and snow, and we slipped into a tunnel at Galera, where icicles hung from the ceiling, engine smoke filled the chamber and the orange light from the western portal receded like a well's mouth as the train leveled out and then, incredibly, started to tilt the other way.

"Did you feel that?" asked Henry Posner. "That was the South American continental divide."

This incredible railroad had been built by another American named Henry, though under considerably different circumstances.

A San Francisco businessman and promoter named Henry Meiggs arrived in Peru in 1868 amid presidential parties and champagne toasts; he was the can-do Yankee contractor who had built a successful railroad in Chile and was now going to stab railroads into the heart of the Andes, reopening big production in the silver mines first dug by the Incas. "Don Enrique," as he was called, built himself a fabulous house in Lima and became close with the tight ring of Peruvian grandees who dominated the shipping business.

Meiggs's biggest patron was President José Balta, a cavalry colonel with a trim mustache who was determined to "make of Peru the leading nation of Latin America" but was hampered by his own crude temperament and an intolerance of any dissent. "On the lightest contradiction," wrote an acquaintance, "he would flush, stamp the floor with his foot and threaten to deliver a blow." Balta was not prone to making speeches; private threats were his favorite method of communication. If he heard talk of dissenters, his customary response—which would become a running joke in Lima's political class—was to scream, "Let him be given four bullets!" Once he ordered his police to build a brick wall inside the doorway to an offending newspaper, which would have sealed the editor and his family inside, as in an Edgar Allan Poe story. The order was countermanded, but not until a portion of this wall was actually built.

He liked Henry Meiggs, though, and recognized within him a sense of the expeditious that he admired and shared. Plans for an Andean railway were hatched, and one of the best assets Peru had to mortgage were the dried mounds of bird droppings off its southern coast. These guano deposits, many of them first passed during medieval days, were rich in nitrates and made excellent powdered fertilizer, the Miracle-Gro of its day. Agricultural newspapers had been singing its praises as a rejuvenator of tired soil, and President Millard Fillmore in the United States gave permission for American adventurers to seize unclaimed islands piled high with the white gold.

The frosted rocks poking above the surf were dug out by laborers with shovels and wheelbarrows, who loaded the excremental gift from the birds into burlap sacks for ultimate spreading on faraway fields in Sussex and Illinois. Balta secured heavy foreign loans off the dung and handed the cash over to Meiggs for the railway projects, which he hoped would break the nation's dependence on bird droppings. "The amount seems at first thought large," Meiggs's brother gloated in a private letter, "but if security amounts to anything, we have the *whole of Peru Boots and Breeches.*"

What Henry Meiggs also failed to mention was that he had left behind a disaster in San Francisco and that the authorities were after him.

He had moved there from Brooklyn in 1849, hoping, like many other young men that year, to get rich on the traffic associated with the gold rush. His garrulous manner made him popular, and his new friends helped elect him to the city council several times. Meiggs believed he could make his fortune by building roads into the unsettled area northwest of Telegraph Hill called North Beach, and his biggest achievement was extending a shipping pier almost half a mile into San Francisco Bay from a weedy shoreline that has today been swallowed up in the Fisherman's Wharf tourist district.

Meiggs's sense of hope outstripped reality; his cash flow became shaky, and while he maintained an outward show of calm and cheer, he filched a book of blank promissory notes from city hall and made them out to his creditors to pay interest on his debts. When the fraud was uncovered, he took a bag of ten thousand dollars in gold coins and fled the city as a last-minute passenger on board the brig *American*, bound for the South Seas just ahead of a pursuing mob.

He disembarked in Chile and tried to start his life afresh. But his crime had been splashed all over the San Francisco newspapers—the *Bulletin* had called him "a black-hearted villain of the deepest dye"—and the story of betrayal had been juicy enough to be picked up by the world press. "After the body of Henry Meiggs shall be worm-eaten," commented the London *Daily News*, "the memory of his deed will remain as another confirmation of that proverb that honesty is the best policy." After the United States demanded his extradition, Meiggs found his way to Peru, where Balta gave him a contract to build a line to Arequipa. But the bigger project he had in mind was the Trans-Andean Railway, which would connect the seaport at Callao to the mining settlement of La Oroya, which lay 12,287 feet above sea level. But the real treasure was the silver at a place called Cerro de Pasco, exploited on the surface by the Spanish in the sixteenth century but never truly developed because of a lack of heavy equipment.*

Going "up the hill," as the local saying went, was an expensive

---

* A curiosity: these same Andean silver mines had enticed a middle-aged Richard Trevithick, the luckless inventor of the railroad, to come to Peru in 1816 and experiment with steam pumping.

undertaking. Meiggs and his chief engineer, Ernest Malinowski of Poland, had decided to follow the course of the Rímac River, a thin stream of snowmelt which nevertheless led almost all the way to the crest, with a green line of mud settlements and banana farms winding upward between a dizzying series of enfolded V's.

When an engineer protested that he couldn't blast a safe right-of-way through a precarious stretch of sliding shale, Meiggs replied, "Can't, eh? Well, young man, that's just where she's got to go, and if you can't find room for her on the ground, we'll hang her from balloons." He also bragged that his railway could go anywhere a llama could walk.

Dozens of tunnels would have to be blasted into the mountain walls, and they often fed straight onto wooden bridges thrown hundreds of feet over the Rímac below. A writer from Chicago's *Railroad Gazette* concluded that the man who built this idiotic thoroughfare would be sentenced to hang by any reasonable jury.

The death toll was predictably high. Not nearly enough Indians had signed up for the labor, so Meiggs hired a contingent of guest workers from Chile to break rocks and lay tracks. They died from dynamite accidents, crushing by locomotives, altitude sickness, fever boils, mosquito-borne plague, falls from the precipice, verruga peruana, many suicides. They died and died and died. A few of them were said to have dug their own graves and lain in them, waiting to die. After reports of the mayhem began to appear in Chilean newspapers, Meiggs retorted that people died in his Andes project "as in any other region on the globe."

When the remaining group of workers grew unruly and some began to desert, he looked to Chinese migrants, as had the builders of the Central Pacific in California less than a decade prior. The company made arrangements to buy labor contracts and rations of tea, rice and bread for as many as six thousand coolies, mostly small-town men from the provinces around Canton and a few toughened veterans of the CP who wore peaked hats and pantaloons. These workers, and the wives they would eventually bring with them, formed the first nucleus of the extensive Chinese community that calls Peru home today. Most of the wooden ties, however, he had shipped down from California mills, and all of the locomotives were top of the line from American factories.

Peru nearly destroyed itself on this railroad. The guano collateral made it possible for the nation to spend four times as much as its real income, but Balta's ministers knew that the supplies of bird droppings were finite, and the insanely corkscrewing railroad represented an all-or-nothing bet on unlocking the inorganic mineral development of the Andes, under the popular name of "public works." Before the operating funds ran out, Meiggs's crews were able to get the road up the Rímac canyon as much as eighty-seven miles from the sea yet short of the goal of La Oroya, which would have made it a genuine mineral-hauling road and capable of paying off the debt. He had to stop work and fire all his laborers.

Newspapers accused him of having given kickbacks to Balta's inner circle, including even the president's wife, to whom he gave $150,000, and his young daughter, who received a $5,000 cash bonus on her birthday. He died in his Lima mansion on September 30, 1877, but only after donating some of his money to California in a failed attempt to clear his name in the long-ago embezzlement scandal. President Balta was jailed during a coup and then shot as he lay in his cell bunk. When Chilean troops invaded Lima during the War of the Pacific in 1881, the bankrupt government was too weak to mount an effective defense.

Though it had been a boondoggle, leaving the railroad half finished was not an acceptable policy, and the new government turned the tracks over, along with 3 million tons of bird droppings, to the Irish-American financier William R. Grace. He finished Meiggs's insane project, pushing the railroad over the summit and into the mining zones in 1904, but not before earning the nickname the "Pirate of Peru" for his extensive plantations of sugar, lumber and coffee, as well as dealing in rifles and cannons during the War of the Pacific. He also inherited mining rights to Cerro de Pasco, one of the highest cities in the world and one of the bleakest, which happened to sit astride thick fingers of silver that the Spanish conquistadores had only begun to tap in the sixteenth century, and also copper, whose surface they had barely scratched. Grace's Peruvian Corporation, registered in London, ran the railroad and a wide belt of mining spurs well into the twentieth century.

In its currupt origins—and nakedly exploitative operations—the Ferrocarril Central Andino was not unlike the sugar-hauling railroads built in neighboring Brazil, which propped up a society of plantations and economic backwardness for generations after their completion. "The tracks were laid not to connect internal areas one with another, but to connect production centers with ports," wrote Eduardo Galeano in his angry and brilliant history *Open Veins of Latin America*. "The design still resembles the fingers of an open hand: thus railroads, so often hailed as forerunners of progress, were an impediment to the formation and development of an internal market."

The only monument erected for Henry Meiggs in the decade after his death was a giant boulder rolled over his tomb, which was said to have been carved out of the final tunnel on the Pacific side of the slope—the one underneath the fez-shaped peak that had been named Mount Meiggs in his honor. Shortly thereafter Dr. Fernando Casos, a Peruvian intellectual in exile, published a sarcastic book titled *Los Hombres de Bien!!* (Men of Good Deeds!!) about the Meiggs folly and the "sudden fortunes" made on guano and railways. There were also those who said that the financial mess in Peru was the real monument to this San Francisco con artist.

But even those who despised his legerdemain had to marvel at what a striking creation he had affixed in the Rímac canyon, one that indeed opened the Andes to the exploitation of its wealth. Concluded his biographer, Watt Stewart, "The most charitable summation that can be made of his life is to say that he was a product of his era—the era that produced Vanderbilt, Astor, Brady and Barnum—and that while he was in many ways a scoundrel, he built some remarkable railways."

The primary control on any diesel locomotive is the throttle, which on most models is a handle that can be set into nine different notches. One of them puts the engine in neutral. The other eight represent increasing grades of power.

Setting the throttle into Notch One will connect the main generator with the motors located in each axle and create a gentle start that is barely discernible. Clicking to Notch Two will raise the speed to about ten miles per hour, and opening it up to Notch Seven on a flat surface creates a truly intimidating display of momentum that can eventually result in a speed of over seventy miles per hour that takes upwards of a mile of track to brake to a full stop. Anything in that path gets pulverized. But the grades of the Ferrocarril Central Andino are so steep in places that any setting below Notch Three will result in a three-thousand-ton train rolling helplessly backward.

I was sitting in the locomotive cab with the driver, Gerberto Llerena, as we backed up through another zigzag. The throttle was opened to Notch Seven, and we were creeping forward by inches. "I can only operate like this for about fifteen seconds before burning out the motors," he explained. Our speed moved up to just about a walking gait and then to a trot before Llerena eased it down with a tug on a lever labeled *freno*, brake.

When going downhill, Llerena keeps the throttle at Notch Zero—neutral—and his hand always on the dynamic brake, which feeds the electric current generated by the motors back into a resistor, saving wear on the wheels and brake shoes. These Trans-Andean locomotives are unique in that they have four different braking systems in case one should fail—the dynamic, the hand brake, a conventional air brake and a "straight air" brake of the sort first invented by George Westinghouse in 1869 and almost never seen on today's trains.

This means the cars have to be connected by two hose couplings instead of one, because a runaway on these tracks is to be avoided at all costs. Stopping on downhill grades requires precise timing, and because the air brake is limited to ninety pounds of pressure, the driver cannot use it for more than one or possibly two short pulls before the compressor must recharge it. And by then it is too late. "What you have to worry about is not what you're doing now but a mile from now," said Llerena. Sheep and llamas sometimes wander into his path; the only thing he can do is wipe away the blood later.

A pianist's interplay between throttle and brake is necessary in places like a summit near Condorcocha on the high tableland of the Andes, approximately 13,500 feet above sea level. An eighteen-car train running up the summit needs a Notch Eight, but there are curves ahead and the speed has to be almost immediately trimmed with both the dynamic and air brakes. Taking those curves at anything above twenty-five miles per hour will throw the train off the tracks. A summiting train is a marvelous puzzle of physics, for the locomotive is accelerating *downhill* at the same time that its back end is still being tugged *uphill*, which requires a judicious sprint tamped quickly by a staccato of brakes. Doing this incorrectly results in the couplers breaking and the train ripping apart.

In defiance of all U.S. safety procedures, Henry Posner allowed me to ride as long as I liked on the front railing of the locomotive, a generosity that probably would have given his risk-management department a heart attack. Out in the sun and the freezing wind, the horn blasting overhead, we crested the summit perfectly and began the sharp descent into the town of Condorcocha. This track was built only four years ago as part of a deal with Cemento Andino, SA, which has operated a plant in this side valley of the Andes since 1958.

We went around one more bend, and the cement plant came into view: a colossal tower, with pipes and flues bulging like giant furnace bellows from its midsection. Tall as a cathedral, it stood at the far end of the valley, dominating a company town at its feet that was barely five decades old but still managed to look ancient. The flat-roofed houses seemed coated in a permanent layer of dust, as though sandblasted with it. A high ridge above town had been squared off into crop rows, and above those was a burned strip; setting grass fires was a way of flushing out the guinea pig known here as *cuy* and served up like Sunday chicken. The noon light was alpine clear, the wind tearing at my face, and for me the view of that industrial needle pinned inside the saddle of the brown peaks was a sight to rival Machu Picchu. I have never seen anything like it.

The train chugged down toward the cement plant in the bed, a deep L-shaped gash on the side of the hill. We were heading toward the yard and the chutes, where each car would take on a hundred tons of building material for eventual use on the coast, as well as in Korea, China and Indonesia.

We hopped off the train so the cars could be filled with the pulverized grit of the Andes, and it occurred to me I was watching an act that was as close to the heart of railroading as it ever came: this blunt function, the carting of stone to where it could be sold for higher sums, the insistent rearrangement of the physical world.

Freight rail is enjoying a profitable comeback across most of the world in the early twenty-first century, mainly because it's a bargain.

One statistic that the American Association of Railroads never gets sick of quoting is that a freight train can move a single ton of freight 463 miles using only a gallon of diesel, which is nearly double the fuel efficiency of twenty years ago, thanks to more advanced locomotives. Perhaps the biggest shot of confidence was administered by Warren Buffett, who paid $26 billion in cash for a controlling interest in the Burlington Northern Santa Fe in November of 2009.

"It's a very efficient way of moving goods," he told a reporter. "I just believe this country will prosper, that you'll have more people moving more goods twenty or thirty years from now, and that the railways will prosper." This was the single biggest purchase ever made by his Omaha-based Berkshire Hathaway company, which is no stranger to large acquisitions. In another statement e-mailed to ABC News on the morning of the announcement, he called the decision to buy the railroad "an all-in bet on the future of the United States."

"He needs to finish that sentence," said Henry Posner III when I asked him about it. "What he also means to say is that he's making a bet that the United States will continue to be a producer of commodities for the Chinese market, such as grain and coal and lumber." Some of these products flow back as manufactured goods for discount stores. And indeed, one of the economic transformations of the last thirty years is that of American railroads' becoming the enablers of a Pacific Rim economy.

One triggering spark for this rail revolution came as far back as 1937, from Malcolm McLean, the owner of a small North Carolina trucking company, who got angry waiting for longshoremen in New Jersey to load his cotton onto a ship. McLean knew nothing about boats, but he recognized inefficiency when he saw it. The waterfront was full of rackets; shipowners told him it cost more to move cargo a thousand feet across the wharves than it did to move it halfway across the world.

He did some tinkering with a blowtorch and built an aluminum container that could be detached from a truck chassis and loaded by a crane onto the deck of a freighter. The contents were locked and would never be touched by the longshoremen. And on October 4, 1957, on the same day that the Baltimore & Ohio canceled all passenger service north of Baltimore, the vessel *Gateway City*, the first ship in McLean's Sea-Land Service, left the Port of Newark heading for Miami with 226 containers stacked aboard.

This was the beginnings of the box boat, or, as the industry calls it, "intermodal freight transport," which would fill ocean ports all over the world, from Savannah to Singapore, with rectangular containers stacked high like Legos. These brightly colored modules filled with T-shirts and auto parts and soccer balls and beer would have to be moved inland, so the railroads built a new type of gondola car into which containers could be locked together.

The container is, as historian Marc Levinson has noted, "a soulless aluminum or steel box held together with welds and rivets," with "all the romance of a tin can." Yet the railroads made it cheap to ship these ungraceful boxes from the ports to the gates of an inland distribution center. "The shift of manufacturing to Asia hurt many segments of the American economy, but not its railroads," wrote the journalist Fred W. Frailey.

A prime corridor for box-boat containers is the Southern Transcon, the link between Chicago and Los Angeles completed in 1887 by the Atchison, Topeka and Santa Fe and now one of the many possessions of Warren Buffett. It follows the old Route 66 for a good part of the way, and it currently services approximately one hundred freight trains per day, many of them more than a mile long and stacked with containers full of Asian merchandise loaded onto the rails by crane at the Port of Los Angeles in San Pedro, as well as cars full of cotton and grain heading the other way. While not truly transcontinental, it functions second only to the Trans-Siberian as the busiest freight route on the globe.

I went out for a look in the high desert town of Winslow, Arizona, in the company of Pat Hiatt, a spokesman for the BNSF. The rail yard happens to sit near one of the finest Harvey Houses in the Santa Fe system, a chandeliered Spanish Revival hotel called La Posada, which was closed in 1957 and then reopened forty years later as a boutique hotel and restaurant. Hiatt showed me the recently installed tracks full of fresh ballast, the control panel that kept track of each train approaching the yard, the gondola cars stacked high with Malcolm McLean's creations: containers labeled HANJIN and MAERSK, their contents and destiny a mystery to us.

Here was the new face of American railroading. Trains could take materials two-thirds of the way across the continent to a centralized warehouse. Doing the same thing solely by truck from a Pacific port would have been phenomenally expensive in gasoline; an average train can carry the loads of 280 trucks. While the old Santa Fe had concerned itself with luxury passenger service and the cattle trade from Dodge City, it was now taking loads of imported Chinese products—"Grandma's pajamas" Hiatt called it—to discount stores and retail outlets across the Midwest, a landed bridge into the interior. There has been a 48 percent increase in this Pacific trade in the last decade.

"We're now in the logistics of twenty-first-century industry," Hiatt said. "No matter what you buy or wear or use, there was a train somewhere."

A freight train network is like "an Internet of things," in the words of Keith Dierkx, director of the IBM Global Rail Innovation Center in Beijing. Even in a data-driven era, the physical world is still preeminent. Raw materials and finished goods will always need a heavy-bore method of transport, and railroads have an important role in the physical structures that make an information economy possible.

To name just one example, the Denver oilman Philip Anschutz in 1988 acquired the Southern Pacific Railroad, which came with a curious inheritance: a vast kingdom of rights-of-way through the West, many of which had first been deeded over as "Indian land" to the corrupt tycoon Collis Huntington in the 1880s. A century later the railroad was a struggling carrier losing its fruit business and looking to diversify. Southern Pacific realized that its many city-to-city spokes could also be convenient routes for long-distance telephone cable. A baby concern called Southern Pacific Railroad Internal Network Telephones, or "Sprint," was spun off, and it became a major telecom player.

Now the Southern Pacific formed a joint venture with Norfolk Southern called FiberTrak after an assistant vice president for real estate named Douglas Hanson had the idea of burying fiber-optic cables* next to the tracks at a depth of four feet. Hanson later became the first CEO of Anschutz's telephone giant Qwest, whose origins were in the rail-

---

* Thin wires of glass through which data can be sent in bursts of light.

roads. This put a new spin to an old business maxim: so many railroads tended to go bankrupt because they thought they were in the train business, not in the transportation business. Now they had to think even more creatively about their physical legacy and how it might fit within the global economy.

The CEO of BNSF is Matthew K. Rose, who started in the trucking business, switched to railroads and was quickly promoted through the ranks. "The traditional view of rail is one where you take raw materials into a plant site, pick them up as finished goods and send it all out to retail," he told me. "Now the railroad of today picks up the raw materials, takes them to the coast, ships it to manufacturing facilities in Asia, where they are taken back to the continental United States and put back on the train. The average American consumes forty tons of stuff per person per year. We don't have the capacity on the highway system to handle that."

But even beyond our national passion for "stuff," there was a second angle to Warren Buffett's wager on cargo rail. It was about America's twenty-first-century energy strategy, which is still tied up in coal, a mineral that had been flowing in the railroad's bloodstream since the days of the Stockton & Darlington and the industrial revolution. And its modern face is best seen south of the city of Gillette, Wyoming, in a region called the Powder River Basin.

Coal mining on an Olympian scale takes place here, at volumes that would have staggered the imagination of the pit owners of northern Britain in the 1820s. Back then the total national production was just over 10 million tons per year. In northeast Wyoming today, that equivalent is dug up in nine days.

Most of it is going to a series of generating stations in the Midwest and the South owned by the big utilities with hieroglyphic names— Xcel, DTE, Westar, NRG—providing electricity to America's grid. China has also been a recent new customer, shipping Wyoming coal via train and then ocean freighter from Canadian ports. And no part of this stupendous resource economy would be possible without the railroad to move the dark diamonds.

The 106-mile line down the spine of the basin, co-owned by Union Pacific and BNSF, is said to be the busiest stretch of rail anywhere on the planet. Wyoming state law makes it a crime to store coal on the ground—the piles tend to catch fire, especially when drying in the sun after a rain—so it is shipped almost as soon as it is mined, and the trains must be kept moving constantly, at every hour on every day of the year. I went here on a bright October day to meet with Will Cunningham, the genial coal-marketing manager for BNSF. We got into his sport-utility vehicle, and he took me over to where two empty trains awaited dispatch to the mines.

Painted on the sides of the cars were four-letter codes, signifying which utility owned the car, and Cunningham translated for me as we drove alongside. Coal trains are by necessity extremely long trains, and this took a while. "KCLX—that's Kansas City Power and Light," he said. "JHMX, that coal is going to Alabama Power. TXNX, Texas Utilities. TGNX, I believe that's going to Houston. Hmmm, PNJX, that's NRG Reliant at Princeton, New Jersey. UCEX means Union Electric in St. Louis." The cars were made mostly of aluminum, which reduces the weight and the stress on the tracks, and were remarkably clean of the graffiti flora that usually decorates rolling stock.

The coal itself is mined by giant electric shovels with walking drag-lines that strip away everything in their path after the earth has been loosened with explosives. These four-hundred-ton beasts lurch like military walkers from *The Empire Strikes Back*. Driving one is said to be like sitting on the toilet of the upstairs bathroom of a two-story house—and then using a steering wheel to drive the whole house. The sagebrush plains south of Gillette have been sliced into giant cuts, most of them as geometric as a sports stadium and all of them about two hundred feet deep.

We stopped at the bottom of a prairie swale that had been trenched down the middle by the railroad tracks and scrambled up a hill. Beyond the barbed wire to the west was a spectacular view of the Caballo Mine, owned by Peabody Coal, and a BNSF train nearly two miles long, creeping forward at a steady rate toward a white columnar building that looked like a grain elevator. This is called a "load-out."

I could hear the faint rumble of coal dropping onto metal.

"It doesn't stop?" I asked.

"If we stopped to load every car, this would take eight hours," said Cunningham. "I can't imagine loading a car that way. It'd be a foreign language."

The whole process takes about an hour and a half and requires a bit of artistry. A man in a glass booth above the tracks uses a joysticklike device to lower a pyramid-shaped nozzle into a hopper car as it creeps before him, a bit like a line worker aiming to fill a moving pastry crust with pie filling. At the right moment, he hits a button and approximately 120 tons of coal tumbles into the bottom of the car in the space of about a second. The car is then inched forward to a scale for weighing. The first dump is typically off the mark by about five hundred pounds, plus or minus, and so a second corrective loading is made at a chute called the "top-off," which shapes the mound into something that looks like a bread loaf.

There is a terrible contradiction at the heart of this enterprise. Since the 1990s the nation's railroads have been trying to position themselves as the more environmentally pure method of transportation when compared to their exhaust-spewing, gas-guzzling brethren in the trucking business. "We help ease gridlock by taking trucks off the road, saving you time and fuel that are being wasted in traffic" is a line from a television commercial put out by Freight Rail Works, a group sponsored by the American Association of Railroads. But they are playing an enabling role in a business responsible for chuffing more than 2 billion metric tons of carbon dioxide into the atmosphere every year, thickening the layer of greenhouse gases above us, not to mention emitting heavy plumes of lead, mercury, methane, uranium and sulfur dioxide.

I asked Matt Rose, the chief executive of BNSF, about this apparent contradiction, and he responded, "My personal belief is that if we go on the path of eliminating coal, there's not an easy substitute and it'll move up the cost of manufacturing." He also pointed out, a bit defensively, that it was his job to transport the material, not question it.

Coal and the railroad are locked in an intractable embrace here in the Powder River Basin. The superscale reach of the endeavor—this long-distance electric wiring of America—would be unthinkable without the power of the railroad. More than 70 percent of the nation's consumption of coal is now shipped on the rails. So a material that has lain undisturbed in the earth for more than 25 million years is frequently dug, loaded, hauled and burned into ash within two days of its resurrection. Cunningham told me that BNSF crews have had the experience of rolling under an empty load-out and then being told by the foreman, "Hold on. We need to mine a little more coal this afternoon so we can load you up."

The sociopathic urge of the railroad to haul as much coal as possible can occasionally create tension. Cunningham told me a story about a contract negotiation with a power-plant manager who grew exasperated with BNSF's insistence on a particularly aggressive coal-delivery schedule.

"Seems like all you guys want to do is run them as far as you can for as fast as you can," said the executive.

Cunningham's response: "Well . . . *yeah!*"

Though the sun was sinking and the dry wind was becoming painful, I made myself stay on the prow of Henry Posner's locomotive almost all the way across the Andean highlands. I was wearing every piece of clothing that I'd brought—four layers of cotton—plus earplugs against the blasts of the horn, which was about three feet above my head. This is how a Viking slave trophy might have felt.

We passed through dust-ridden towns with pitted wooden balconies, looking like the scene of a western gunfight. Out on the plains, flock of llamas were herded up by old Quechuan women in peaked wool hats and rainbow shawls. Cumulonimbus clouds, high and dark, mingled around the far mountains, and sun slanted through them at refracted angles.

The tracks were knife straight for forty miles. There were a few corridors of wire strung from sticks to keep the animals away. But in most parts it was wide-open range with clumps of grass amid alluvial rocks. We stopped for fifteen minutes while a crew added six new cars, and then we ascended a curve on the side of a broad mountain. Our altitude was now about fourteen thousand feet, and once again we were climbing.

A light snow began to fall, and my hair began to freeze. And what I felt when we were moving was some close cousin to joy, an utter forgetfulness of physical space.

On the other side of the mountain, the security lights of a copper mine lit a valley far below, the tailings ponds glowing like coins, and we hugged the edge of a canyon before starting a descent into a valley that I could no longer see in the darkness. This was the mineralized region where the Spanish had made Indians sink silver diggings in the late sixteenth century, where Richard Trevithick had tried and failed to make his steam pumps work, and where Henry Meiggs had been aiming to lay track. It was also where Alberto Benavides de la Quintana liked to roam around on his donkey, looking for the perfume traces of zinc in the hills.

Too soon our headlamp was drowned into the lights of Cerro de Pasco, once called the "Royal City of Mines" and today one of the most polluted places in the world, with a giant open-pit mine at its center. The ground has been thoroughly contaminated by heavy metals, and the national congress gave the zinc producer Volcan Compañía Minera,

SA (which happens to be an important railroad client), permission to expand the pit and swallow up what is left of the town's old colonial plaza. The locomotive pulled up into a yard, across the street from what looked like a customshouse, and I reluctantly climbed down.

When I was back in Lima two days later, I went to lunch with Juan de Dios Olaechea, whom Don Alberto had persuaded a decade ago to help him run Peru's premier mineral-hauling railroad. He is married to the sister of José Ignacio de Romaña Letts, the director of the Volcan zinc company (another example of the tightness of the Peruvian ownership class). He has a wide grin and a teenager's mad exuberance.

On the tracks near Río Blanco, I had watched him and Henry Posner play a little game of chicken in a "gravity car" they took out for special occasions. It was an open cart with wheels, designed for track inspectors in Henry Meiggs's time. There was only one controlling device: a hand-operated lever brake on either side. We had flown down the dizzying slopes and through the tunnels in a ride that felt like a manic Disneyland attraction, a Mr. Toad for grown-ups. Juan had worn a Red Baron–style leather pilot's cap with goggles for the occasion, and he had dared Henry with his smile to apply the hand brake. We were soon whipping along at twenty-five miles per hour, a near-derailment speed on the curves for any locomotive on this line.

With a fifty-dollar plate of sushi now in front of him, Juan spoke in expansive terms about future potentials: a railway line to Rondônia in Brazil to tap into the new soybean farms, another line to the copper bonanza at Antamina. There were studies being done right now to chart the feasibility of building spur lines to new zinc properties. All of it was so much more attractive because of the growing minerals trade with China. "We used to be on the wrong side of the Pacific—now we're on the right side," he had said.

"I used to know nothing about trains," de Dios said. "But they are the infrastructure of the future. As the world gets more populated, guided systems are the only means of transportation, whether we like it or not. There's going to be an oil scarcity in the next twenty or thirty years. The liberty and flexibility of the car are suited for a planet of three billion people, not six billion."

Yet he acknowledged that the roots of the train are still grounded in what it does best, which is to move bulk goods for long distances— especially the output of mines.

I asked de Dios about what people in Peru thought of the new system that he and Don Alberto had helped create, and he conceded that there had been criticism, particularly from truckers who felt that their business had been taken away. But the country was better off with a fixed link into the Andes, he said.

"Everyone thinks those who run trains are a robber baron: a Rockefeller, a Vanderbilt, a Gould. And a trucker is a poor guy with a mortgage. But it is not like that," he said. And later, "You may think *sewers* are dirty, but you'll keep building them. We live where everything is moving."

FASTER

Barcelona to Madrid

The earliest train travelers were often afraid of what they saw. The speed of the locomotive seemed inhuman and sinister—as if mankind were pushing a barrier of nature that ought never be breached.

"It is really flying," said Thomas Creevy of an 1829 journey in which the top speed was twenty miles an hour. He confessed that he couldn't let go of the idea that he and the rest of the passengers would be immediately killed if there were even the slightest mishap under the wheels. This was in an era when mechanized transportation was in its infancy, when the nearest comparable sensation was riding a horse at full gallop.

I experienced a taste of that cognitive shock while on board the AVE, an acronym for Alta Velocidad Española that happens also to mean "bird." This is Spain's high-speed train that gets you from Barcelona to Madrid in less time and for less money than a commercial airline flight. The AVE is also one hell of a ride, because the sense of traveling at two hundred miles per hour while still rooted to the ground is truly disorienting.

I paid about a hundred ten dollars for the fare at Barcelona's Sants station and, after passing through a metal detector, went out to the platform to board the AVE, which looks like a pencil-thin version of the old Concorde supersonic jet. The beak of the locomotive car is pointed and curved slightly downward; each trailing car is like an airplane fuselage inside with padded blue bucket seats and carpet in a gray-green checkerboard pattern.

The doors closed behind me with a discreet hiss. An electronic glass screen displayed the time, outside temperature and velocity. I watched this last number creep steadily upward as we left the station via a high-walled corridor and through green San Francisco–like peaks terraced with glassy houses. Before long we were out of the lush coastal area and into an arid plain. That's when the unseen engineer opened the throttle and turned all of Aragon into a smeared blur.

The blast of velocity hurts the eyes after a few minutes: dry riverbeds, truck depots, olive trees, power substations, blast furnaces, vineyards and rambling stone estates rocketed by in an indistinct splash of watercolors. No object could be held in focus for long, not even the trucks on the highway next to us, whose speed by comparison was a pathetic joke.

I almost never get carsick, but looking too long out the window was conducive to nausea. I tried the old sailing trick of focusing on the horizon instead of anything nearby, and it didn't seem to help. Eventually I had to turn away from the window, and it occurred to me that the fuselage—though made of high-quality steel—could probably crumple like a stomped-on beer can. When going full speed on level ground, a train like this needs approximately four miles to come to an emergency stop.

Well, we're all toast, I thought, *if this thing ever hits a car. Just as bad as a plane crash.*

The interior of the train, meanwhile, was as sedate as an insurance office. There was no engine noise, only a quiet electrical hum, an exhaling *ahhhhhh* when we went through tunnels and an ominously soft rattle when we passed another AVE train. A uniformed attendant—dressed for travel glamour, like a Pan Am stewardess from the sixties—

handed out iPod-like earpieces for those who wanted to watch the movie, which was an animated feature called *The Clone Wars*.

"Very fast, easy," said a man across the aisle from me, whose name I learned was Gracian García. He was a veteran of the AVE, and the speed no longer bothered him, if it ever did. "My wife doesn't like to fly. This is worth it." He gestured out the window. "Here you can see Spain. In a plane you can't see anything."

For most of the twentieth century, Spain had a horrible fleet of trains. They were notoriously late and dirty, usually without toilets, and not even connected with the rest of Europe.

The first builders in the 1850s had decided to use a gauge of six Castilian feet,* which made it impossible for Spanish trains to carry on past the border with France. This was partly a military decision, as the rails couldn't be used against Spain in a land invasion, but also a protectionist economic strategy, as it would add an additional burden to imported goods. It certainly accomplished this, but it had the effect of walling off trade and travel for generations and deepening the isolationist tendencies that still resonate today. Napoleon Bonaparte's famous dismissal of the Iberian Peninsula—"Europe ends at the Pyrenees"—was true in a railroading sense as well.

But Spain has now laid more high-speed rail track than any other country except for China. Its domestic train-set manufacturer, Talgo, has consequently emerged as a top supplier to the rest of the world.

Domestic aviation has taken a nosedive since Spain made this expensive wager on trains. After the Barcelona-Madrid link opened, the Iberia Airlines service between those two cities (once the busiest route in Europe) lost nearly 2 million passenger journeys per year, a 40 percent decline. The drop was noticeable almost immediately after it opened in 2008. Travelers liked the dependability of the train, as well as not having to go out of

---

* The equivalent of 5 feet, 5⁵/₁₆ inches.

the city limits to an airport and wait around at a gate. There is very little fuss about it—certainly nothing compared to the elaborate convolutions of the airport—and most of the AVE stations in Spain have been grafted directly onto existing depots, which already enjoy proximity to the cathedral squares and shopping districts, as they have for a hundred fifty years.

The Spanish high-speed experience is frequently cited as a model by heads of state who see infrastructure as a key to building an economy. Visiting politicians are routinely taken on tours of the Talgo factory. The AVE has also become a point of reference for U.S. president Barack Obama, who cited it favorably in an April 16, 2009, speech in which he described his own plan to bring a similar system to the United States.

"In Spain a high-speed line between Madrid and Seville is so successful that more people travel between those cities by rail than by car and airplane combined," he said, adding, "There's no reason why we can't do this. This is America. There's no reason why the future of travel should lie somewhere else beyond our borders."

I wondered about this as I rocketed toward Madrid. There were obvious dissimilarities between Spain and the United States. This was a country that could tap rich reserves of European Union money and was also a smaller area in which the distance between premier cities was measured in hundreds of miles instead of thousands. Citizens here are more generally willing—or at least historically conditioned—to tax themselves for big-ticket projects. And even despite the bad reputation of trains in Spain, there was at least a basic cultural comfort with them that the United States has lost somewhere along the way.

Obama's spending program was called, cautiously enough, "a vision" for high-speed rail in which an initial $8 billion commitment would be barely enough to get a hundred miles constructed on its own. The cash was intended as public fertilizer to be spread out in ten strategic places, which the White House identified as Pacific Northwest (Portland-Seattle), South Central (Dallas–San Antonio), Gulf Coast (Mobile-Houston), Chicago Hub Network (St. Louis–Chicago–Minneapolis), Southeast (Atlanta–

Charlotte–Washington, D.C.), Keystone (Philadelphia-Pittsburgh), Empire (New York–Buffalo), Northern New England (Boston-Montreal), California (Los Angeles–San Francisco) and Florida (Tampa-Orlando).

All of these strips were teeming with affluent commuters, and the White House planners saw high-speed rail as the next incarnation of the nineteenth-century steam railroads that had boosted the commuter villages like Hinsdale, Lake Forest and Hyde Park that formed the stool pegs of the megalopolis called "Chicagoland." Only the high-speed train, with its ability to telescope space as never before, would make it easy to be a citizen of Chicago while living in a former cornfield in Iowa or Missouri or to be a Bostonian while taking mail in Vermont. Railroads had once destroyed the old order of American space. They could do so once again.

"All of you know this is not some fanciful, pie-in-the-sky vision of the future," Obama said. "It is now. It is happening right now. It's been happening for decades. The problem is, it's been happening elsewhere, not here."

Four states—Ohio, Wisconsin, Florida and California—stepped forward as the lead contenders for the initial share of the money. Nobody concerned thought it was going to be an easy ride: high-speed rail was an untested vision on American soil, and many believed it to be a Disneyland toy that would never be embraced by the public. The nation was in the midst of a terrible credit squeeze, and building just one of the regional networks in California was going to cost at least $50 billion in borrowed money. The Tea Party movement was railing against exactly this kind of spending, and Americans of all political stripes were wondering the same thing about high-speed trains. How can we afford this? The fear was almost enough to kill it.

Spain had a distinct opening advantage: the decision to build AVE was made when the government had a lot of loose cash and a leader willing to take a risk.

When Spain joined the European Union in 1986, it received an immediate windfall from the currency revaluation. Prime Minister Felipe González then immediately proposed a high-speed railroad, a local version of a Japanese-style "bullet train" that would connect Madrid to Seville, which happened to be his birthplace.

His enemies in the Cortes Generales—the Spanish parliament—scoffed at the obvious hometown pork. And they also feared the price tag. Popular Party spokesman Felipe Camisón called it "the irrationality project." The pushback was vigorous, acknowledged Julio Hermida Gayubas, a spokesman for the national rail company RENFE, whom I met for coffee inside a railroad station.

"The people said, 'It's a lot of money,'" he recalled. "'We have education and roads and health care expenses, and why are you building a pharaonic building project. For what?'"

I complimented him on his reference to Egyptian pharaohs, and he laughed.

"This word 'pharaonic' became very popular in Spain for a while," he said. "For years people thought it was pharaonic and it was quite crazy to spend money on this Japanese-style thing. The government said in response, 'Let us decide what the future is and what has to be mandatory.'"

In the early 1990s, up to half the nation's transportation budget would go to laying high-speed track between Madrid and Seville that indeed proved awesomely expensive: an average of $10 million per mile, which was five times what ordinary track would have cost. The total bill soared to $3.8 billion, far beyond what the president had promised. And tricky safety problems had to be solved in field tests.

When a train is passing through a tunnel at a speed of two hundred miles per hour, there must be a lot of ceiling space. If the aperture is too tight, the wave of air pressure in front of the leading car will reverberate with the temporary equivalent force of a hurricane, possibly strong enough to blow the train off the rails. Tunnels therefore had to be built with a rather generous circumference.

There was also the matter of rock ballast on the tracks: it would be sucked upward by air pressure and bang the bottom of the train. The solution was to use concrete sleepers and no ballast. A series of electric catenaries had to be strung overhead. And sensitive monitoring equipment would put the immediate brakes on the trains if a car or a stray cow tumbled onto the tracks.

The train opened in 1992, and RENFE publicized it with an unprecedented deal. If you were more than five minutes late, you received a full refund immediately—cash put into your hands as you disembarked. This was almost never necessary. The train has achieved an on-time record of 99.7 percent. Opposition to the train melted away, and now even conservative legislators have supported expansions.

The safety systems worked beautifully until July 24, 2013, when an apparent human error caused a bloody wreck on the line outside Santiago de Compostela. The injured driver was pulled from the wreck moaning, "We are all human, we are all human." He had reportedly been zooming around a curve at a velocity more than twice that of the posted speed restriction. Local journalists reported that he had previously posted a photo to his Facebook page of a dashboard speedometer with its needle almost ticked to the endpoint. The caption: "I'm at the limit and I can't go any faster or they will give me a fine."

The crash was a reminder that even closed-loop systems have room for human error (as the driver seemed to acknowledge in his first thoughts). And even as Spanish politicians vowed to get to the bottom of the crash and made new safety guarantees, the political commitment to high-speed rail remained solid.

The AVE will never pay for itself, but reducing highway congestion has had a noticeable effect, said Juan Matías Archilla, RENFE's director of international projects, who met with me in his office. On the wall was a painting of a locomotive shaped like a camel's nose plowing through the narrow streets of a village.

The largest benefits of high-speed rail have been social benefits, which do not show up on a classic balance sheet, he told me. One example he likes to cite is Ciudad Real, a shabby city that now has an energized bedroom community simply because of its AVE stop.

I went to go see it for myself. Cuidad Real is what people here call "deep Spain"—the traditional bedrock of La Mancha where family farms struggle and many think that Generalísimo Francisco Franco was not such a bad guy after all. The city is effectively becoming a new suburb of Madrid, now just an hour away when it used to be three. A thousand tract homes have been built near the station. The Don Quixote International Airport on the edge of town, meanwhile, now sits abandoned. Bright yellow X's have been painted on its runways to warn pilots away from landing. Opened in 2009, it was built for about a billion euros and even featured an AVE stop, but it was a victim of Spain's housing meltdown, which was in many ways worse than the one in the United States.

On the train out to Ciudad Real, I met Pamela Zamberk, a dermatologist who bought a house there because of the AVE. She has a long-term contract to work at a hospital in Madrid, but she was tired of her tiny apartment. "I know many people who do this," she told me. "The quality of life is better, cheaper. I have a good job, even more money. You can go to Madrid in an hour or to the coast in an hour and a half." Her mortgage on a home is about the same as what she was paying in rent, after deducting what she spends on the regular train fare.

The local branch of the Universidad de Castilla has scheduled its classes around the AVE, and enrollment has leaped upward because of the influx of students from Madrid—a trend not in line with the traditional Spanish habit of staying close to home. "This university was transformed because of the train," said Juan José Pastor, a music-theory professor who was wearing square glasses and an ivory suit when we met. "This fantasy of travel has created a new reality."

On the train back to Madrid, I thought that this could easily be the picture of a careworn Texas town that would suddenly burst with new money if a convenient daily link to Houston could be laid down.

Time shapes the land. This has been the iron law of the railroads ever since the Camden & Amboy began to expand the reach of New York City in the 1830s. It now also works at two hundred miles an hour. But there is another durable truth: the benefits come only to those towns lucky enough to get a station, where the real estate goes crazy as a result. The jockeying almost always involves backroom dealing and a little corruption. And the promised benefits don't always materialize, particularly if the choice was unwise from the start.

The maps of France's high-speed network, the Train à Grande Vitesse, or TGV, include just such an embarrassment. The planners created a station in a rural area in hopes of spurring growth. But it never came. The station at Haute-Picardie is now called "the beetroot station" because of the fields full of beets that still surround it.

Spain's own embarrassment is a town nine miles from Guadalajara, called Yebes, where local boosters planned an instant town they christened "Avelandia" near the new station. But then journalists reported that nearby properties were owned by family members of Esperanza Aguirre, who was the president of the Autonomous Region of Madrid, and the land had ascended in value by a factor of a thousand in the space of twenty years.

During a call-in program on SER radio, Aguirre herself dialed the station to make the following on-air denial: "Neither me, nor my husband, nor my in-laws, nor my brothers- and sisters-in-law, nor my mother, nor my brothers and sisters have an inch of land in Yebes." When the host asked her if her family owned land in nearby Chiloeches, she said, "That's all I have to say," and hung up. The new city near the AVE station became a failure; the streets are largely deserted.

Building new stations inside established cities has its own set of problems, including the high costs of land, angry neighbors and the bull-in-a-china-shop disruption to cultural treasures. One of RENFE's goals has always been to connect the high-speed train to France's TGV network and thus pierce the long-standing wall of railroad isolation

from the rest of Europe. But this required drilling a tunnel underneath
Barcelona that would pass within a few centimeters of the pillars of the
eye-achingly beautiful Sagrada Familia Church, the greatest achievement of the architect Antoni Gaudí and one of the nation's top tourist
attractions.

Gaudí had devoted the latter part of his life to building the hyper-
boloid church before he was struck and killed by a railed streetcar in
1926. Preservation groups were afraid the tunneling could create a sinkhole and trigger an all-out collapse. A federal committee of experts
spent several months reviewing the geology before declaring it safe, over
the objections of most Barcelona residents, who polls showed were 60
percent opposed to the underground extension.

This is not the only political problem with the AVE. The opposition
to it touches a lasting wound in the Spanish psyche, one that has nothing
to do with the technology of the train but rather with what it represents.

I went to go see Germa Bel, a professor at the University of Barcelona
who had written a sarcastic article about the train for the newspaper *La
Vanguardia*, entitled "Welcome, Mr. Marshall!" This was the same title
as that of a 1953 film comedy about a village in rural Spain that tries to
win foreign aid by sucking up to American diplomats. And what Bel was
saying was that the train is based more on emotional appeal than on real
economics.

Bel is a balding man who wears his glasses on a leash and has the
half-bemused, half-grumpy look of a tenured academic, and indeed he has
done time teaching at Cornell and Harvard. He once served in the Spanish parliament and calls himself a "Scandinavian socialist" without apology. He is also unapologetic about his opposition to the high-speed-rail
project, which he thinks is a boondoggle.

"It's cool, quick, nice," he said. "But this is not a cost-benefit analysis. To me the train is best for the city metro and for freight transportation. It is not particularly good for a journey where you have planes
or even other trains that happen to travel less than a hundred fifty

kilometers per hour. And Barcelona's airport now has seven times the passenger seats as the AVE. This is not the train replacing the stagecoach! This is the train replacing another train. This is a new, cool and very expensive offer for trips that were already being offered. A small offer for huge costs."

We had been talking for nearly half an hour before a deeper question surfaced. He mentioned that one of the former prime minister's deputies had outlined a vision to link all the provincial capitals in Spain to high-speed rail, putting them all within about three hours' distance of Madrid, which sits near the heart of the country like a hub among spokes.

"Can you imagine," he asked me, "what would happen in your country if Obama had said, 'I want to put all the state capitals—Springfield, Illinois, and Albany, New York, and all of them—less than four hours from Washington'?"

I told him it would probably not go over well with those in America who feared excessive reach from the federal government.

This sentiment also exists in Spain, where suspicion of centralized structures has a long history.* Struggling for autonomy is a running theme for Catalonia, which was a hotbed of republican and anti-Catholic fervor during the Spanish Civil War of 1936–39. Generalísimo Franco had ordered the army to bomb targets in Barcelona as well as torture the dissidents and crush the use of the Catalan language. Franco's ironhanded rule came to symbolize everything about the capital that still arouses resentment: taxes, inequality and the enforced use of the Spanish language.

The old anger still rises when it comes to big-ticket adventures like the AVE, which is viewed among many Catalonians as a straw through which to suck money to Madrid, as well as a rope to lasso everyone closer to the *federales*.

* In the most visceral example, Basque fringe groups in the north like ETA have spent fifty years in an underground terror-driven fight for independence.

"This is not just a train," said Bel. "This is an ideology."

The train as ideology: this same equation had been made in America multiple times over. Intellectuals of the 1830s first saw the British-born railroad as a welcome agent of "technology," the word coined by Harvard medical professor Jacob Bigelow. He described it as a fusion of artistry and science, and the elegance of the locomotive seemed to perfectly embody that idea. The merchant princes of Philadelphia and Baltimore viewed the trains not as art but as tools of commerce, while military tacticians saw them as hammers for westward expansion and Indian removal.

But within fifty years railroad companies would be pilloried for their greed, and the locomotive would assume popular Thoreauvian comparisons to the devil. And in the twentieth century, the chief heroine of Ayn Rand's novel of fierce individualism, *Atlas Shrugged*, is Dagny Taggart, the vice president of a transcontinental railroad, and the novel's famous original cover was of a train barreling down on the reader. This was anachronistic, because after World War II trains had turned into popular symbols of postindustrial backwardness and floundering socialism, which is roughly where they reside today.

Therefore this irony: born in a bare-knuckle era of laissez-faire capitalism, the train is now seen—especially by conservative intellectuals—as a creeping menace designed to exert tyrannical control.

George F. Will in a column entitled "Why Liberals Love Trains" wrote, "Forever seeking Archimedean levers for prying the world in the directions they prefer, progressives say they embrace high-speed rail for many reasons—to improve the climate, increase competitiveness, enhance national security, reduce congestion and rationalize land use." But the plot behind trains, says Will, has to do with "diminishing Americans' individualism in order to make them more amenable to collectivism."

This is all nonsense, argues Glenn Bottoms, who has a somewhat lonely role as the head of the American Conservative Center for Public Transportation, which might seem a contradiction in terms, but he explained his own belief that infrastructure is the starting point for building a robust economy.

"The Republican Party has been taken over by ideologues, and they have this litmus test on spending that doesn't make sense," he told me. "The Tea Party has a point that spending is out of control, but the idea that the federal government has to get rid of *every single project* is kind of mindless. Trains give people an alternative, and they foster economic development. They will reduce our dependence on foreign oil. They provide an economic spark to neighborhoods, which bolsters conservative values like strong families. If we let all our institutions go to hell, we won't have an economy to preserve. It's common sense."

But is it? In Barcelona I went to go talk with Joan Trullén Thomas, who sees this liberal-versus-conservative train argument from a completely different perspective.

Trullén was the secretary of industry during the first government of Prime Minister José Luis Rodríguez Zapatero and is now a professor of applied economics at the Autonomous University of Barcelona. Framed on the wall of his glassy office were abstract geometric squiggles. He was dressed in black, with rimless glasses, and wore a chronometer the size of an apricot on his wrist. Although he had the bearing of a diplomat, his style was more like that of a racing cyclist.

Trullén had been a supporter of the AVE and had argued that the external benefits would increase the quality of urban life in Spain in ways that go far beyond a straight economic calculus. He drew for me on a piece of typing paper the very same conceptual drawing, oddly enough, that Germa Bel had described: Madrid in the center, with linear rays emanating to Zaragoza, Badajoz, Valencia, Barcelona and other regional centers. (All Spanish thinkers, it seems, have to master this cocktail-napkin map of their country.)

"This is like a bicycle wheel," he told me. "If there are no strong spokes, the economy collapses. And this is not a zero-sum game. It is an increase of wealth. We are turning places into 'open cities.' This can't create an economy out of nothing. But it can enhance an existing economy."

One universal rule of the high-speed-train era is that the sweet spot for revenue is in journeys between two hundred and six hundred miles. Expressed in time, that's between one and three hours—about what it would take to get from Chicago to Minneapolis or London to Manchester. From the customers' perspective, any time shorter than an hour feels like a waste of resources and sitting on a train longer than three hours strains the patience. There are deep psychological factors at work in this equation.

The Italian physicist Cesare Marchetti has documented a "cave instinct" throughout world cultures that seems to limit the amount of time people are willing to spend roaming away from their homes at just over one hour. In premodern times, this meant that a person on foot could cover about seven square miles looking for food and making alliances with neighbors. Today that means that a dual-income family with jobs in downtown Chicago would consider buying a home in Naperville but no farther out.

Marchetti's constant helped determine the size of ancient cities— Rome, Venice and Persepolis had city walls that were no more than five kilometers apart, about the distance a person could cross in an hour by walking leisurely. Later studies cited by urban-design expert Peter Newman show that the circumference of British cities conformed to this rule through six hundred years of history. These borders expanded only in the mid–nineteenth century, when the advent of the railroad made it possible for people to live farther out but still get to work within one hour. Writing in 1994 of European businessmen who flew to meetings without staying overnight, Marchetti said, "They take the plane because it permits them to come back at night to sleep in their beloved cave, with family, cultural, and status symbols in place."

Our sense of comfort with new technologies has its own time borders. They adapt to our hidden desires as if by magic. Symphonies last about an hour, movies for two hours, a popular song for about three minutes, a television comedy for a half hour, a mystery novel around eighty thousand words. Daily commutes, as we have seen, are about an hour. A one-day business-trip commute might conceivably last up to three hours, about equal to the cab and flight time of the New York–Washington shuttle. It is also, not coincidentally, how long it now takes the AVE to get from Barcelona to Madrid.

In Trullén's view, one hour is the critical slice of time that will set the boundaries of a twenty-first-century city. He described for me, in lavish terms, the archipelago of bedroom communities that could surround a major city such as Barcelona—like colorful planets in orbit around a star. Between each village was plenty of open green space and forest, and all were about an hour (or two hundred rail miles) from the primary city core.

"High-speed rail is the condition to build a polycentric region," he said. "You use these links to create natural places for cities. This is not American-style growth."

He was referring to the heedless spread of motel towns and car-dealer promenades outside most American cities that create massive traffic snarls and have ever since the end of the Second World War, to the frustration of state governments who keep issuing bonds for new overpasses and highways that never seem to make the problem go away.

Transportation analysts like to talk about a concept called "latent demand," which explains why building highways generally does not relieve congestion. A new road only encourages more people to drive, people who would otherwise be seeking out alternative modes of travel or not traveling at all. A movement called New Urbanism calls for an enforced return to the walkable "human-scale" villages full of store-front retail—usually clustered around rail depots—that used to be common in the United States before the 1920s. Its backers call for zoning codes and tax spending that would stimulate small boutiques to open around high-speed rail stations instead of in highway strip malls.

As it turns out, Barcelona had an experience with something quite similar to this in the nineteenth century. Ildefons Cerdà was hired to design new gridded neighborhoods to extend the city's reach beyond the alleyway maze of what is now called the Gothic Quarter when medieval defensive walls were torn down in 1860. An extension called the Eixample was built with the edges of the corner buildings shaved off so that intersections became like octagons, all the better to enable railroad carriages to make easier turns. Motion was a part of the expectation. "Man is, man moves: that is all there is," Cerdà wrote. "And these two elements, as one would expect, have in the city the two corresponding means or instruments for their practice." The Eixample became fashionable and is now as much a part of Barcelona's civic identity as is Manhattan's grid of streets and avenues above Fourteenth Street.

"Cerdà was the first person to see that the railroad should be used to create new forms of life," Trullén told me. "He saw that the railroad could make city life look like country life. These ideas are still relevant. We are still having debates about the ways that cities organize themselves around the railroad. An archipelago of cities connected by high-speed rail can function as *one* city."

I wondered as I left Trullén's office and got back on the commuter train for Barcelona whether this "train archipelago" could ever work in the United States. The conversation had made me remember a monstrous city of ten thousand baked-tile homes far out in the desert an hour north of Phoenix, a master-planned place called Anthem at the base of some dead volcanic peaks and linked to the outside world by no roads except Interstate 17.

Like most of the way Arizona lives—like most of the way America lives—the place was made possible by cheap gas. Foreclosures near the end of the decade had hit Anthem harder than almost any other place in the nation; rising fuel prices had made it undesirable. But what if it had been connected instead by a high-speed train, the same way that the tidy commuter villages on the north shore of Lake Michigan or up in Westchester County, New York, were created by railroads in the latter part of the nineteenth century? Would Anthem be more durable to oil shocks? Less physically ugly? Could America ever again build a town like Ridgewood, New Jersey, where storefronts and parks are within a five-minute walk of the station?

Urban planners like to use the word "seamless" when talking about this problem. The train is by its very nature an inflexible machine—it goes only from point A to point B. Once you get to B, there has to be a way to move onward to the next place you're going. This is why beetroot stations didn't work in France or Spain, and they wouldn't work here. The station should ideally be in the middle of an existing city core and with lots of pedestrian-themed businesses around it, as well as connections to a city subway or a regional commuter train.

There would be little point, as one architect told me, of speeding to a city on a fast train only to have to wait for a slow bus. And so any investment in high-speed trains has to be linked to more money for local bus and light rail. And also—believe it or not—airports.

One intriguing by-product of the AVE service, noted by authors John D. Kasarda and Greg Lindsay, is how it unlocked a demand for international air travel even as it destroyed the domestic market. Madrid's airport *expanded* in size and volume because of the AVE, because it was now easier for passengers to get to the airport without the burden of a car. Barcelona's long-distance traffic went up by a factor of two.

Here is another defining fact about the train that makes it both incredibly useful and incredibly inconvenient at the same time: the train does not belong to you. You don't have to worry about keeping the tank full of gas or fixing its valve seals. You don't have to worry about parking it on the street. All you do is pay for your ticket and get on. You can even drink a beer or fall asleep. But again, it isn't yours. The train is running on somebody else's schedule and going along a route bounded by steel. You are always in a passive role. You can't get on the train at

3:00 A.M. or take it to Plano, Texas, on a whim. You can't even take it
to the mall.

An independent streak in the American character hates the idea of
being told what to do and when to do it. That is exactly the surrender
expected when you buy a ticket and take a seat. Even worse: regional
commuter trains and the lumbering Goliath of Amtrak are run by
bureaucrats and are poorly equipped to handle complaints. Yet American visitors to Europe often come back wondering why those nations
have seemingly ubiquitous trains that take you anywhere you want to
go—even internationally—and for only a few euros.

The reasons for Europe's rail superiority* date to the aftermath of
the Second World War. The tracks had seen heavy shelling. Flush with
money from the Marshall Plan, the continental governments put an
emphasis on railroad repair as a means of getting people back to work—
a European New Deal of the 1940s. Monopolies like Deutsche Bahn in
Germany and SCNF in France were able to make command decisions
with generous subsidies, whereas in the United States the political
emphasis (and the federal stimulus money) went toward building the
Interstate Highway System.

American railroads were never nationalized during the war, and
they also suffered the perverse disadvantage of never seeing their tracks
bombed. They were free to run as private businesses within a nation
joyfully embracing the car and the diesel truck. Rates of car ownership
weren't nearly as high in Europe, where transporting the masses was
given primary attention. Breaking apart European railroad ministries—
with all their political muscle—today would be extremely difficult, if
not impossible, even though car ownership is now roughly on a par in
Western Europe and the United States. So the superior rail infrastructure of Europe lives on an antebellum legacy, both in mass psychology
and as a physical reality.

---

* For passengers and not freight, in which European performance tends to be dismal.

By contrast, America was turning its back on the passenger train and making it an antique by the 1950s, at about the same time that a remarkable technological advance was being made in Japan.

The Shinkansen trains that now crisscross Japan had been the late-life vision of a bureaucrat named Shinji Sogō, whom his employees called "Old Man Thunder" for his habit of yelling at them when things didn't go his way.

At the age of seventy-one, Sogō was settling into the retirement that he had craved. Before World War II, he had followed the orders of his employer, Japan National Railways, to build and operate a coal-hauling road in occupied Manchuria. His reputation as a hard taskmaster had followed him, though, and after he suffered a stroke and left his mid-level job in 1954, he was asked to come back and steer the agency through a difficult period. Japan was facing a crossroads; its rail system was aging, and a new four-lane expressway was being built between Tokyo and Osaka. Car manufacturers were gearing back up from the bomb damage they had suffered in the war, and the nation seemed ready to take a direction similar to the one being taken in the United States—the gradual retirement of its tracks.

Sogō accepted the job, but his bosses had misjudged him. He was one of the old-line JNR men with an obsessive faith in the rails. He hired a talented engineer named Hideo Shima, who convinced him that a light-weight electric train could function at top speeds. Sogō thought this was the right tool to reinvigorate the corridor between Tokyo and Osaka, pro-saically called *shinkansen*, which means "main trunk line." But a whole new set of tracks would have to be built, with concrete ties and an overhead bundle of wires that would feed power to the train through a folding contact device called a pantograph. A centralized train control system in Tokyo would remove almost every decision from the driver. No locomotive either—power would be routed directly to each wheel. The key to speed was the straightest track possible—there could be zero road crossings.

Sogō worked like a man ablaze. To his accountants he was a bully ("When he was angry, he roared like a lion," remembered a secretary), and to politicians he became a garrulous annoyance, practicing the passive-aggressive art of what is called *youchi asagake*, calling on important people at their homes early in the morning and late at night when they had no other excuse not to listen. The customs of Japan required that they give the old director their ears and accept the pamphlets he pressed upon them. "Transportation will lead the economy, not follow it," he liked to say.

What really sold the project, however, was flat-out deception. Sogō deliberately misled his superiors about the actual cost of the project. This was an act that required "the chutzpah of a robber baron," according to his biographer, Bill Hosokawa, for he knew that the cost would be well over $1 billion but his reports consistently promised less. His tireless lobbying had paid off by this point, and the Japanese parliament began to accept the project as inevitable. Sogō pushed the fattened budget a little lower by calling his carriage contractor and bluntly demanding a 10 percent discount; the chairman later confessed he thought Sogō a "terrible man" but expressed gratitude for the opportunity to sell his train sets overseas.

Old Man Thunder was appointed for a second term as director, which was nearly unheard of, as tradition dictated that the man in this position was obliged to resign in apology after train crashes. The World Bank took an interest in his project and granted a loan big enough to cover the land acquisition and train procurement. Sogō was there to swing the hoe at the ceremonial ground breaking, though not at the opening on October 1, 1964, presided over by Emperor Hirohito. By that point the gigantic budget shortfall had been discovered, and Sogō was eased out quietly. In his good-bye speech, he read a haiku he had composed. *Spring thunder / rolling along / twenty thousand rail road lines.* His successor called the train a "spoiled baby" as he took over JNR and prepared to smother the project.

But the train proved an astonishing success with the public. Journalists fell in love with the hypermodern fuselage that covered the distance between two of Japan's major cities in less than two hours, the near-silent running of the wheels, the "bullet-shaped nose under a rakishly slanted windshield," in Hosogawa's words, so much like an airliner and seemingly just as fleet. The term "bullet train" gained popularity. Photos and films of it zipping past Mount Fuji were circulated all over the world. The train had become, like the 1964 Summer Olympics, a symbol of the New Japan, free of the dark stain of militarism and defeat.

Today the Shinkansen runs as frequently as a subway, about three hundred trains per day between all major cities, and the ticket cost is typically about two-thirds that of an airline ticket. The average delay in arrival is about ten seconds. No crash fatalities have ever been recorded, and the only person who ever died on one got caught in the sliding doors.

The next nation to try high-speed rail also enjoyed the benefit of a state authority that could afford huge overhead costs in pursuit of a long-range vision. SCNF, the French national railway, started investigating high-speed technology in the early 1960s after it became clear, in an era of highway building and cheap cars, that citizens would be abandoning the rails forever unless they could be enticed to stay. The oil shocks of the early 1970s also convinced SCNF to abandon a prototype that blasted itself across the countryside on gas turbines—basically a jet aircraft on rails—and switched to the Japanese-style electric model. The Train à Grande Vitesse service made its debut in 1981 between Paris and Lyon, running on a combination of regular tracks and high-speed corridors. The service paid for itself within a decade; SCNF president Louis Gallois called it, without exaggeration, "the train that saved French railways." Today just 9 percent of domestic intercity travel in France is done by airlines; the rails handle slightly over half the traffic, with the remainder using highways.

Russia is now operating trains capable of speeds of 220 miles per hour between Moscow and St. Petersburg. The line was built by the German company Siemens at a cost of approximately $1 billion and was named the *Sapsan* by the government of Vladimir Putin, "sapsan" being the word for a breed of peregrine falcon. The line is intended for business and elite passengers. "The Russians are very proud of themselves," the Siemens project manager David John told me over breakfast at Moscow's Metropol Hotel. "But the reality is, they hinder themselves with all these regulations. There were certain mentality issues that had to be overcome. But at the end of it, they appreciated us."

America's own best try was an expensive disappointment. In 1996 Amtrak announced it would be spending $661 million for what it called the *Acela*,* which would travel between Boston and Washington, D.C., at 150 miles per hour. But strict federal design standards caused the train to be built twice as heavy as its European counterparts. French Canadian engineers at the carriage plant in Barre, Vermont, nicknamed it *le cochon*, "the pig," while a frustrated Amtrak official called it "a high-velocity bank vault."

The design had other problems: motor failures, broken bolts, feeble brakes. A tilting mechanism intended to prevent rocking did not work correctly after Amtrak officials added four inches to the width of the carriage. If the tilt failed when two trains were passing at balls-out speed, trains could brush against each other and cause a spectacular wreck. And there were curving sections on the tracks, which had been laid in an era of gunpowder and bowler hats. Add all the degrees of the curves between New York and Boston, for example, and you get something like five complete circles.

The speed restrictions make *Acela* less than pulse-pounding. Only on an eighteen-mile straightaway near the Rhode Island border does the train achieve maximum velocity, and only on a good day. High-speed

---

* Like Amtrak's own name, a mash-up of two words, in this case "acceleration" and "excellence."

trains cannot run* at top speed on almost any of the track between New York and Washington, and Amtrak didn't have the billions of dollars it would take to lay down the kind of exclusive concrete corridor that would be free of lumbering freight trains, grade crossings and other such nuisances. So average total speeds on the *Acela* are sixty-eight miles per hour, which is about what the cars are doing on the neighboring New Jersey Turnpike.

This also happens to be slightly below the average speed of the old coal-powered *20th Century Limited* between New York and Chicago in the 1920s, which had a much better on-time performance. Historians call this sort of thing "technological regress"—which is when perfectly good ways of building or making things are discarded or forgotten.

The science fiction authors of the past could not have known that the real advances of the early twenty-first century would be in tiny things— microchips and genetics—and not into big, powerful ships. Yesterday's fantasies of tomorrow had a distinct fetish for transportation.

In H. G. Wells's *War of the Worlds*, the Martians use landing craft that look like giant stools. An omnipresent character in *Star Trek* was the USS *Enterprise* herself, and even the weak cartoon show *The Jetsons* spent loving care on schlumpy George Jetson and his commute to work in an airborne plane-saucer. Before we learn that the *Millennium Falcon* did the Kessel Run in twelve parsecs—in fact, before a single line of dialogue is spoken in *Star Wars*, we are treated to a shot of the underside of a moving star destroyer. Donald Fagen satirized this urge for utopian motion in his 1982 song "I.G.Y.": *On that train all graphite and glitter, / Undersea by rail. / Ninety minutes from New York to Paris.*† Fantasies of interplanetary life are always centered on vessels we'll need to get there.

---

* As a general rule, it takes a high-speed train about 2.5 miles to navigate a right-angle turn.
† Slightly less than the time it now takes to get from London to Paris, undersea by rail.

Walt Disney understood this and made sure the Mark II monorail was threaded through Tomorrowland.

The future—and its annuities—was at the heart of the 2010 U.S. High Speed Rail Association's conference at the Hilton on Destination Drive in Orlando, Florida (thirteen miles from Walt Disney World). This gathering was a potential feed sack for the dozens of consultants and contractors prowling the carpet outside the speakers' hall. Within a few weeks of the president's announcement of the $8 billion commitment to high-speed rail, the number of lobbyists for the industry had shot up three times. In its own way, it was like the frenzied speculation of the 1830s, when investors could get rich off railroads even if no train ever materialized.

The unofficial celebrity of the event was Nazih Haddad, the chief operating officer of the Florida High Speed Rail Authority, which had been formed to dispense the federal money.

Florida was the ideal place for the nation's first bullet train, he said. The Orlando-to-Tampa route already had a ready-made "envelope" of Interstate 4, a table-flat landscape with no bridges or tunnels needed. There were plenty of tourists who would ride it to Disney World, and the state's retired population was old enough to remember the days when trains were king. A bonus: all the environmental permits were in place, because Florida voters had already approved the project during flusher times back in 2000. Governor Jeb Bush killed the plan four years later, citing worries about cost overruns. But the Obama administration was giving it a $1.25 billion grant of stimulus money, bringing it back from the dead, and Haddad laid out the authority's hope of creating the hourlong Tampa link as the prelude to a southward connection to Miami, creating a boomerang-shaped corridor by 2020.

The ambition of this route—even the improbability of it—made me think of Henry Flagler, an old partner of John D. Rockefeller, who had retired to Florida but couldn't quell his passion for making money and turned the sleepy Florida East Coast Railroad into a juggernaut in the 1890s. Flagler used the railroad to turn town after town into beach-front resorts. His greatest civic creation was Miami, an obscure trading post in the sawgrass that he endowed with hospitals, churches and the five-story Royal Palm Hotel. But then he became fixated on building a railroad to, of all places, the tip of the Florida Keys in order to take advantage of Panama Canal shipping. "It is perfectly simple," he reassured a skeptic. "All you have to do is build one concrete arch and then another, and pretty soon you will find yourself in Key West."

And so he did. Eight Mississippi River paddle wheelers were hired as mobile bases for the equipment; metal barges served as mixing stations; flatboats served as floating dormitories; and the whole fleet was a clanging, cursing, coal-belching swarm as it inched forward toward Key West, methodically connecting islands with the arched bridges until the first trains ran on January 12, 1912. But the 1935 Labor Day hurricane wiped out large sections of the track. Key West resident Ernest Hemingway—he called his adopted town "the St. Tropez of the poor"—went out to look at the mangled bodies and the damage to Flagler's railroad. "The railroad embankment was gone and the men who had cowered behind it and finally, when the water came, clung to the rails, were all gone with it," he wrote. The Florida Department of Roads bought the right-of-way and used it as a path to build U.S. 1, which hopscotches between the sand barrier islands and the coral reefs in a rebuke to nature, just as Flagler's express across the water had ensured that the eccentric port of Key West would always be hugged to Florida.

This proposed high-speed-rail boomerang seemed like a newer kind of Sunshine State audacity, only one that would be paid for by the taxpayers instead of by a vainglorious billionaire. The state bureaucrat Nazih Haddad had barely made it down from the dais before I saw him mobbed with people in suits trying to shove business cards into his hand. This wasn't because of his brilliant oratory. He is the man who has oversight of the bidding process in which consortiums get contracts.

"They smell blood in the water," said an economic-development official from Polk County, and he himself was trying to figure out whom to lobby for a station in his town.

"The glass isn't just half full—it's overflowing," added Nathan Heisler, a railroad-supply salesman from Kansas. "There's a lot of money to be made here." For the first time in American history, high-speed rail seemed like a real possibility. But within the year something unexpected happened.

Three of the four eligible states elected Republican governors on a wave of Tea Party enthusiasm. Wisconsin was supposed to receive $810 million to start the connection between the premier cities of Milwaukee and Madison and lay the grounds for an eventual Chicago-to-Minneapolis link. The Democratic governor, Jim Doyle, was a big supporter, and Talgo already operated a factory there. But Scott Walker was elected governor in 2010 with Tea Party backing and immediately delivered on a promise to return the Obama grant. "It's great news that Wisconsin taxpayers won't be fleeced for many decades to come by paying for a liberal pipe-dream in high-speed rail," enthused State Representative Steve Nass. "Unfortunately, the $810 million will now be wasted on high-speed boondoggles in other states."

Not as many as he thought. Ohio planners had talked for years of a "3C's" route to parallel the heavily used highway spine between Cleveland, Columbus and Cincinnati, and labor unions saw it as a golden jobs creator, but Governor John Kasich had promised it would be "dead" if he got elected, and he delivered on the threat. And so did Governor Rick Scott of Florida, who wrote in a letter to the U.S. Department of Transportation, "Put simply, the proposed high-speed rail line is far too uncertain and offers far too little long-term benefit for me to consider moving forward."

That left California as the sole beneficiary of the federal bequest and the only state in the country that seemed willing to gamble on a train in the midst of a recession.

I was beginning to get used to the time-bending speed of the AVE, and I could understand how regular riders would become blasé. The novelty of going faster than a horse eventually wore away for the early Victorians, and looking down on cornfields from a height of thirty-six thousand feet is a matter of boredom for most business travelers.

The people across the aisle told me they rode the Madrid train frequently and used it to get work done. They were writers for a television soap opera called *Ventdelplà*, whose title is a Catalan word for "wind across the plain" and told the turbulent story of a small-town veterinarian and her many loves. Jordi was a thirtyish man with an owlish face and square glasses. "This is an improvement of the kinds of trains we had before," he said dryly. The difference between the AVE and the wretched Spanish trains of his youth was nothing short of astonishing.

He was sitting in a modular seat next to a lithe woman about his age, in jeans and a woolen sweater. She looked up from her book and smiled at me. Her name was Anaïs, one of Jordi's writing colleagues on the show. She had chocolate-colored hair and passionate opinions about how the AVE was just as much an ideological tool as it was a glamorous way to do business travel.

"This is a very nice train, of course," she said. "I cannot deny that. But it cost an amazing amount of money. We are overtaxed in Barcelona already, and this was done without regard to how we feel about it. There are a lot of politicians who got rich. And corruption, of course."

They were headed off to a hacienda outside Madrid to shut themselves away and get at least three episodes on *Ventdelplà* written. Anaïs talked to me about writing as the vineyards and the highways bulleted past. Her English was excellent and even slightly antiquated—she used the word "truculent" to describe someone who was angry at her—with impressively few mistakes, and even those charmed me. At one point I mentioned that my birthday had been the day before. I'd spent it in the company of friends in Barcelona.

"Are you married?" she asked.

"No," I said.

"So you are a spinster, then?"

I laughed. "The male equivalent is 'bachelor.'"

She smiled and looked away, a little embarrassed. "I am single, too."

That came as a surprise. I had first assumed she and Jordi were more than colleagues, but I can misread situations with the best of them. She put a finger in her place in the book, then closed it entirely.

Before much longer, the hum of the electricity started to falter and the placement of the houses on the side of the tracks grew thicker, and sunny yellow slopes rose around us. We were coming into Madrid's Atocha station. The trip was 324 miles long, and it had taken two hours and forty-five minutes. And it seemed much shorter.

Jordi and Anaïs and I walked down the platform together. They had a hired car waiting at the curb outside the station to take them to their retreat, and I reluctantly told them good-bye as other passengers bustled and streamed around us. Another train friendship ended as quickly as it had started.

Anaïs hung behind for a minute. "Here is my card," she said, and then asked for my e-mail address. "We should get together for a drink before you leave Spain," she told me. I wrote it down for her, as my insides pleasantly turned over in that familiar anticipatory roll, the one first felt in early adolescence.

A train. A stranger. A random meeting. How many times in history? This was wholly unoriginal. And it was not the woman I had first seen across the aisle in the Pennsylvania snowstorm. But it felt right.

"See you soon," Anaïs called over her shoulder, smiling, and I walked happily into the waiting room of Atocha station, an old red palace of a terminal built in 1851, which had been reconstructed with a sparkling glass roof and a grove of palm trees at the center and what felt like misty tropical clouds gathering in the air. An architectural critic had said this renovation evoked "the imperial grandeur of a modern-day Persepolis."

Perhaps I was still glowing from the exchange I'd just had, but the atmosphere of the room made me think of a Portuguese word that I'd once read about: *jeito*, which means a heavy object that is given an improbable lightness, a free-flowinginess. Sunlight poured down from the skylights. A crowd of passengers mingled near the AVE gates, waiting for high-speed departures to Barcelona and Seville. There was also an easy connection to the underground metro, but the Plaza del Emperador Carlos V was right outside the front doors, the very doorstop of Madrid.

I walked out into the city and thought once again, *Why not in America?*

Only a few dozen hard-core advocates showed up for the U.S. High Speed Rail Association's conference in May 2012, which took place in a donated studio above San Francisco's Market Street. There were a lot of empty chairs and a noticeable lack of the contractors who had so aggressively made their presence known in Florida. The bonanza seemed to have come to an end, and a defensive mood permeated the room.

The news was not good. The California Senate was faltering on a proposal to take on another $2.6 billion in debt to pay for the first phase of construction in the Central Valley, and there were many question marks about where the rest of the money would come from—especially in a state with crumbling public schools and deteriorating highways. If this bill failed, it was the probable tombstone for high-speed rail in America.

The head of the Mineta Transportation Institute, Rod Diridon, urged the audience to go out and lobby a California politician immediately, and his arguments veered toward the apocalyptic. He asked everyone to consider a future of a sun-baked earth wrecked by climate change and a child asking a question: " 'Grandpa, what did you do to protect us? Did you think that trains would be part of the solution?' Or, 'Grandpa, mammals are dying off, and food is hard to grow.' "

Diridon then looked out into the audience. "Are you going to be good ancestors?" he demanded.

The environmental argument is a favorite among high-speed-train backers, even though they do not mention that powering the California project would require about 2.7 million kilowatt hours of electricity each day, which would require about six hours of work for a large coal-fired plant. But it is still vastly kinder to the atmosphere than automobiles. One trainload of passengers equals about a hundred city blocks of cars. The figures are even more attractive when compared to airplanes. A high-speed train would produce about one-tenth of the carbon dioxide emissions created by a flight to the same destination and doesn't dump Jet A exhaust directly into the upper troposphere.

If the Spanish example is any guide, the airlines and not private cars would be the main economic competitor to a high-speed train. Journeys such as those between San Francisco and Los Angeles—known as "short-haul routes"—are exactly where the airlines are at their most wasteful. No matter if the plane is going fifty miles or around the world, there are fixed costs that must be paid: maintenance, labor, bag loading, taxes, landing fees and cleaning. And there is the fuel it takes to launch the jet into the air, which is the same no matter what the destination. Planes typically burn the bulk of their petroleum during takeoff and landing; a comparatively smaller amount is consumed once they are at cruising altitude. Even for all the inefficiency, short haul is still the sine qua non of American air travel: about two-thirds of domestic flights are less than seven hundred miles long, and about 35 percent of those are less than three hundred fifty miles long. We are a continental nation, but we don't fly as if we are.

And so this question arises: in an era of declining oil reserves, does it really make sense to keep running dozens of daily scheduled flights between cities that are so close*—Chicago to Milwaukee, Phoenix to Tucson, Dallas to Houston, Portland to Seattle? Shouldn't this more properly be a job for a train?

---

* Candidates for the most absurd scheduled flight in the United States would include Detroit-Toledo, Boston-Manchester and Los Angeles–Orange County, each of which takes about twelve minutes—less time than it takes to taxi out to the runway.

Nowhere is this question more relevant than down the spine of California, where about five thousand passengers travel between Los Angeles and San Francisco each day, with still more going to and from the airports in San Diego and Oakland. The flight times are generally a little over an hour, but this is nevertheless the busiest short-haul airline corridor in the nation, served by no fewer than nine carriers.

No sane person would ever take Amtrak between L.A. and the Bay Area on anything but a leisure trip—it is a twelve-hour slog—so I had to take one of those flights to the rail conference to hear the multiple lamentations, including one from U.S. House Minority Leader Nancy Pelosi, who said that jitters about borrowed government money did not stand in the way of other big-ticket California projects. She cited the San Francisco Bay Bridge, built at the nadir of the Depression.

"I don't fully understand," she said, "why we would do something to stand in the way of a twenty-first-century economy."

A California bullet train had been the dream of futurist thinkers ever since the Shinkansen debuted, but official support was always shaky. After a spike in train ridership following the September 11 attacks, Governor Grey Davis reluctantly funded a study, but only after calling it a "Buck Rogers fantasy." His successor, Governor Arnold Schwarzenegger, was much more enthusiastic, encouraging the state's voters to tax themselves $9.95 billion in a 2008 ballot initiative to create a high-speed service with tracks in the shape of a salad fork from Los Angeles up to Sacramento and San Francisco. The new law says the train must be built to cover this distance in two hours and forty minutes. In other words, it won't be the *Acela*. It will be built right or not at all.

Schwarzenegger made repeated appeals to American exceptionalism in his drive to get the train built. "How much longer do we need to travel the same speed as we did a hundred years ago?" he said in a video made for train lobbyists. "I mean, that's *embarrassing*. I know there are some trains that go a little faster now, but it's really Mickey Mouse, let's admit it. . . . It makes me mad we don't have it in the United States. I mean, what is that? We are supposed to be the leaders, we are supposed to be the number-one country in the world!"

He was in opposition to many members of his own party, who saw the high-speed train as part of an insidious plot to rewrite the "California Dream"—to pull the state away from its post-WWII roots as a freeway-driven paradise of detached single-family ranch homes with swimming pools and *Sunset* magazine style and remake it into more of a European apartment-dwelling greenbelt where docile citizens were forced to take the train. "This is entirely social policy," Assembly member Tom McClintock told the *Los Angeles Times*. "It is all about the far left's fever dream to get Mother Earth back to a pristine condition by elbowing us into these dense urban cores."

Others objected for aesthetic reasons, noting the likely need for mammoth concrete pillars to support ninety-foot-high viaducts through downtown Bakersfield and Fresno. The effect would be similar to the elevated freeways rammed into cities in the 1960s that created urine-smelling slashes that damaged vibrant neighborhoods like Boston's North End, Brooklyn's Williamsburg and San Francisco's Embarcadero, among other places. After studying the fine print in a series of environmental-impact statements, the Train Riders' Association of California concluded that at least 40 percent of the tracks would be up on stilts. That's about twenty-two thousand concrete pillars laid in a dotted line across California. It would eliminate the need for most grade crossings, as local roads could just pass under the elevated tracks. But it would have the aesthetic charm of an oil pipeline.

After President Obama made his announcement of White House support, the newly formed California High Speed Rail Authority had a huge bankroll and some difficult decisions to make. The entire thing would cost an estimated $42 billion—later revised to $68 billion—and probably so much more than that. Nervous planners wondered if the high-speed trains could share track with Union Pacific and BNSF for part of the way in order to save money. This was a particular concern inside the peninsula south of San Francisco—a tough operating area even for nineteenth-century railroads—where arriviste money and dot-com McMansions abound and the residents were known to be lawsuit happy. The authority soon called for a "blended system," which would have the train running on dedicated AVE-style tracks out in corn country but use cargo rail track close to big metro areas. The ride would be physically slower but politically easier.

The California bullet train needed to demonstrate quick progress, and the authority surprised everyone in December 2010 by announcing that the very first rails would plow through downtown Fresno on viaducts and connect the two obscure Central Valley farm towns of Borden and Corcoran. The latter place, most famous for hosting the state's super-maximum-security prison where Charles Manson and Sirhan Sirhan currently reside, actually campaigned against being one of the stops, citing worries about noise. "We would prefer that it not go through town," Mayor Raymond Lerma told the *Visalia Times-Delta*. A state assemblyman complained that taxpayers were being asked to pay for "a train to nowhere." The initial ridership estimates of 14 million people per year were also derided as fantasy.

But the authority wasn't crazy: it had deliberately picked a spot with Floridian flatness to make the sixty-five-mile construction as quick and cheap as possible, as well as bring a jobs infusion to the depressed alfalfa towns that some have called "California's Appalachia," where fewer people were likely to bring property or environmental lawsuits. (Two farm bureaus sued anyway.) This was also a way of creating "facts on the ground," similar to Israeli settlements on the West Bank, that would be difficult to contradict later on. Once even a small portion of it was built, the train would have a strong political claim for continuing streams of cash. Nobody wants to be blamed for coloring the elephant white.

The White House money depended on the state's putting up its own cash, so advocates created a $5.6 billion bond package deliberately bundled with other noncontroversial rail improvements, especially $2 billion to build overhead electrical wires for the Caltrain commuter rail that serves the peninsula. This was a sop to opponents, said Assembly member Fiona Ma. "They wanted the bond money and the electrification, and they didn't want the high-speed rail, but they voted for it anyway," she said. "We're politicians. We need political cover. Everyone thinks they're going to be recalled if they make a wrong move." Labor unions, especially the powerful State Building & Constructing Trades Council, leaned heavily on Democrats to vote for it, above the objections of budget-conscious Republicans and even some liberal Democrats who feared environmental lawsuits over the multiple wetlands and hills the tracks would have to traverse.

The vote appeared doomed. For opponents it was an arena for rehashing the historic doubts—too destructive, too expensive, a liberal social tool, destined to be obsolete on arrival anyway. "Trains and bikes are not twenty-first-century transportation," Republican assemblywoman Diane Harkey complained. But then a miracle for supporters arrived as the midnight arm-twisting by the unions paid off: the Senate passed it 21–16, and President Pro Tem Darrell Steinberg hailed "a turning point in California, a time when we decided to say yes to hope, yes to progress, yes to the future."

Governor Jerry Brown had worked the phones hard on behalf of the train, and he made a point of signing the bill inside Los Angeles' Union Station, where the first bullet train was expected to arrive in 2028. By that point a population equal to that of New York State was expected to migrate into California, and freeways could no longer bear the burden, he said. "I know there are some fearful men—I call them declinists— who want to put their head in a hole and hope reality changes," Brown said. "I don't see it that way. This is a time to invest, to create thousands of jobs." He called those standing in the way "fraidy cats." California leads the nation in courageous big thinking, he said—like aqueducts and bridges and first-class universities—and this train was no different.

The authority still couldn't answer a nagging question. Completing the project was going to require at least six times the available cash, and every single mile was going to cost at least $190 million, which would run two public high schools for a year. Where was the money supposed to come from? "I wouldn't be surprised if the costs double again, and that's not a reckless estimate," said Martin Wachs, a transportation expert from the RAND Corporation. "It will probably die of its own weight." A revised business plan, created under pressure from the legislature, called for "investments of capital from the private sector" in the construction, without providing specifics. Authority head Jeff Morales has said the project will be actively courting the overseas-state investment pools called sovereign wealth funds, which means an oil-rich Middle Eastern state might have a large stake in America's first real high-speed train. Others have suggested that a revenue stream might come from leasing condemned land to create mini-mall villages at the new stations.* A firm plan was years away, even as the first construction contracts were bid out and ground was broken.

Brown reached into American historical romance for an explanation. "When Abraham Lincoln, in the middle of the Civil War, started the intercontinental railroad, he didn't know where the money was coming from."

His comparison was effective, but less than elegant. Lincoln knew the money would come from the sale of Indian lands, and the financing of the Union Pacific turned out to have been one of the most corrupt public-private adventures of the history of the U.S. Congress, involving a shell corporation, wild spending and stock kickbacks to more than thirty elected officials.

But the tracks did get laid.

The most expensive segment will be over the crest of the Tehachapi Mountains. I went to drive that section armed with an engineering map of where the tracks were expected to go (but not *too* precise: rail officials

* A scheme that recalled the gifts of former Indian land to the Illinois Central and other large western railroads in the middle of the nineteenth century.

kept secret the actual land they want to purchase, lest somebody try to make a play).

Bakersfield is an oil-patch city in the midst of corporate farms, one of the largest cities in America to lack an interstate highway. But it is a station stop for the bullet train, whose tracks will follow Truxtun Avenue on the way south out of town, passing a freight yard and a shambling wreck of a Southern Pacific depot, built here in 1874 out of spite. The SP had asked for a deed of two downtown blocks, but Bakersfield's town council agreed to only one. The railroad then built itself a competing town called Sumner, which has since withered. But these old tracks—the souvenir of another century's arrogance—now determine the route of the high-speed rail south of Bakersfield. The new electrified rails will parallel the existing tracks, and lumbering freight trains are going to get passed by a blue-and-yellow projectile going 220 miles per hour up on Chinese-style concrete viaducts.

I drove alongside this grubby rail corridor out of town, past sun-weathered homes, tank-fabrication plants, an RV resort, a shallow canal, dingy apartment blocks with stairs like insect vertebrae, a business called Born Again Auto Works, the occasional palm tree sticking proudly upward as a reminder that this, after all, is California. Then the dwellings peter away and the train will emerge onto the potato fields and the grape arbors for ten miles before encountering the first escarpment of the mountains, their leather-colored folds dotted with chaparral and looking threatening. From a distance, they looked like sand dunes in an Arabian hallucination.

The Tehachapi range was always a natural barrier between the two halves of California. And these mountains were a formidable challenge to the Southern Pacific in 1874. There was no other logical entrance to the Los Angeles Basin, but the northern slopes were far too steep to run ordinary track. So the SP's chief engineer, William Hood, devised an ingenious solution. Trains made a horseshoe turn to the left and then executed a perfect pi-ratio curve to the right,* passed over a bridge and then curved left again in an exit horseshoe: a 580-degree spin in a perfect circle that left the train seventy-seven feet higher as a result. It must be seen to be believed.

Chinese laborers were brought in to do the shoveling. The "Tehachapi Loop" was regarded as an engineering marvel of its day, and it still gets heavy use. About seventeen Union Pacific and BNSF trains still pass through it daily, as this is the main freight line between the Intermodal Container Transfer Facility near the port at San Pedro and the J. R. Davis Yard in Roseville. The high-speed-rail line will pass within a mile of it, on the other side of Highway 58.

The elevation isn't far above sea level here, only twenty-six hundred feet, but the high-speed rail faces exactly the same Tehachapi problem as Hood faced in 1874. Even a high-speed train cannot ascend a slope with a grade much steeper than 4 percent, and the gentle rises and easy curves required by an electric bullet are in many ways a genetic inheritance from its ancestor, the steam train. Laying slab track up to the summit was going to be phenomenally costly.

"There's going to be lots of bridges and tunnels and cuts and fills," a project engineer told me. "Probably several miles of tunnels, in fact. We're going to plow through those hills." The tracks that aren't in a tunnel will likely be hanging over the hills on bridges up to three hundred feet high. "The project of the century," as a civil-engineering professor at the University of California at Berkeley called it.

I got out of my car on the shoulder of Highway 58 and looked at the foothills where the train was supposed to climb and where earthmoving equipment would one day be tearing it apart. And it occurred to me that making way for a new railroad was one essential American art form that had fallen out of favor and not been widely practiced since the presidency of Woodrow Wilson.

---

* A particularly long train's caboose might be inside the underpass while the engine was traveling directly over it, a serpentine effect never before seen in railroading.

Perhaps this alien idea is what separates us from our recent ancestors. The countryside—its soil, its raw physicality—has been completely divorced from our ideas about what makes a nation rich. Our economy is now far more oriented toward what is microscopic than what is large: aimed more toward digital information than at the rearrangement of actual land. Data travels instantly, coast to coast and overseas, through satellite connections and T1 cable, annihilating space more thoroughly than anything before it. Airlines glide over the forgotten knucklebones of the country, making it abstract and picturesque and nearly irrelevant.

But the train would always be different. The train had to have an intimate relationship with land, because it was anchored to the land and has depended on it since 1825, even as it reshaped the world into its own peculiar geography that we live in today, a Train Sublime writ large.

This chaparral valley did seem to provide a gentle approach to the pass if the platform was level and continuous. As Henry Flagler might have said, you just put in one pillar after another until you reach the top. From this plateau it would be an easy descent to the town of Mojave and then on to Los Angeles, a steel bridge clicked in place that could unite California.

Once envisioned, the conclusion was hard to ignore. How many others had stood at this prospect thinking the same thing that I was?

Yes, this would be a good place for a railroad.

ACKNOWLEDGMENTS

I am grateful to many people not already named in these pages for their support on the rails and at home while this book was being written. This is only a partial list: Greg Cullison, Dick Eisfeller, Gus Melonas, Don Pease, Kim Libby, Jan Moorlag, Bob Etter, Michael Downs, Trevor Horner, Jane Brown, Katy Lederer, Gabrielle Giffords, Jim Runde, Emily Curtis, Shagun Mehrotra, Kate Krauss, Carol Raulston, John Wetzel, Juliet Eilperin, Jonathan Lowet, Joshua Coran, Lisa Zhang, Steve Apkon, Rachel Wall, Emma Reichert, Henry Posner III, Richard Bausch, Charles Bohi, Mary Tolan, Mercé Baida, Lyndsay Duncombe, Sarah Gouldsbrough, Leona White, John Bromley, Mark Magliari, Beth Skinner, Annette Pollert, Ann Walter, Ilanna Bavli, Ken Winkenwader, Grady Gammage, Greg Lindsay, Terry Hermsen, Doug Merlino, Joanna Levin, Anna Leahy and Crystal Murphy. A special mention to Gail and Ivyl Kenning. Marc Herman supplied perceptive insights and enthusiasm; he and his wife, Nuria, were also gracious hosts to me in Spain. Brad Tyer, H. Roger Grant, Monica Rico, Sugi Ganeshanathan, Ellen Ruark and Shannon Craigo-Snell read early portions and made invaluable suggestions. Brettne Bloom was my literary agent and persistent champion. Kathryn Court and Allison Lorentzen believed in this project from the start and edited the manuscript with care and expertise. The quiet heroes of the publishing business work in the production department. Kate Griggs did a wonderful job of line editing this book, Daniel Lagin designed the interior and Nick Misani designed a striking jacket. Kevin Gass traveled with me to Peru and was always a friend nonpareil. My family in Arizona was a source of constant love and support. I offer heartfelt thanks to everybody.

New York City–Los Angeles, September 2009–May 2013

NOTES

INTRODUCTION

ix **Train Sublime:** I owe inspiration for the phrase to the book *American Techno-logical Sublime*, by David Nye (Cambridge, MA: MIT Press, 1996).

x **13 trillion:** *Rail Freight: Global Industry Guide* (London: Datamonitor, 2010).

xii **"unusual spectacle":** *Scientific American*, vol. 2, no. 3, Oct. 10, 1846.

xii **"fever and ague":** *History of the Illinois Central Railroad Company and Representative Employees*, William K. Ackerman (Chicago: Railroad Historical, 1900).

xii **"fiery speed":** Quoted in *Railways of India*, J. N. Westwood (London: David and Charles, 1974).

xiii **"holy prophets":** *The Encyclopedia of North American Railroading*, by Freeman Hubbard (New York: McGraw-Hill, 1981).

xiii **"railway spine":** *The Railway Journey: The Industrialization of Time and Space in the 19th Century*, Wolfgang Schivelbusch (Berkeley: University of California Press, 1977).

xiv **envied:** "Back on Tracks," Michael Grunwald, *Time*, July 9, 2012.

xiv **never set foot:** *Waiting on a Train: The Embattled Future of Passenger Rail Service*, James McCommons (White River Junction, VT: Chelsea Green, 2009).

xx **Central Branch:** "Atchison and the Central Branch Country, 1865–1874," George L. Anderson, *Kansas Historical Quarterly*, Spring 1962.

xx **woman crying:** If this brief remembered scene could have had a sound track, it would have been the "Aquarium" movement from *Carnival of the Animals*, by Camille Saint-Saëns.

BEGINNINGS

2 **"wished to swagger":** *Among the Railway Folk*, Rudyard Kipling (New York: Doubleday & McClure, 1899).

9 **"whirl through":** Quoted in *The Power of Steam,* Asa Briggs (Chicago: University of Chicago Press, 1982).

9 **Bizarre-looking plants:** *Coal: A Human History,* Barbara Freese (New York: Penguin, 2004).

10 **temperature and time:** *Coal: Its Properties, Analysis, Classification, Geology, Extraction, Uses and Distribution,* Elwood S. Moore (New York: John Wiley & Sons, 1922).

10 **dizzying series:** *Our Coal and Our Coal-Pits and the People in Them and the Scenes Around Them,* J. R. Liefchild (London: Longman, Brown, Green, and Longmans, 1856).

11 **labyrinths underground:** *Coal,* Freese.

12 **dropped hints:** "A Case Study of Sabotage by the British Royal Society: Liebniz, Papin and the Steam Engine," Philip Valenti in *21st Century Science and Technology,* Summer 1997.

13 **"though I was obliged":** *Historical and Descriptive Anecdotes of Steam Engines and of Their Improvers and Inventors,* Robert Stuart (London: Wightman, 1829).

13 **James Watt:** This era is covered extensively in Briggs, above, as well as in *James Watt and the History of Steam Power,* Ivor Hart (New York: Henry Schuman, 1949); *A Brief History of the Age of Steam,* Thomas Crump (New York: Carroll & Graf, 2007); *James Watt and the Patent System,* A. N. Davenport (London: British Library Board, 1989); and *Rail Steam and Speed: The "Rocket" and the Birth of Steam Locomotion,* Christopher McGowan (New York: Columbia University Press, 2004).

14 **1787 map:** *Catalogue of Maps, Prints, Drawings, Etc. Forming the Geographical and Topographical Collection Attached to the Library of His Late Majesty King George the Third and Presented by His Majesty King George the Fourth* (London: Trustees of the British Museum, 1829).

14 **wooden sets of rails:** "Sketches of Our Information as to Railroads" (Newcastle, UK: Edward Walker, Pilgrim Street, 1826) quoted in *Tracts Relating to Railways, 1826–80* on file in the British Library, London.

14 **flagstones of ancient cities:** *The Museum of Science and Art,* Dionysus Lardner (London: Walton and Maberly, 1854). See also *Early Railways,* by J. B. Snell (London: Weidenfeld and Nicholson, 1964).

15 **Late-medieval miners:** *De Re Metallica,* Gerogius Agricola, Herbert Clark Hoover and Lou Hoover, trans. (repr. Whitefish, MT: Kessenger, 2003).

15 **act that would enchant:** *Lives of the Engineers,* Samuel Smiles (London: John Murray, 1904).

17 **silences could be excruciating:** *Railway Journey,* Schivelbusch.

19 **In those days:** *First in the World: The Stockton to Darlington Railway,* John Wall (London: Sutton, 2001).

20 **"concourse of spectators":** Quoted in *The Origins of Railway Enterprise: The Stockton and Darlington Railway, 1821–1863,* Maurice Kirby (Cambridge, UK: Cambridge University Press, 1993).

21 **elderly laborer:** *George and Robert Stephenson: The Railway Revolution,* L.T.C. Rolt (London: Longmans, Green).

23 **decrepit old row house:** For a firsthand account of their relationship, see *The Diaries of Edward Pease* (repr. London: Headley Bros., 1907).

24 **former metallurgist:** "Britain's Most Hated Civil Servant," Tom Geoghegan, *BBC News Magazine,* Oct. 1, 2008.

25 **regional monopolies:** *Off the Rails: The Crisis on Britain's Railways,* Andrew Murray (London: Verso, 2001).

28 **crude system:** *Red for Danger: A History of Railway Accidents and Railway Safety,* L.T.C. Rolt (London: David & Charles, 1955).

29 **vivid account:** *Fanny Kemble: A Performed Life,* Deirdre David (Philadelphia: University of Pennsylvania Press, 2007).

30 **Another disaster:** *A Biographical Study of the Father of Railways George Stephenson,* Hunter Davies (London: Weidenfeld and Nicholson, 1975). See also *Fire and Steam: How the Railways Transformed Britain,* Christian Wolmar (New York: Grove Atlantic, 2009).

31 **"Arabian Nights' vision":** *The History and Antiquities of Cleveland,* John Walker Ord (London: Simpkin and Marshall, 1848).

32 **primary task:** *The Railway Navvies: A History of the Men Who Made the Railways,* Terry Coleman (London: Pimlico, 2000).

34 **leering morality:** The *Morning Chronicle,* n.d. On file at the British Museum, London.

34 **hired chaplains:** *The Railway Navvies,* Coleman.

36 *Ye Gods!:* Quoted in *The Machine in the Garden: Technology and the Pastoral Ideal in America,* Leo Marx (Oxford, UK: Oxford University Press, 1964).

39 **visited his capital:** *Fire and Steam,* Wolmar.

39 **mysteria of churches:** *The Railway Station: A Social History,* Jeffrey Richards and John M. MacKenzie (Oxford, UK: Oxford University Press, 1986). See also *The Impact of Railways on Victorian Cities,* John R. Kellett (London: Routledge & Kegan Paul, 1969), and *The Railway Age,* Michael Robbins (London: Routledge & Kegan Paul, 1962).

41 **wrote in his diary:** *Isambard Kingdom Brunel: A Biography,* L.T.C. Rolt (London: Longmans, Green, 1957).

41 **Art Deco posters:** *Go GWR: A History of Great Western Railway Publicity,* Roger B. Wilson (Newton Abbott, UK: David and Charles, 1970).

44 **son of a mine engineer:** *Richard Trevithick: Giant of Steam,* Anthony Burton (London: Aurum Press, 2000).

44 **workshop notes:** "Papers and Correspondence relating to Richard Trevithick, c. 1771–1833," On file at the National Railway Museum, York, object 2002-8348.

45 **He got distracted:** *The Oblivion of Trevithick,* Philip M. Hosken (Camborne, UK: Trevithick Society, n.d.).

46 **Simón Bolívar:** *Brute New World: The Rediscovery of Latin America in the Nineteenth Century,* Desmond Gregory (London: British Academic Press, 1992).

46 **Broke and frustrated:** *Richard Trevithick: The Engineer and the Man,* H. W. Dickinson and Arthur Titley (Cambridge, UK: Cambridge University Press, 1934).

47 **"roast goose and proper drinks":** Ibid. This incident is well known among even casual readers of British rail history. When Prince Charles visited Camborne for a Trevithick festival, he asked Hosken, "I hear he enjoyed a pint, did he?"

THE PEOPLE, AND ALL THE PEOPLE

53 **eighth-largest:** "Which Is the World's Biggest Employer?" Ruth Alexander, BBC News, Mar. 19, 2012.

54 **seven hundred job categories:** *Exploring Indian Railways,* Bill Aitken (New Delhi: Oxford University Press, 1994).

54 **a World Bank study:** *Highway and Railway Development in India and China, 1992–2002,* Clel Harral, Jit Sondhi and Guang Zhe Chen (Washington, DC: World Bank, May 2006). See also "Encouraging Signals," S. D. Naik, in *The Hindu Business Line,* Mar. 15, 2006.

56 **brittle when pushed:** " 'Spirited' Mamata Has Sonia in Splits," *Indian Express,* Feb. 24, 2010.

57 **cultish following:** "An Unlikely Figure on the Big Stage," in *Economist,* July 29, 2006; "The New Face of Indian Railways," Arpita Agnihotri, in *IUP Journal of Business Strategy,* vol. 6, nos. 3 and 4, 2009; and "Brand Lalu Ruling Bihar Markets," from zeenews.com, June 18, 2006.

58 **took the microphone:** *Bankruptcy to Billions: How the Indian Railways Transformed,* Sudhir Kumar and Shagun Mehrotra (New Delhi: Oxford University Press, 2009).

63 **rearranging force:** *Building the Railways of the Raj,* Ian J. Kerr (Oxford, UK: Oxford University Press, 1995).

63 **spice and opium trades:** *The Decline and Fall of the British Empire, 1781–1997,* Piers Brendon (London: Jonathan Cape, 2007).

64 **his pet cause:** *Railways of the Raj,* Kerr. See also *History and Development of Railways in India,* Aruna Awasthi (New Delhi: Deep & Deep, 1994).

64 **would be private:** *Blood, Iron and Gold: How the Railroads Transformed the World,* Christian Wolmar (New York: Public Affairs, 2010).

65 **crossed with a metal bridge:** *Engines of Change: The Railroads That Made India,* Ian J. Kerr (Westport, CT: Praeger, 2007).

65 **Clouds of mist:** *Railways: Glorious 150 Years,* R. R. Bhandari (New Delhi: Ministry of Information and Broadcasting, 2005), and *Railways of the Raj,* Kerr.

66 **before it could continue:** "Fall of a Viaduct on the Great Indian Peninsular Railway," *Illustrated London News,* Sept. 21, 1867.

66 **villages in Nottingham:** *Among the Railway Folk,* Rudyard Kipling (New York: Doubleday & McClure, 1899).

67 **British bankroll:** "Railway Development in India," Daniel Thorner, *Far Eastern Quarterly,* Feb. 1955.

67 **romantic hyperbole:** "Representation and Representations of Railways of Colonial and Post-Colonial South Asia," Ian J. Kerr, in *Modern Asian Studies,* May 2003.

67 **expressed some pleasure:** Ibid.

68 **time fabric:** "The Railroad Introduces the Country to Uniform Time," Ajit Dayal, *India Abroad,* Mar. 28, 1997.

68 **"as far as Hooghly":** Ibid.

69 **"I tell you, I was permitted":** *The Essential Gandhi: An Anthology of His Writings on His Life, Work and Ideas,* Louis Fischer, ed. (New York: Random House, 1962).

70 *caused* **the famines:** *Hind Swaraj and Other Writings,* Anthony J. Parel, ed. (Cambridge, UK: Cambridge University Press, 1997).

70 **Indian dependence:** *Mahatma Gandhi and the Railways,* Y. P. Anand, ed. (Ahmedabad, India: Navajiven, 2002).

70 **grew sharper:** Ibid.

71 **mistaken prediction:** "The Future Results of British Rule in India," Karl Marx, *New-York Daily Tribune,* July 22, 1853.

71 **"set a limit":** *Mahatma Gandhi,* Anand.

72 *loved* **the railways:** Ibid.

74 **a metal pot:** "India Failing to Control Public Defecation Blunts Nation's Growth," Jason Gale of Bloomberg News Service, Mar. 4, 2009.

75 **excreta:** Ibid.

83 **effective technique:** "Thermite Welding Gets High School Chemistry Class on Track," Anthony L. Feliu, *Journal of Chemical Education,* Jan. 2001.

84 **a letter:** Quoted in *Fanny Kemble: A Performed Life,* Deirdre David (Philadelphia: University of Pennsylvania Press, 2007).

85 **bad information:** "Safety on Indian Railways: Prolonged Neglect and Warped Priorities," in *Economic and Political Weekly,* Feb. 26, 2000.

89 **dismal safety record:** "Driver Fatigue Causing Rail Accidents," Srinand Jha, *Hindustan Times,* Jan. 23, 2010. See also "Save Elephants from Speeding Trains, Says People for the Ethical Treatment of Animals," *Times* of India, July 4, 2008.

89 **crushing price:** "Overloaded and Unsafe," *Indian Express,* Nov. 16, 2009.

93 **Temples jammed:** "East Indian Railways," Frank G. Carpenter, *Boston Daily Globe,* May 29, 1910. See also "Night-Train Glimpses of India," Cameron Barr, *Christian Science Monitor,* Mar. 9, 1992; and "Sacred Benares Is Weird Place," George A. Dorsey, *Chicago Daily Tribune,* Aug. 28, 1909.

BOUND FOR GLORY

96 **a strange effect:** The original quote is in *George Gershwin: A Study in American Music,* Isaac Goldberg (New York: Frederick Ungar, 1931). See also *George Gershwin,* Rodney Greenberg (London: Phaidon, 1998), where there is some speculation that the thought was at least partly embroidered by Goldberg.

97   **American Train Sublime:** A variation on the phrase from *American Technological Sublime,* David Nye (Cambridge, MA: MIT Press, 1996).

100 **master plan:** *Conquering Gotham: A Gilded Age Epic—the Construction of Penn Station and Its Tunnels,* Jill Jonnes (New York: Viking, 2009).

100 **crowned with eagles:** *The Late, Great Pennsylvania Station,* Lorraine B. Diehl (New York: American Heritage, 1985).

110 **"more than a machine":** *American Technological Sublime,* Nye.

110 **"my eyes put out":** In Thoreau's *Walden* and also quoted in *The Machine in the Garden: Technology and the Pastoral Ideal in America,* Leo Marx (Oxford, UK: Oxford University Press, 1964).

111 **towns conjured:** *Railroad Avenue,* Freeman Hubbard (San Marino, CA: Golden West, 1945).

111 **towers and bins:** *American Towns: An Interpretive History,* David J. Russo (Chicago: Ivan R. Dee, 2001). A technological approach to the historiography of the American map can be found in *The North American Railroad: Its Origin, Evolution and Geography,* James E. Vance Jr. (Baltimore: Johns Hopkins University Press, 1995).

112 **The city fathering:** *Names Upon the Land,* George Rippey Stewart (New York: Random House, 1945). Other specific examples are in *A History of the Origin of Place Names Connected with the Chicago and North Western and Chicago, St. Paul, Minneapolis and Omaha Railways,* by an anonymous author who called himself "One Who for More Than 34 Years Has Been an Officer in the Employ of the System" (Chicago, 1908). Also illustrative was *1001 Kansas Place Names,* Sondra Van Meter McCoy and Jan Hults (Lawrence: University Press of Kansas, 1989).

113 **a relatively gentle footprint:** *Allies of the Earth: Railroads and the Soul of American Preservation,* Alfred Runte (Kirksville, MO: Truman State University Press, 2006). See also *The Great Road: The Building of the Baltimore and Ohio, the Nation's First Railroad, 1828–1853,* James D. Dilts (Palo Alto, CA: Stanford University Press, 1993).

115 **dark seams:** *Appalachia: A History,* John Alexander Williams (Chapel Hill: University of North Carolina Press, 2001).

115 **Their names were eccentric:** *Night Comes to the Cumberlands: A Biography of a Depressed Area,* Harry M. Caudill (repr. of 1962 version: Ashland, KY: Jesse Stuart Foundation, 2001).

117 **One Granger resolution:** *The Story of American Railroads,* Stewart Holbrook (New York: Crown, 1947).

117 **"War . . . is the natural state":** *Hear That Lonesome Whistle Blow,* Dee Brown (New York: Henry Holt, 1977).

118 **muscular rhythm:** "The Gandy Dancer Speaks: Voices from Southern Black Railroad Gangs," Maggie Hotzberg-Call, in *Alabama Folklife: Collected Essays* (Birmingham: Alabama Folklife Association, 1989).

123 **a Chicago tradition:** *The Railroad Tycoon Who Built Chicago: A Biography of*

William B. Ogden, Jack Harpster (Carbondale: Southern Illinois University Press, 2009).

124 **took out advertisements:** *Story of American Railroads,* Holbrook.

124 **colorful assortment:** *Railway Journey,* Schivelbusch.

125 **chain of slaughterhouses:** *Nature's Metropolis: Chicago and the Great West,* William Cronon (New York: W. W. Norton, 1992).

125 **these abattoirs:** *Chicago's Pride: The Stockyards, Packingtown and Environs in the Nineteenth Century,* Louise Carroll Wade (Urbana: University of Illinois Press, 1987).

125 **packers consolidated:** *The Iron Horse and the Windy City,* David M. Young (DeKalb, IL: Northern University Press, 2005).

126 **ten-hour shift:** *Nature's Metropolis,* Cronon.

126 **demanded fresh meat:** *Railroads Triumphant: The Growth, Rejection and Rebirth of a Vital American Force,* Albro Martin (Oxford, UK: Oxford University Press, 1992).

127 **fitted with tubes:** *The Great Yellow Fleet: A History of American Railroad Refrigerator Cars,* John H. White (San Marino, CA: Golden West, 1986). See also *How Great Cities are Fed,* W. A. Hedden (New York: D. C. Heath, 1929).

129 **thirty hours:** "Freight Train Late? Blame Chicago," John Schwartz, *New York Times,* May 7, 2012.

130 **big trunk line:** *Story of American Railroads,* Holbrook.

130 **epochal human movements:** The best study of the Great Migration is *Land of Hope: Chicago, Black Southerners and the Great Migration,* James Grossman (Chicago: University of Chicago Press, 1991).

131 **depot in Savannah:** *Black Protest and the Great Migration: A Brief History with Documents,* Eric Arnesen (Boston: Bedford/St. Martin's, 2003).

131 **came from a newspaper:** *The Lonely Warrior: The Life and Times of Robert S. Abbott,* Roi Ottley (Chicago: Henry Regnery, 1955).

131 **Sympathetic black porters:** *Selling the American Dream: The Chicago Defender and the Great Migration of 1915–1919,* Alan De Santis, a dissertation for Indiana University in the Department of Speech Communication, Sept. 1993.

132 **"hundreds of houses":** *The Chicago Race Riots, July 1919,* Carl Sandburg (Mineola, NY: Dover, 2013), a reprint of some of Sandburg's groundbreaking stories for the *Chicago Daily News.*

132 **"but the kitchen stove":** *Land of Hope,* Grossman.

133 **white fellow traveler:** Ibid.

134 **difficult home:** *The Promised Land: The Great Black Migration and How It Changed America,* Nicholas Lemann (New York: Vintage, 1992).

137 ***"where the Southern cross' the Dog":*** *Long Steel Rail: The Railroad in American Folksong,* Norm Cohen (Urbana: University of Illinois Press, 1981).

138 **wail like a locomotive:** *The Railroad in the African American Experience,* Theodore Kornweibel Jr. (Baltimore: Johns Hopkins University Press, 2010).

142 **captive workers:** *Railroads Triumphant,* Martin.

145 **That's my Middle West":** *The Great Gatsby,* F. Scott Fitzgerald (New York: Scribner, 2004 reissue).

147 **instant centers:** *Railroad Avenue,* Hubbard. See also *Great American Railroad Stations,* Janet Greenstein Potter (New York: John Wiley & Sons, 1996).

148 **the *Superior Express*:** Disclosure: I was once an employee.

150 **wrote of his childhood:** *Because I Was Flesh: The Autobiography of Edward Dahlberg,* Edward Dahlberg (New York: New Directions, 1959).

152 **the old song:** *History of the Atchison, Topeka and Santa Fe Railway,* Keith L. Bryant Jr. (New York: Macmillan, 1974).

152 **custom in most towns:** *Story of American Railroads,* Holbrook.

154 **people still groused:** "The Day of Two Noons," a speech given by Carlton J. Corliss of the American Association of Railroads at an annual meeting of local watch inspectors at the Chicago Towers Club, Aug. 26, 1941.

157 **easy commerce:** "Motel Town," Bernard DeVoto, *Harper's,* Sept. 1953.

158 **reckless colonization:** *Railroaded: The Transcontinentals and the Making of Modern America,* Richard White (New York: W. W. Norton, 2011).

160 **on the border:** "Minus Its Backbone, Amtrak Makes a Tempting Target," Fred W. Frailey, *Trains,* Aug. 2010.

160 **"Freight doesn't complain":** *Appetite for America: How Visionary Businessman Fred Harvey Built a Railroad Hospitality Empire That Civilized the Wild West,* Stephen Fried (New York: Bantam, 2010).

161 **wispy beard:** Ibid.

162 **"promiscuous peddlers":** "Railroad Workers Demand Protection of Their Daytime Sleep," Marna Grubb, Green River Historic Preservation Commission, cityofgreenriver.org.

163 **the carrier of choice:** *All Aboard for Santa Fe: Railroad Promotion of the Southwest, 1890s to 1930s,* Victoria Dye (Albuquerque: University of New Mexico Press, 2005).

164 **"triumph of a proconsul":** *Twentieth Century,* Lucius Beebe (Berkeley, CA: Howell-North, 1962).

164 **blankets and pots:** *Inventing the Southwest: The Fred Harvey Company and Native American Art,* Kathleen L. Howard and Diana Pardue (Flagstaff, AZ: Northland, 1996). See also "The Atchison, Topeka and Santa Fe Railway and the Development of the Taos and Santa Fe Art Colonies," Keith L. Bryant Jr., *Western Historical Quarterly,* Oct. 1978.

170 **free to make investments:** *Getting There: The Epic Struggle Between Road and Rail in the American Century,* Stephen B. Goddard (New York: Basic Books, 1994).

171 **"absolutely disgusting":** *The Wreck of the Penn Central,* Jospeh R. Daughen and Peter Binzen (New York: Little, Brown, 1971).

171 **government troubles:** "Trains vs. Trucks," Jim Giblin, *Trains,* May 2007.

172 **result was disaster:** *Wreck of the Penn Central,* Daughen and Binzen.

172 **ceremonial first run:** *The Amtrak Story,* Frank N. Wilner (Omaha: Simmons-Boardman, 1994).

173 **"You may be surprised":** "Amtrak . . . The Continuing Saga of the Vanishing American Passenger Train," Joseph Zucker, *Elks,* Oct. 1971.

173 **operating losses:** *Amtrak: The History and Politics of a National Railroad,* David C. Nice (Boulder, CO: Lynne Rienner, 1998). See also the splendid *Waiting on a Train: The Embattled Future of Passenger Rail Service,* James McCommons (White River Junction, VT: Chelsea Green, 2009), and *End of the Line: The Failure of Amtrak Reform and the Future of the American Passenger Train,* Joseph Vrancich (Washington, DC: American Enterprise Institute Press, 2004) for a discussion of agency dysfunction.

173 **stanch the bleeding:** "Next Stop: Independence: Amtrak Is Getting There, but Uncle Sam's Ward Still Faces Steep Hill," James Peltz, *Los Angeles Times,* June 16, 1996.

173 **more public money:** "Evaluation Report E-08-02: Public Funding Levels of Euro- pean Passenger Railroads," Amtrak Inspector General's Office, Apr. 22, 2008.

174 **days of clover:** "Frustrations of Air Travel Push Passengers to Amtrak," Ron Nixon, *New York Times,* Aug. 15, 2012.

175 **hard-core train fanatics:** For a quirky academic take on the subject, see *British Railway Enthusiasm,* Ian Carter (Manchester, UK: Manchester University Press, 2008).

179 **branching from the depot:** *Walt Disney's Missouri: The Roots of a Creative Genius,* Brian Burnes, Robert W. Butler and Dan Viets (Kansas City, MO: Kansas City Star Books, 2002).

180 **unbridled happiness:** *Walt Disney: Hollywood's Dark Prince,* Marc Elliott (New York: Birch Lane Press, 1993), as well as the more complete biography *Walt Disney: The Triumph of the American Imagination,* Neal Gabler (New York: Knopf, 2006).

180 **elaborate miniature railroad:** *Walt Disney's Railroad Story: The Small-scale Fascination That Led to a Full-scale Kingdom,* Michael Broggie (Virginia Beach, VA: Donning, 1997).

180 **"in the workshops":** "Disneyland, 1955: Just Take the Santa Ana Freeway to the American Dream," Karal Ann Marling, *American Art,* Winter–Spring 1991.

180 **favorite snack:** *Walt Disney: Hollywood's Dark Prince,* Elliott.

181 **Chicago Railroad Fair:** *Walt Disney's Railroad Story,* Broggie.

182 **"already forming":** Ibid.

183 **reached only by car:** An irony noted in "Disneyland, 1955," Marling.

184 **"an open patio":** "An Architect's Impression of the New Los Angeles Union Railroad Station," Paul Hunter, *Southwest Builder and Contractor,* July 14, 1939. Quoted in *The Next Great American Station: Union Station and Downtown Los Angeles in the Twenty-first Century,* Jaymes Phillip Dunsmore, master's thesis, Massachusetts Institute of Technology, June 2012.

184 **background for movies:** "Hollywood Is All Aboard Union Station," Richard Verrier, *Los Angeles Times,* Sept. 1, 2010.

BLOOD ON THE TRACKS

188 **"side of the road":** *Railway Journey,* Schivelbusch.

189 **annex the east:** *Conquest of a Continent: Siberia and the Russians,* W. Bruce Lincoln (Ithaca, NY: Cornell University Press, 2007). See also *Gulag: A History,* Anne Applebaum (New York: Random House, 2003).

190 **bullied and bluffed:** *Road to Power: The Trans-Siberian Railroad and the Colonization of Asian Russia, 1850–1917,* Stephen G. Marks (Ithaca, NY: Cornell University Press, 1991).

190 **"natural abundance":** Ibid.

191 **diverted for the project:** Ibid. See also "Siberia's Iron Road," Paul Richardson, *Russian Life,* May–June 2001, and "The Trans-Siberian Railway," Igor Slepnev, *History Today,* Nov. 1996.

192 **most boring jobs:** *The Trans-Siberian Railway: A Traveler's Anthology,* Deborah Manley and Bryn Thomas, eds. (Oxford, UK: Signal, 2009).

192 **debut party:** Ibid.

193 **splashy train:** *Yet There Isn't a Train I Wouldn't Take: Railway Journeys,* William D. Middleton (Bloomington: Indiana University Press, 1999).

193 **red carpets:** *Orient Express: The Birth, Life and Death of a Great Train,* Garry Hogg (London: Hutchinson, 1968).

193 **King Boris of Bulgaria:** *A Book of Railway Journeys,* Ludovic Kennedy, ed. (New York: Rawson, Wade, 1980).

194 **"capital fellows":** *Trans-Siberian Railway,* Manley and Thomas.

194 **journalists of that period:** Ibid.

195 **"sun shines weakly":** Ibid.

199 **towerlike monument:** Ibid.

200 **kept them hostage:** *The Last Days of the Romanovs: Tragedy at Ekaterinburg,* Helen Rapaport (New York: Macmillan, 2009).

201 **"whore is to love":** *The Structure of Anna Karenina,* Sydney Schultze (New York: Ardis, 1982).

201 **His inspiration came:** Ibid.

203 **French scientific encyclopedia:** *Railway Journey,* Schivelbusch.

203 **"It is a puzzling fact":** Quoted in *Eleven Minutes Late: A Train Journey to the Soul of Britain,* Matthew Engel (London: Macmillan, 2009).

204 **cartoon trope:** "Adventures in Space: Victorian Railway Erotics, or Taking Alienation for a Ride," Peter Bailey, *Journal of Victorian Culture,* Spring 2004. See also "They Knew Their Station in Life," Matthew Sweet, *Independent,* Nov. 21, 1999.

204 **"I kept my eyes on her":** *My Secret Life,* Anonymous (repr. New York: Signet Classics, 1996).

205 **"a favorite actor":** *The Tender Passion: The Bourgeois Experience from Victoria to Freud,* Peter Gay (Oxford, UK: Oxford University Press, 1986).

205 **morning train:** *Tolstoy,* A. N. Wilson (New York: W. W. Norton, 2001).

206 **"Please delete":** "Some Wild Creature," James Meek, *London Review of Books,* July 22, 2010.

206 **"the olive branch":** "Peasants Kneel at Tolstoy's Bier," *New York Times,* Nov. 21, 1910.

207 **"fir boughs":** "Czar Deplores Tolstoy's End," *Boston Daily Globe,* Nov. 22, 1910.

207 **"gun carriages":** *The Sebastopol Sketches,* Leo Tolstoy (repr. New York: Penguin, 1986).

207 **a flash of insight:** *The Grand Crimean Central Railway,* Brian Cooke (Cheshire, UK: Cavalier House, 1990). General background is in *Railways at War,* J. N. Westwood (London: Osprey, 1980).

208 **"fight to the end":** *To the Finland Station,* Edmund Wilson (New York: Harcourt Brace, 1940).

208 **"war by timetable":** *War by Timetable: How the First World War Began,* A. J. P. Taylor (New York: American Heritage, 1969). The thesis of this book—that the technology of warfare can hamstring its users—found special resonance among nuclear protesters when it was published.

209 **Railway Carriage 2419:** *The World the Railways Made,* Nicholas Faith (London: Bodley Head, 1990).

210 **pointed letter:** "A Public Enterprise in the Service of Mass Murder: The Deutsche Reichsbahn and the Holocaust," Alfred C. Mierzejewski, *Holocaust and Genocide Studies,* Spring 2001.

210 **punch-card machines:** *IBM and the Holocaust: The Strategic Alliance Between Nazi Germany and America's Most Powerful Corporation,* Edwin Black (New York: Random House, 2001).

211 **"many of us broke down":** *Shadows of Treblinka,* Miriam Kuperhand and Saul Kuperhand (Urbana: University of Illinois Press, 1998).

211 **daily efficiency:** *Nazi Germany and the Jews, 1939–1941: The Years of Extermination,* Saul Friedlander (New York: Harper, 2007).

212 **"Tell me, Pless":** "A Public Enterprise in the Service of Mass Murder," Mierzejewski.

212 **"not to concern myself":** Ibid.

212 **to the chassis:** *World the Railways Made,* Faith.

215 **fifteen pounds of dynamite:** "Russia Train Wreck Tied to Terrorist Bomb," Clifford J. Levy and Ellen Barry, *New York Times,* Nov. 28, 2009.

THE ROOF OF THE WORLD

217 **near-imperial expansion:** "China's Rail Plans: Awesome or Awful?" Kathleen E. McLaughlin, in *Far Eastern Economic Review,* June 2009. See also "Is China's Economy Speeding Off the Rails?" Michael Forsythe, *New York Times,* Dec. 22, 2009.

218 **eat up the distance:** "How Fast Can China Go?" Simon Winchester, *Vanity Fair,* Oct. 2011.

220 **"all this trouble":** *China's Great Train: Beijing's Drive West and the Campaign to Remake Tibet,* Abrahm Lustgarten (New York: Times Books, 2008).

221 **"route from Yunnan":** Ibid.

222 **Overseeing the project:** "Boss Rail," Evan Osnos, *New Yorker,* Oct. 22, 2012.

222 **wool blankets:** *China's Great Train,* Lustgarten.

222 **"They had no time":** *An Auspicious Road: The Qinghai-Tibet Railway,* Li Chunsheng, ed. (Beijing: China Pictorial, 2006), the government's official English-language history.

223 **oil shale:** "China Discovers 600 Sites of Copper, Iron Ore Deposits on Qinghai-Tibet Plateau," *People's Daily,* Feb. 14, 2007.

223 **"praising the railroad":** *Tracking the Steel Dragon: How China's Economic Policies and the Railway Are Transforming Tibet,* International Campaign for Tibet, Washington, DC, 2008.

223 **formally opened:** *China's Great Train,* Lustgarten.

223 **benevolence of the Han people:** "Tibet Through Chinese Eyes," in *Atlantic,* Feb. 1999.

223 **a different view:** 2006 Annual Report of the Congressional-Executive Commission on China, Washington, DC, co-chaired by Senator Byron Dorgan and Representative Sander Levin.

228 **town of Woosung:** *The Dragon and the Iron Horse: The Economics of Railroads in China 1876–1937,* Ralph William Huenemann (Cambridge, MA: Harvard University Press, 1984).

228 **peasant way of life:** *China: Railway Patterns and National Goals,* C. K. Leung (Chicago: University of Chicago Press, 1980).

228 **"crow of the rooster":** *Dragon and the Iron Horse,* Huenemann.

229 **"suddenly introduced":** Ibid.

229 **construction loans:** *Railway Problems in China,* Mongton Chih Hsu (New York: Columbia University Press, 1915).

229 **"clocks and toys":** *China,* Leung.

230 **debt to foreign contractors:** *Railway Enterprise in China: An Account of Its Origin and Development,* Percy Horace Kent (London: Edward Arnold, 1907).

230 **foreign control:** *Modern China: The Fall and Rise of a Great Power, 1850 to the Present,* Jonathan Fenby (New York: Ecco, 2008).

231 **secretive and conservative:** "Industrial Involution" in *How China Works,* Jacob Eyferth, ed. (London: Routledge, 2006).

232 **hit a signal box:** "Wenzhou Crash Report Blames Design Flaws and Poor Management," Han Qiao, *International Rail Journal,* Jan. 30, 2012.

232 **driver had been warned:** "Boss Rail," Osnos.

232 **"D301, be careful!":** "Wenzhou Crash Report," Qiao.

233 **"Do not question":** "Boss Rail," Osnos.

233 **illegal subcontracting:** Ibid.

233 **luxury house:** "China Steps Up Efforts to Keep Officials from Leaving Country," Barbara Demick and David Pierson, *Los Angeles Times,* June 6, 2012.

234 **slowed down:** "High-speed Trains in China to Run Slower, Ministry Says," Ian Johnson, *New York Times,* June 13, 2011.

234 **potential problem:** *Tracks from the Past, Transport for the Future: China's Railway Industry 1990–2008,* World Bank, Washington, DC. See also the bank's report *Future Plans and Possibilities,* Richard Bullock, Jitendra Sondhi and Paul Amos, Mar. 2009.

235 **loan documents:** *People's Republic of China: Preparing the Nanking-Kunming Railway Capacity Enhancement Project,* Asian Development Bank, 2007.

237 **"melting permafrost":** 2006 Annual Report, Dorgan and Levin.

248 **"old-fangled and pleasant":** *Riding the Iron Rooster: By Train Through China,* Paul Theroux (New York: Penguin, 1989).

OVER THE MOUNTAIN

250 **bad joke:** Some trade-journal coverage of the Ferrocarril Central Andino is in "Doing Good, in Spite of the Odds," a Mar. 2004 special report produced by Argentina's *Latin Tracks* magazine, as well as, in the same publication, "Mining Spurs Rail Projects," Daniel Thomas, Apr. 2010, and "As Open as a Road," October–November 1999.

251 **rail legacies:** "Back on Tracks: A Nineteenth-Century Technology Could Be the Solution to Our Twenty-First-Century Problems," Phillip Longman, *Washington Monthly,* Jan.–Feb. 2009.

255 **children of La Oroya:** "Poisoned City Fights to Save Its Children," Hugh O'Shaughnessy, *Guardian,* Aug. 12, 2007.

255 **largest single residence:** "Poison Playtime," Chuck Bennett, *New York Post,* Nov. 22, 2010.

256 **can-do Yankee contractor:** *Henry Meiggs, Yankee Pizarro,* Watt Stewart (Durham, NC: Duke University Press, 1946).

257 **mounds of bird droppings:** *Twilight Rails: The Central Railway of Peru and the Cerro de Pasco Railway,* Donald Binns (North Yorkshire, UK: Trackside, 1996).

257 **disaster in San Francisco:** *Henry Meiggs,* Stewart.

259 **Rímac River:** *Railways of the Andes,* Brian Fawcett (London: Allen & Unwin, 1963).

260 **kickbacks:** *Henry Meiggs,* Stewart.

260 **over the summit:** "The Grace Contract at Close Quarters," London's *Pall Mall Gazette,* Feb. 22, 1898.

261 **sarcastic book:** *Henry Meiggs,* Stewart.

265 **triggering spark:** "The Containership Revolution," Brian J. Cudahy, *Intermodal Container Era: History, Security and Trends,* a special report of TR News, published in Sept. 2006.

265 **contents were locked:** *The Box: How the Shipping Container Made the World*

Smaller and the World Economy Bigger, Marc Levinson (Princeton, NJ: Princeton University Press, 2006).

267 **fiber-optic cables:** "Fiber Optic Valuation: The Need for Conformity," Gary Valentine and Thurman Hodges, *Right-of-way,* July–Aug. 2011.

271 **Coal and the railroad:** *History of Wyoming,* T. A. Larson (Lincoln: University of Nebraska Press, 1990). See also *Powder River Coal Trains,* Jeremy Taylor (Telford, PA: Silver Brook Junction, 1997).

273 **colonial plaza:** "Peru Town Copes with Being Devoured by Mine," Andrew Whalen of the Associated Press, Apr. 18, 2010.

FASTER

275 **"It is really flying":** *Railway Journey,* Schivelbusch.

277 **taken a nosedive:** "Spain's Bullet Train Changes Nation—and Fast," Thomas Catan, *Wall Street Journal,* Apr. 20, 2009.

278 **his own plan:** "Remarks by the President and Vice President on a Vision for High-speed Rail in America," Apr. 16, 2009, available at whitehouse.gov.

279 **commuter villages:** *Railway,* George Revill (London: Reaktion Books, 2012).

282 **Cuidad Real:** "Spain's Bullet Train," Catan.

283 **call-in program:** "Aguirre Calls the SER to Rectify and Hangs Up," *El País,* Mar. 20, 2009, translated for me by Mercé Baida.

284 **create a sinkhole:** "Safety Concerns over Barcelona Church Awaiting Benedict XVI," Sinikka Tarvainen, published on earthtimes.com, Oct. 27, 2010.

284 **lasting wound:** Other opposition to the AVE is documented in the following articles, translated for me by Mercé Baida: "Why Doesn't the Expression 'Rating Change' Exist?" Benjamín Prado, *El País,* Oct. 5, 2006; "The Government Considers the 33 Percent Rise on the Price of the Madrid-Seville AVE Reasonable," José María Castro, *La Vanguardia,* Dec. 18, 1991; "Iberia Is Afraid of Losing 35 Percent of Its Barcelona-Madrid Passengers Due to the AVE," A. Trillas, *El País,* Oct. 19, 2007; "Train Is More Comfortable, More Punctual and You're Not Too Surprised," A. Mars and P. del Llano, *El País,* Jan. 25, 2010; and "Long Live the Infrastructure," Patricia M. Liceras, *El País,* Dec. 16, 2009.

285 **three hours' distance:** *Spanish Steps: Zapatero and the Second Transition in Spain,* David Mathieson (London: Policy Network, 2007).

286 **plot behind trains:** "Why Liberals Love Trains," George F. Will, *Newsweek,* Feb. 27, 2011.

288 **"cave instinct":** "Anthropological Invariants in Travel Behavior," *Technological Forecasting and Social Change,* vol. 47, 1994. Tom Vanderbilt also wrote about this phenomenon in his excellent *Traffic: Why We Drive the Way We Do (and What It Says About Us),* (New York: Knopf, 2008), as did Peter Newman in "Why We're Reaching Our Limits as a One-Hour City," *Sydney Morning Herald,* Apr. 26, 2004.

290 **"Man is, man moves":** "A Saint-Simonian for Nineteenth-Century Barce-

lona," Ramon Grau of the Arxiu Històric de la Ciutat de Barcelona, and archived
in Sept. 2009 at barcelonametropolis.cat, which also includes "An Innovative
Plan Turned into a Grand Reality," Joan Busquets.

291 **unlocked a demand:** *Aerotropolis: The Way We'll Live Next,* John D. Kasarda
and Greg Lindsay (New York: Farrar, Straus & Giroux, 2011).

293 **late-life vision:** *Old Man Thunder: Father of the Bullet Train,* by the legendary
Denver Post columnist Bill Hosokawa (Denver: Sogō Way, 1997).

294 **man ablaze:** Ibid.

295 **"saved French railways":** "TGV High Speed Hero," Keith Fender, *Trains,*
Aug. 2010.

296 **federal design standards:** "Acela, Built to Be Rail's Savior, Bedevils Amtrak at
Every Turn," James Dao, *New York Times,* Apr. 24, 2005; and *Amtrak,* Brian
Solomon (St. Paul, MN: MBI, 2004).

297 **"technological regress":** "Stop This Train! Are Trains Slower Now Than They
Were in the 1920s?" Tom Vanderbilt, *Slate,* May 15, 2009.

298 **potential feed sack:** "Can High-speed Rail Get on Track?" Michael Grunwald,
Time, July 19, 2010.

298 **shot up:** "Washington's Newest Gravy Train: High-speed Rail," Matthew
Lewis, Center for Public Integrity, Nov. 30, 2009.

299 **town after town:** *Last Train to Paradise: Henry Flagler and the Spectacular Rise
and Fall of the Railroad That Crossed an Ocean,* Les Standiford (New York:
Crown, 2002), as well as the biography *Henry Flagler: The Astonishing Life and
Times of the Visionary Robber Baron Who Founded Florida,* David Leon Chandler (New York: Macmillan, 1986).

299 **paid for:** "High-speed Railroading," *Economist,* July 24, 2010; additional
details are in "American Express," James Glave and Rachel Swaby, *Wired,* Feb.
2010.

300 **"liberal pipe-dream":** "High-speed Rail Funds Scatter to Other States," Larry
Sandler, *Milwaukee Journal-Sentinel,* Dec. 9, 2010.

300 **"long-term benefit":** "Florida's Rick Scott Sends High-speed Rail Packing,"
Michael Grunwald, *Time,* Feb. 16, 2011.

302 **"modern-day Persepolis":** *Architecture of Rail: The Way Ahead,* Marcus Binney
(London: Academy Editions, 1995).

304 **powering:** "The Full Cost of High-speed Rail: An Engineering Approach,"
David Levinson, Jean Michel Mathieu, David Gillen and Adib Kanafani of the
Institute of Transportation Studies at the University of California–Berkeley,
published by the *Annals of Regional Science,* May 1996.

304 **fixed costs:** *The Southwest Way,* Jody Hoffer Gittell (New York: McGraw-Hill,
2002).

305 **spine of California:** *When America Flies, It Works,* the 2010 annual economic
report from Air Transport Association, Washington, DC.

306 **"entirely social policy":** "A Collision of Visions," Ralph Vartabedian, *Los
Angeles Times,* Mar. 8, 2012.

306 **up on stilts:** "Red Army Construction Battalion Arriving Soon?" Richard F. Tolmach, *California Rail News,* Apr. 2012.

306 **share track:** "Union Pacific Railroad Scoping Comments for Joint EIR/EIS," Feb. 23, 2009, letter to the High Speed Rail Authority from Union Pacific general manager of network infrastructure Jerry Wilmoth.

307 **"go through town":** "Corcoran, Hanford Not Thrilled About High-speed Rail Plan," Valerie Gibbons, *Visalia Times-Delta,* Dec. 4, 2010.

308 **"fearful men":** "Jerry Brown Signs Rail Bill, Avoids Central Valley Opponents," David Siders, *Sacramento Bee,* July 19, 2012.

309 **revised business plan:** "California High-speed Rail Program Revised 2012 Business Plan: Building California's Future," Apr. 2012, available at www .cahighspeedrail.ca.gov/Business_Plan_reports.aspx.

309 **"When Abraham Lincoln":** " 'Thank God' for High-speed Rail Funding, Gov. Jerry Brown Says," Chris Megerian on latimes.com, July 9, 2012.

311 **Tehachapi problem:** "Rail Line's Big Dig," Ralph Vartabedian, *Los Angeles Times,* Nov. 13, 2012.

INDEX